A PARENT'S SURVIVAL GUIDE TO THE PUBLIC SCHOOLS

Sally D. Reed

Published by the
National Council for Better Education
Alexandria, Virginia

*A special thanks to Mike Costigan
for his technical and editorial
assistance on this project*

Cover design by Theresa Sheldon

Text design, typesetting, and production by
AAH Graphics, Seven Fountains, VA 22652
(703) 933-6210

Published by the
National Council for Better Education
101 North Alfred Street #202
Alexandria, VA 22314

Printed in the United States of America

First printing March, 1991

DEDICATION

This book is dedicated to my parents, William Howard and Sally Gibson.

To my father who spent his evenings, after long days at work, teaching me my numbers and how to read phonetically with flash cards and a feather.

To my mother who provided a positive example for reading by always having her nose in a book.

CONTENTS

V

ACKNOWLEDGMENTS

Many friends, family members and colleagues have contributed to (unwittingly in some cases) and encouraged me in writing this book. I would like to acknowledge:

My loving husband, David, who unselfishly shared the computer with me during his law school finals.

My grandmother, Eula Maude Anderson, who must have been the inspiration for Henry Ford's immortal words, "If you took all the experience and judgment of people over fifty out of the world there wouldn't be enough brains and talent left to run it."

My aunts, Joyce and Janie, and my uncle Fred, for always encouraging me to shoot for the moon knowing the worst I could do was hit a star.

My brothers, Mike, Grady and Bill, who have stood by patiently for years as I practiced my parenting and teaching skills on their children, in anticipation of my own.

My loyal and highly capable staff, especially John Campbell and Mike Costigan, the two who are most responsible for this book ever making it out of my office and into print.

And last but certainly not least, the ever faithful, loyal members of the National Council for Better Education. Without them public education would not stand a chance.

INTRODUCTION

I never remember making a clear cut decision to enter the teaching profession. My aunt had been a teacher, my grandmother had always wanted to be one, and I idolized them both. It was always understood that was why Sally was attending college—so she could be a teacher.

To this day, I believe it was one of the best decisions I have ever made. I loved teaching—imparting knowledge to eager, impressionable students and watching them grow up—fervently praying I'd had a positive, lasting influence on their lives.

The first time I was asked what was the most disillusioning incident I had ever had as a teacher, I had to think long and hard. Being the eternal optimist, it is hard to disillusion me, but one incident came to mind above all the rest.

There I was, my first day teaching a senior civics class at Killeen High School, one of the largest public high schools in the state of Texas. Fort Hood, the largest military installation in the free world, was practically on our doorstep. My class was filled with young people who had been brought up in regimented households where paying homage to our great nation was a daily ritual as they watched their parents go to work daily for Uncle Sam. I, quite naively, expected the class to do very well on a pop test. The questions were ridiculously easy: Who is known as the father of our country? Name two men considered founding fathers? How long is a presidential term? How many senators does a state have? And, finally, what is the American dream?

I was disappointed at how ill-informed my students were on basic American history and government, but the single most disillusioning thing about the test was their collective inability to tell me what the "American Dream" is. Some had heard the term even though they did not understand it, but most looked at me as if I was from the Cro-Magnon era.

This same scenario was repeated in subsequent classes later in the day. Not only was I disillusioned, I was depressed. Something as basic to our heritage as this concept had been conveniently left out of their almost completed formal education.

I looked through the civics text I would be using for the year and I saw no mention of it anywhere.

I took a deep breath and delivered the following discourse on the "American Dream": America is the great land of opportunity; it is the proverbial pot of gold at the end of the rainbow for millions of people throughout the world. Here each of us is free to work out our own individual destiny; to carry out God's plan for our lives to the best of our ability. But to do so each of us must be able to know how to read, write and communicate in a logical manner so we can absorb or transmit knowledge to and from our fellow man. This is all part of the striving to achieve our destiny. I told them it was my job and responsibility to help young people learn to do this so they can stake their own place in our free society. This will not come easily—success never does, but with a good education it is within each of all of us. I told them it takes hard work and perseverance to succeed, but that is part of the wonder of America. Here you can be whatever you want to be. Your dreams can come true if you are willing to work hard for them.

The Pilgrims understood this, as did millions of immigrants from Italy, Germany, China and Ireland as their boats rounded the bend in New York harbor and they caught their first glimpse of the Statue of Liberty. It is the reason millions of Europeans, Central Americans and Asians flock to this country yearly in droves. In America, they have a chance to realize the "American Dream."

I reiterate this story to give the reader insight into the sad state of demise our public school system is now in. Each of us must try our best to positively influence the education system whether it be from Washington, D.C. or Galveston, Texas. I assure you that same pop test was given at the end of the semester, and not only did my students know what the "American Dream" was, they realized and appreciated its significance.

X

This book is written primarily for parents who have children in the public school system—either by choice or financial limitations. It should be used as a tool by parents to find out what is going on in their child's school. If they do not like what they find—and they probably will not—the book is meant to empower them with the knowledge to either change it, or find alternative ways to educate their children.

I am calling for nothing short of a parent's revolution. But before you go on the offense, know the nature of your enemy. Prepare for battle. Nothing less than the future of your children and your country is at stake.

A good start might be a healthy dose of righteous indignation. After all, your are **forced** to support the public school system with your tax dollars, whether or not you have children enrolled, and, furthermore, you are **forced** to send your children there unless you can afford the double burden of taxes and private tuition.

What happened to the public in "public schools"? Should they more appropriately be named "state schools"? Do parents not have ultimate rights over their own children? Yes! You, not the state, have the primary, God-given responsibility of educating your children. When you send them to a public school you delegate authority to teachers, never do you abdicate that authority.

It must be understood that everyone employed by your school district ultimately works for you. Your tax dollars pay the bills, which includes their salaries. They are public servants—not public masters.

Educators have traditionally been considered nothing more than an extension of the parent and home. They are not supposed to do anything in the context of the public school that would undermine parental authority or infringe on family integrity. But today, chances are they do.

As parents, you must seize the control that is rightfully yours and see to it that your schools reflect community standards. We should not necessarily expect schools to reflect parental knowledge, but they can and should reflect parental values. This is basic to the concept of local control of public education.

Local control ensures a proper education for your child, but several things must be done before this can be achieved. First, we must begin working immediately to get the federal government out of the education business. Most people do not realize that the federal government only funds approximately 6-9 percent of a school district's overall budget. Only 6-9 percent: but the strings which accompany that small amount of financing are devastating to the philosophy of local control. Keep in mind, that this money is not handed over to the school board in the form of discretionary funds where decisions are made locally on how best to spend the money. Instead, it is sent to your school district, if they accept it (and they do not have to), the federal government will tell them exactly—penny by penny—how to spend it. Often times, federal funding requires local funds to be supplemented with it to carry out the mandates dictated by the federal government. In this way, the government conveniently positions itself to oversee practically every aspect of your school's operations by virtue of making sure your district is ''complying'' with rules and regulations attached to the federal money.

Make no mistake about it, federal involvement and local control are not just incompatible—they are mutually exclusive. The federal government does not ask for your opinion and you have no recourse to complain to them when something goes wrong.

When federal funding initially began, prior to the 1960s, public education was in much better shape. It was better because the local communities were in control of their respective schools. In fact, when this country was founded, education was a function of the family and church. A treatise written in 1800 at the request of Thomas Jefferson shows a literacy rate in America that puts today's figures to shame: ''Most young Americans can read, write and cipher. Not more than four in a thousand are unable to write legibly, even neatly . . . ''

Later, when public schools were established in the 19th century, they depended upon local communities controlling their own schools, even though they were funded to a considerable extent by the state governments. Once again, local control enabled them to work.

Today, after decades of "federalized" education headed by the National Education Association (NEA), we see a painfully different picture. The inability of our public schoolchildren to perform even the most rudimentary functions was first exposed in 1983, when the Department of Education (DOE) released the report "A Nation At Risk." Its findings shocked most Americans and the call for change could be heard from coast to coast.

But after seven years have we really witnessed any change? Yes and no. Yes in the sense that we have seen mass increases in spending on education, and NEA-developed curriculum reforms. According to the 1989 Digest of Education Statistics since 1983, teachers' salaries have increased from an average of $20,000 to almost $30,000, and the NEA has implemented anti-nuclear and death sensitivity courses to "strengthen" the school curriculum.

In the most important area, however, the answer is a resounding NO! Despite sharp increases in funding for education and reforms adopted by the NEA, a 1990 Department of Education study reports that "the reading and writing skills of American students remain dreadfully inadequate." The study goes on to say that the performance of 9, 13, and 17-year-olds remained virtually unchanged since the last assessment was reported in 1984. This is shameful and should serve as an indictment of the NEA-controlled federal system of education. Unless parents regain control of their children's education, they are doomed to failure.

Throughout my tenure, I have frequently been labeled by the NEA, People for the American Way (PAW), and other far-leftist groups as anti-public education and anti-teacher. Nothing could be further from the truth. I believe the public education system is salvageable, but only if parents get back in the driver's seat. I have always contended that teachers are manipulated by the left to promote their own social agenda. So, I have some advice for America's school teachers. If you are for federally funded abortion, affirmative action for homosexuals, nuclear freeze, the ERA, cutting parents out of the education loop, banning handguns and cutting off aid to the Nicaraguan contras, you will find your niche as a member of the NEA. Personally, I think most teachers are more responsible than that. Even if they personally are sympathetic to many of these issues, they do not care for their so-called professional association to be using their dues money to promote such a political agenda on their behalf. So, if you are a teacher who is against these things and for parents, local control and traditional moral values being encouraged in the classroom or if you are weary of being a social worker and anxious to return to teaching in your classroom, then you need to get out of the NEA.

Forget collective bargaining and all the goodies you think you are getting. Yes, public school teachers have a lot of problems, low pay in some school districts being one of them, but any help you get from the NEA is help you can live without. For example, one reason many teachers purport to be NEA members is because the union offers malpractice insurance. What they do not realize is that for approximately $12-25 annually, they can have a malpractice rider attached to their homeowner's insurance. Many other advantages of being an NEA member are similarly insignificant.

What advice do I have for you as a parent? You must first do everything you can, as individuals and as a group, to reshape your public school's environment. Your children cannot thrive under the destructive influence of the NEA and their immoral philosophy of secular humanism. Insist on having input, get on the school board, work on textbook adoption committees if you can. In short, get involved, and do not let school officials dismiss you as an over-protective parent or troublemaker.

This book was written with one objective in mind. Knowledge is power and if parents become knowledgeable about the problems and solutions in the public education system, this newfound empowerment will help them to restore normalcy and excellence to an otherwise bankrupt system. Use the information I have provided and make a difference. Not only for your children, but for all our children.

If your public school is totally unresponsive, then the best thing to do is get your children out of there as fast as you can—at least until a climate is established that will permit meaningful reform to take place. Alternatives include private or parochial schools and, if you are really serious, home schooling or private tutors. You do not have to be a genius or even a college graduate to do a good job home schooling your children. All it takes is a real commitment on your part.

Be prepared for a struggle, for the NEA will be completely unwilling to relinquish its control of public education. But we must not get discouraged. Over the last year we have all seen remarkable changes throughout the world—the forces of freedom overcoming the forces of socialist and communist tyranny. While the Cold War may be over, there remains a "covert war" raging in America's public schools. The agents of this war, namely the NEA, seek to drive a moral and psychological wedge between you and your child. However, this war, like the Cold War, can be won. We must never forget that if we, as a society, clearly define the duties we wish our public schools to fulfill, and if we steadfastly support those ideals, not only with money but with faith and personal involvement, we will once again have a good, viable system of public education which can and should be the envy of the free world.

Sally D. Reed

CHAPTER 1

GENERAL SYMPTOMS

As all of us begin our journey into the 1990s we find that one of America's most cherished institutions—public education—is in real trouble. Incredibly, not only can't our sons and daughters read, write, or think for themselves, but many of their teachers can barely read or write, as evidenced by shockingly high percentages of teachers failing competency tests in every state in the union.

The educational situation in this country has increasingly deteriorated during the last few decades in spite of the billions of dollars ploughed into it and the most modern of educational theories utilized in the classrooms. Statistics bear this out: Financial spending per student has risen from an average of $1274 in 1950 to $4,724 in 1989 (both measured in 1988 dollars), but the increase in spending has not prompted an increase in standards. [1]

In 1963, when SAT (Standardized Achievement Tests—college admissions exam) scores were at their highest (Math: 502, Verbal: 478), and in 1983 when they were at their lowest (Math: 468, Verbal: 425), real dollars spent per student rose by 70 percent. [2]

Much to the dismay of liberal lobbying groups, like the NEA, this decline in standards coincides with an increase of state and federal funding. In 1950, 57 percent of education funding was local, states contributed 40 percent and the federal government 3 percent. In 1981, local governments contributed 43 percent, the states 47 percent and the federal 9 percent. [3]

With an increase in state and federal intervention comes an increase in federal regulations that are ill-suited to local educational needs. It is quite obvious that this pork-barrel approach to education has shifted

1

the emphasis from providing a quality education to establishing a larger educational bureaucracy, and the result has been a steadily deteriorating public education system.

Columnist Patrick Buchanan aptly puts his finger on the ills of our education system when he continually asserts that today's public high school graduates are the dumbest ever produced by our schools. Mr. Buchanan has not indulged in fancy either. The 1983 report of the National Commission on Excellence in Education catalogued the dwindling state of American education.

The bipartisan commission warned that "The educational foundations of our society are being eroded by a rising tide of mediocrity that threatens our very future as a nation and as a people."[4]

Among the numerous signs that America's public education system is in dire straits, the report cited:

—Some 23 million Americans are functionally illiterate. Among minority youth this figure is forty percent.

—High school students score lower today on standardized tests than 27 years ago, when Sputnik was launched. In particular, Scholastic Achievement Tests (SAT's) scores declined every single year from 1963 to 1980. Verbal scores fell more than 50 points. Math scores fell nearly 40 points.

— American students, compared on 19 subjects with students of other industrialized nations, did not score first or second in a single subject. To its chagrin, America's students scored last on seven of the 19 subjects (even though the United States spends over half the amount more per student on education than the nation's students who did better than American children.)

—More than half of the students judged to be "gifted" in the U.S. do not score above average in high school. Nor do many of them perform outstandingly in later life.

—Remedial mathematics courses in U.S. colleges increased by 72 percent between 1975 and 1980. Many students enter col-

lege today despite their inability to write a grammatically correct sentence.

—Advanced skills among students are especially scarce. Nearly
40 percent of 17-year-olds cannot draw logical inferences from
written material. Only 20 percent can write a persuasive essay.
Only one-third can solve a multi-step math problem.

—Scientific skills are equally lacking. Science achievement
scores have plummeted in this country. In 1983 they were
lower than in 1977. That year they were lower than in 1973.
The 1973 scores were less than in 1969. As we move towards
the 21st century our knowledge diminishes.[5]

What happened to the average American citizen that he became anxious enough to begin questioning the one institution that up until that
time had been viewed as practically infallible by most Americans? Little Johnny came home and not only could he not read, spell, write or
compute, even more disturbing to his parents was the fact that something did not seem right about the way little Johnny's personality was
developing. His attitudes about society, his family and his classmates
were not in correlation with the way he was being brought up at home.
This problem was more widespread than just with little Johnny. The
parents of his classmates were equally alarmed.

Then, suddenly, it became clear. Johnny had become a cynical, ego-
tistical, callous little boy who chose to remain a recluse from a family
and society that could not understand him.

As time went on, it became evident Johnny was operating from a
completely different mindset than his parents—a mindset where there
are no moral absolutes and no clear distinction between right and
wrong; where authority figures are not merely rebelled against, but
held in contempt; where traditional values are despised and ridiculed
as archaic.

Suddenly parents realized their children were little more than strang-
ers living under the same roof. This was not the way they had raised
their offspring. What had happened that could have so thoroughly un-

dermined the values and attitudes these parents had spent so long trying to instill into their children's thinking and behavior?

Parents began asking questions and started searching for answers. The answers led them directly to the public schools. To the parents' surprise, they discovered that while they had been sitting back naively trusting their school system—to which they had willingly delegated the awesome responsibility of preparing their child for adulthood— there had been a quiet revolution, a silent coup, led by the liberal elite of the education establishment. They discovered that teachers had usurped the parental role in education for the purpose of building a new social order—that is, perpetrating the liberal version of "a better world."

Unfortunately, the traditional version of basic education got lost in the shuffle. The shuffle that occurred was when power shifted from local/state/federal control to federal/state/local control. As Theodore M. Black, one time Head of Regents for the New York school system, said, "I think it is fair to say that through most of the 1950s the authority of the schools rested upon a sense of inner confidence—they believed in themselves because we believed in them . . . "[6]

Writing in *Commentary* magazine, Dr. Joseph Adelson, psychology professor at the University of Michigan, said:

> . . . more than any other institution in American society, the schools have become an arena for the struggle between the values of traditionalism and of modernity. Among the values of traditionalism are: merit, accomplishment, competition and success; self-restraint, self-discipline and the postponement of gratification; the stability of the family; and a belief in certain moral universals. The modernist ethos scorns the pursuit of success; is egalitarian and redistributionist in emphasis; tolerates or encourages sensual gratification; values self-expression as against self-restraint; accepts alternative or deviant forms of the family; and emphasizes ethical relativism . . . In a morally unified and harmonious era, the schools can serve the public

intention readily. In an era marked by multiplicity of aims, or by competing aims, the schools tend to become ambivalent or confused, or inhibited—often all three at once.[7]

Mr. Black continues this line of thinking:

> That struggle [between the modernists and traditionalists] continues and the schools continue to suffer, as do their clients, the children. While modernists contend that their ideas for education have not yet been fully tested, and that post hoc era . . . is not a fair way to judge, the fact remains that as and where modernism has nudged out traditionalism as the governing philosophy of education, the quality of education has suffered. And why should we have expected otherwise? The modernist credo is nothing less than an invitation to mediocrity, in the name of equality.[8]

This modernist version of education is called by many different names—liberal, progressive and socialist—but it all plays on the American dream of giving the best to our offspring—of trying to pass on the best of all worlds, the best of hopes and the best of opportunities to one's children. Unfortunately, the liberal, progressive or modernist version of a "better world" differs considerably from the crystal clear vision of our forefathers. One of the first great tasks undertaken by our guiding forefathers was to create an enlightened citizenry so that self-government might work.

Our forefathers felt they had the key; a system of free education, so that all Americans might secure the blessings of liberty. This was their vision, their best hope for the future of their children and the fledgling nation.

At that time, the curriculum of our nation's public schools reflected the rationale of our forefathers, and besides providing an enlightened citizenry to carry out the requirements of self-government, two other tasks were imposed on America's founders: to create national unity out of diversity and to transmit the skills that would enable every generation of Americans to pursue the American dream. Our schools accomplished these goals.

Out of particularism came nationalism, writers like Cooper and Hawthorne, poets like Bryant and Longfellow, painters like Trumbull and Stuart, historians like Sparks and George Bancroft, and schoolmen like Noah Webster with his spellers and William H. McGuffey with his readers, defined the vision that was America. These and others popularized that familar group of heroes and villains, that common store of stories, images and values that helped to create the national spirit. These men, with the school as their medium, gave to Americans a people's common language with which to voice a heritage.

That heritage rang from children's lips when they voiced passages of the "Concord Hymn" or "Paul Revere's Ride." It shined in their eyes when they learned to recognize such scenes as William Penn making a treaty with the Indians or Daniel Boone pushing his way through the Cumberland Gap.

As a result of our public schools, even new immigrants to our shores were able to accomplish what few in other countries have been able to do: rise from obscure, even poverty-stricken beginnings to become managers, business executives, and experts of every sort. Through our education system, our country absorbed more varied ethnic stocks more rapidly than any other country in history. Education in America became the ticket to economic prosperity and financial independence as well as intellectual prosperity and freedom of thought.

But in the late fifties and early sixties, something happened to change all that. Children came home who did not know who Cooper, Hawthorne, Trumbull and Webster were. They could not read and they could not spell. Their values and images were not only alien, but in many cases were uncomely and unhealthy. They did not have the slightest idea how a representative democracy worked, in what ways free enterprise was different from other economic systems such as communism, or the political history behind the various present-day governments.

Just how much of an effect does the low quality of our system have on the "citizenship" potential of future voters?

> . . . two-thirds of our seventeen-year-olds do not know that the Civil War occurred between 1850 and 1900. Three quarters do not know what *reconstruction* means. Half do not know the meaning of the *Brown decision* and cannot identify either Stalin or Churchill. Three quarters are unfamilar with the names of standard American and British authors. Moreover, our seventeen-year-olds have little sense of geography or the relative chronology of major events. Reports of youthful ignorance can no longer be considered merely impressionistic.[9]

> All great leaders from Thomas Jefferson to Martin Luther King, Jr., have understood the basic fact that a voter is completely disenfranchised when he is illiterate. "Illiterate and semi-literate Americans are condemned not only to poverty, but also the powerlessness of incomprehension. Knowing that they do not understand the issues, and feeling prey to manipulative oversimplifications, they do not trust the system of which they are supposed to be the masters. They do not feel themselves to be active participants in our republic, and they often do not turn out to vote. The civic importance of cultural literacy lies in the fact that true enfranchisement depends upon knowledge, knowledge upon literacy, and literacy upon cultural literacy."[10]

In short, between the 1960s and the 1980s, our children became easy targets for those who would pervert our educational institutions to promote anti-American principles, immoral patterns of behavior, and other tenets and causes damaging to the individual and to the society. Our public school system became the instrument by which future generations would be denied the American dream.

The takeover was actually a bloodless fight, a one-sided war. In the battle between the elitist liberal mentality of the education establishment versus the good, common-sense thinking of the American public, we, the public, lost. We lost by default. Most of us were not even aware a battle was going on. We read books and accepted new theories and newfound experts because we were told they were good. In short, the education consumers were the victims of their own trust—and their children became the casualties.

The public education system in the United States is sick. The symptoms of its sickness are all around us—drugs, violent crime, teenage pregnancy, drop-outs and functional illiterates. You, as parents, like a doctor must be able to recognize the symptoms before the patient can be treated.

Let us turn our attention to some of the easily recognizable symptoms of the disease that rages through our public schools.

CHAPTER 1 FOOTNOTES

1. Heritage Foundation, *The Heritage Backgrounder* (Washington, D.C.: May 11, 1984) pages 5-6.
2. Heritage, page 6.
3. Heritage, page 6.
4. The National Commission on Excellence in Education, A Nation At Risk (Washington, D.C.: U.S. Government Printing Office, 1983) page 5.
5. Nation, pages 8-9.
6. Theodore Black, Straight Talk About American Education, (New York, NY: Harcourt, Brace, Jovanovich Publishers, 1982) page 8.
7. Dr. Joseph Adelson, *Commentary* magazine, March 1981: page 22.
8. Black, Straight, pages 8-9.
9. E.D. Hirsch, Cultural Literacy, (Boston, MA.: Houghton Mifflin Company, 1987) page 8.
10. Hirsch, Cultural, page 12.

CHAPTER 2

BRIEF HISTORY OF THE PUBLIC EDUCATION SYSTEM

The concept of public education was first introduced when the Puritans came to the New World and founded the Massachusetts Bay Colony in the early 1600s. It sprang from the Reformation Protestant rebellion against the authority of the Catholic Church in Europe.

The leaders of this revolt against Rome realized that if their reform movement, which was based on the concept of the Bible as the revealed word of God, was to be the authority for the conduct of man's life, then it was imperative that Biblical knowledge be disseminated on a widespread basis. Only by having educated masses would it be possible for the common man to understand God's word.

Martin Luther, in the early 1500s, had urged the German princes to not only establish public schools, but to require their attendance by all children. He thought this would ensure that coming generations would understand the message of the Bible and, in this way, provide for the continuation of the Reformation.

While Luther laid a solid foundation for public schooling in Europe, the person most influential towards schooling in the New World was the theologian John Calvin.

From his academy in Geneva, Switzerland, Calvin formulated and implemented his version of the Reformation. He realized that the faithful must be educated in Biblical study and interpretation in order for the doctrine to spread and become lasting.

In short, it required an educational system to instruct the followers. For this reason, the town fathers in Geneva created a system of public schools in which the Protestant doctrines of John Calvin were taught as well as reading and writing. After all, if the people could not read or write they would be unable to follow the message of the Scriptures. Thus, it became a matter of necessity in Calvin's view to have a literate society.

Education, Calvin thought, had a very important role to play in a religious order. Due to Calvin's influence and intellectual arguments, the church in Geneva was granted a measure of independence unprecedented in the known world which placed the entire school system under ecclesiastic, not secular, control.

Wiliston Walker, in his biography of Calvin, commented:

> Calvin viewed the office of teacher as of divine appointment, having as its highest duty that of educating "the faithful in sound doctrine" from the Old and New Testaments. But he felt no less strongly that before the learner "can profit by such lessons he must first be instructed in the languages and worldly sciences" . . . In Calvin's judgment, the school was an integral factor in the religious training of the community.[1]

It was this concept—that the school was vital to the church—that the Puritans brought with them to their colony at Massachusetts Bay.

In Calvin's ideal society, civil government would serve the broad purposes of religion, not the other way around. The church was looked upon as a self-governing partner with the civil government. However, both were to bow down and be subservient to the word of God.

The Puritans in the New World attempted to put Calvin's doctrine into practical use and to build a new society from the ground up by creating a civil government that was a working partner with the church.

Following Calvin's emphasis on education, just six years after the colony's founding, it appropriated money to create an educational institute that eventually contributed to the destruction of Calvinism when Massachusetts-Harvard College was born.

In 1642, the colony passed its first educational law concerning the education of children. The law was ahead of its time.

> For as much as the good education of children is of singular behoof and benefit to any commonwealth . . . as not to endeavor to teach, by themselves or others, their children and apprentices as much as learning as may enable them perfectly to read the English tongue, and knowledge of capital law . . . [2]

The Colony's educational laws served two purposes: to encourage learning in general and religious study in particular.

No other English colony had such a comprehensive system of education. They had all been settled by different religious sects and worked under different grants of power from the English Crown. The Puritans had been free to organize and govern as they saw fit. Thus education in the other colonies was left entirely up to the parents, individual religious sects, private teachers and philanthropy.

In 1684, the Puritan's colonial charter was revoked by Charles II and a new one was granted in 1691 that weakened the Puritan's orthodox influence.

This did not, however, mean a loss of interest in education. Private schools flourished and the citizens of Revolutionary War America had "an adult male literacy rate that ran from 70 to 100 percent."[3] This rate compares quite favorably with current literacy rates, especially when one considers that billions of dollars are being spent to "educate" our citizens.

After the formation of the new nation, the United States, Massachusetts enacted the first state comprehensive school laws in the nation. The new laws continued the educational legacy of the Puritans by requiring every town in the state to support an elementary school for six months out of the year.

The city of Boston soon followed suit and passed its own school laws, thus laying the foundation for the first system of public schools in an American city.

Before the law was passed, however, an age-old controversy erupted that is still with us today—who was going to control the schools? One faction wanted to continue the old system under which the elected town councilmen and their appointees controlled the schools. The other faction wanted the control to be by a democratically elected committee that would oversee school activities. The "democrats" won, and the system of elected school boards was established.

With the exception of New England— where tax-supported schools existed, due to the proximity and influence of Massachusetts—the United States had a laissez-faire system of education.

But it would be incorrect to assume that just because the rest of America did not have a formal system of tax-supported public schools children were not being educated.

Noted researcher and author, Sam Blumenfeld points out: "parents educated their children as they wished: at home with tutors, at private academies, or church schools. This did not mean that poor children were neglected."[4]

At that time, some states did what today is vociferously opposed by educational elitists: they paid poor children's tuition which allowed them to go to the private school of their choice.

"Virtually every large city in the country," says Blumenfeld, "had its 'free-school' societies that built and operated schools for the poor and were supported by the community's leading benefactors and philanthropists . . . Thus, there was no need for any child to go without an education."[5]

This system apparently worked quite well for as Blumenfeld notes, in a statement that should indict today's National Education Association's (NEA) union-controlled educational system, "The rate of literacy in the United States then was probably higher than it is today."[6]

This laissez-faire attitude was beginning to eat into the support for public schools in New England. In spite of Massachusetts' public school laws, free market forces were shifting the public away from support of often poorly managed public schools to the large number of efficiently run private schools.

Boston, however, stoutly resisted the growing public support of private schools. This was due mainly to the influence of the Unitarian movement which was becoming ensconced in Boston as a result of its having taken control of Harvard College. Unitarians strongly favored and supported public, not private education.

The Unitarian movement was strongly opposed to doctrinaire Calvinism, and did not get along with other Protestant doctrines either, because both Protestantism and Catholicism were based upon the Trinitarian God-Father, Son and Holy Spirit. Unitarian thought rejected this doctrine of the Trinity and the divinity of Christ.

Theologically, Unitarianism's incompatibility with other Christian religions required either a new concept of God or the creation of a new god, which made them appear more pagan than Christian.

Since the Calvinists viewed education as a means of enhancing the religious nature of the people, they viewed Unitarianism as a most dangerous heresy.

For many years there had been a struggle for control of Harvard between the Calvinists and the more liberal Unitarians. In 1805, the takeover of Harvard by the Unitarians was secured. It was a momentous event as it effected not only education, but also the intellectual history of the United States. In fact, the long journey of secular humanism that dominates American thought today can be traced to this event.

The takeover made Harvard then, as it is today, the center of liberalism. We have all heard the joke: "Do you know how to become a liberal? Go to Harvard and turn Left." This sentiment is even more pronounced today.

The biggest differences between the two religions, arose over the nature of man. Calvinists thought, and Fundamentalist Christians still believe today, that Adam's original sin was responsible for corrupting man. Only by obedience to God's laws could man be saved from the consequences of his corrupt and evil nature. Many non-Fundamentalist Christian sects view the Fall of Man as an ongoing event which re-occurs every time man considers himself separated and apart from God, rather than a single monumental, historical event. These sects viewed the Bible as a divinely inspired treatise on the psychological and spiritual nature of man, not a history lesson. But the seeds of sinfulness, as shown in the story of Adam and the Fall, were thought to exist, however latent, within every individual.

The precepts of secular humanism sprang from the Unitarian perspective which was to view man as innately good, rational, benevolent and cooperative. They believed it was civilization, or in modern terms, his environment, which was the cause of man's corruption. Change the environment, or the external conditions, and you will have solved the problem of so-called sinfulness.

The Unitarians of yesterday and the secular humanists of today believe that all it takes to change man's actions is proper education. Man, a reasonable and rational creature, will respond much more positively to education than he will to a list of do's and don'ts. There is, these two believe, no limit to the good man can achieve using education as its tool.

There was, however, one major intellectual stumbling block for the Unitarians. How do you explain the greater problem of evil?

The leader of the Unitarian movement in the early 1800s, William Ellery Channing, explained the answer to the problem of evil in a letter to a former Harvard classmate, William Shaw. A biographer of Channing describes its contents:

Avarice was the chief obstacle to human progress [Channing] declared. The only way to eliminate it was to establish a

14

community of property. Convinced that virtue and benevolence were natural to man, he blamed selfishness and greed upon the false ideas of superiority of the body over the mind and the separation of individual interest from that of the community as a whole.[7]

In Channing's view, then , as in the modern liberal view today, evil was created by society: Therefore, he reasoned, if you change society, evil will be eliminated.

The Unitarians gave the public school system their unswerving support, and in Boston, Channing and other Unitarians served on the school board.

From their base in Boston the Unitarians launched their crusade for public education throughout the rest of the United States. Their views on education were the rallying cry for a better society.

One Unitarian proponent of public education, George Ticknor, wrote in 1827:

> The grand lever, which is to raise up the mighty mass of this community is education . . . The school holds, in embryo, the future communities of this land. The schools are the pillars of the republic. To these, let the strong arm of government be stretched out. Over these, let the wisdom of our legislatures watch.[8]

That Channing and the Unitarians won the battle of public education is evident today. Their ghosts must be dancing with glee in their Valhalla as they look down upon the fruits of their labor—today's educational system in the United States.

Unfortunately, as an examination of it will demonstrate, education is in a sorry state. Serious steps must be taken to return it to excellence. Why? Let us turn our attention to the current situation. The best place to start is with the NEA, which, in the guise of being pro-education, has wreaked tremendous havoc not only in our schools, but throughout our society as well.

CHAPTER 2 FOOTNOTES

1. Sam Blumenfeld, Is Public Education Necessary? (Old Greenwich, CT.: Devin Adair Publishers, 198) page 12.
2. Blumenfeld, Is. page 17.
3. Blumenfeld, Is. page 20.
4. Blumenfeld, Is. page 27.
5. Blumenfeld, Is. page 43.
6. Blumenfeld, Is. page 44.
7. Arthur W. Brown, William Ellery Channing (Twayne Publishers, Inc., January 1827) page 169.
8. North American Review, Improvement of Common Schools. Article X, January 1827: page 169.

CHAPTER 3

PUBLIC SCHOOLS: INDOCTRINATION CENTERS FOR COLLECTIVISM

By the late 1970s, it became clear that a philosophy known as "humanism" had become the cornerstone of progressive education. From that time on, our public schools increasingly were dominated by a collectivist mentality—collectivism being central to humanistic thought.

The intellectual godfather of the humanist philosophy was John Dewey, the socialist. It was Dewey's dream to create a socialist paradise, and the most viable route, he thought, was through the education system. "The school's ultimate social ideal," said Dewey, "is the transformation of society through a new, socially-minded individualism."[1]

Dewey's writing left no doubt that the socialist state was his ideal, and that as far as he was concerned the school's sole job was to indoctrinate the pupils to accept the new social order. "Apart from the thought of participation in social life the school has no end or aim."[2] According to Dewey, then, the major aim of education was not learning, but indoctrination.

Sam Blumenfeld , an expert on the NEA and John Dewey, writes,

> The NEA's reverence for Dewey borders on deification. In 1929, at age 70, he was made honorary president of the NEA

17

. . . Dewey made the word democracy synonymous with socialism. He used the words interchangeably, creating a good deal of confusion in the minds of many intelligent people who favored democracy but opposed socialism and read little of what Dewey actually wrote. An intimate knowledge of Dewey's writings clearly illustrates the full extent of his commitment to "collectivism" and the educational means he devised to bring it about.[3]

The NEA has become the self-appointed vehicle for realizing Dewey's dream. How is it doing this?

Consider several examples. In the spring of 1981 the NEA sent out a collection of materials deploring American support for the Duarte government in El Salvador. Former NEA head, Braulio Alonso, argued that Salvadoran citizens were being harmed by right-wing death squads and that their union, ANDES, was being suppressed.

With this in mind, the NEA presented materials as an objective analysis of the Central American conflict but they were, in fact, a severe distortion of what was actually occurring there. Little mention was made of the Marxist government in neighboring Nicaragua which funds and arms the Salvadoran rebels, and no mention whatsoever was made of the tyranny the Nicaraguan government has imposed on its own people. This was certainly relevant to the debate since a Nicaragua-style Marxism was what the El Salvador guerrillas wanted, and the Salvadoran government vigorously opposed.

The NEA material on El Salvador was prepared with the assistance of the Committee in Solidarity With the People of El Salvador (CISPES), a pro-Marxist group. This should not surprise anyone, since it seems that NEA president Mary Hatwood Futrell took great pride in being associated with communist organizations. In the March, 1986 edition of *NEA Today*, Futrell was proudly announced as the winner of the Labor Research Association's 10th annual award for outstanding union leadership. This sounds like a wonderful achievement, right? What makes this a dubious honor is that the Labor Research Association (LRA) is a well-documented communist front organization.

This is nothing new, as evidenced in a letter by former Attorney General Tom Clark. In a letter to the Loyalty Review Board on December 4, 1947, Attorney General Clark made the statement that the LRA is a "subversive affiliate of the Communist Party, and an organization that seeks to alter the form of government of the United States by unconstitutional means."[4]

More recently, an April, 1983 FBI Intelligence Division report on Soviet Active Measures was released to the House Intelligence Committee. It said, " . . . The Labor Research Association is a vehicle for Soviet Active Measures, to bring labor groups into the Peace campaign. It is a vehicle for Active Measures in the trade unions."[5]

As you can clearly see, the LRA has been embraced by the NEA trade union, yet another indication that the NEA is not interested in education.

It is interesting that the NEA is so indignant about human rights violations within the democratic Salvadoran government, while blind to the much more blatant violations by the former Nicaraguan government—the foremost being the inherent denial of individual rights within the Marxist-Leninist ideology.

In June 1982, the NEA's weekly newsletter to its members identified thirty "peace resource groups" to which it referred teachers. The purpose was clear: The NEA wanted educators to get materials from these groups and use them in the classroom to "educate" children about defense issues.

One of the groups identified by the NEA was something called Educators for Social Responsibility. It has published a 209 page curriculum guide that deals with issues of nuclear war in the classroom. In fact, the guide reads like an anti-nuclear tirade. It is certainly not an objective presentation of the arguments for and against disarmament. Rather, it encourages teachers to use creative literature to acquaint students with the dangers we might face in a nuclear world.

In other words, show scary pictures and create horrific situations in which children play the victims of nuclear war so they will be frightened into the "peace" camp. This fosters an emotional response to the nuclear issue, rather than an informed one, which runs counter to the basic tenets of education.

NEA sponsored literature often asks questions like, But who are the Soviets?

The NEA feels that the proper answer is found in a short story called 'The Fate of Man,' by Mikhail Sholokhov. It is the story of a Soviet soldier in WWII who spends time in a Nazi prison camp, and returns home, only to find that his family has been killed in a bombing attack. In the NEA's view the WWII setting, when the U.S. and the Soviet Union were allies, may help students 'bypass cold-war distortion' to reach an understanding of the Soviets as people.

'Cold-war distortion'? In other words, teachers are to be silent about gross Soviet abuses—brutal repression of Christians, Jews, dissidents, mentally ill—and focus on the "niceties" of the Soviet Union. Do not mention Stalin's part in starting the second World War and forget that this man is responsible for killing millions of his own people.

The Soviets are people, too. This is the message.

Well, of course, the Soviets are people, but the people are not the ones in control of the Soviet government. And the Soviet government's history shows their leadership to be the collective equivalent of your neighborhood butcher. This is not "Cold War rhetoric": it is simply historical fact. Thirty million Russians killed by Stalin is not "Cold War propaganda;" it is a statistic with which no historians disagree.

This NEA curriculum asks us to remember the U.S.-Soviet alliance in World War II, but not to remember the preceding Soviet-Nazi alliance, which the Soviet opportunists entered into, or the fact the Soviets allowed the Nazis to secretly train their soldiers in Russia, in violation of the treaty ending World War I. This Soviet-Nazi alliance was in force until the Germans got the bright idea of attacking their socialist partner, Russia.

Another section in the teacher's curriculum guide explains to children that "Inflammatory Words Can Teach You to Hate." Students are asked to study the memoirs of Lt. William Calley to see how his simplistic grasp of the inflammatory word "communism" led to his killing spree at My Lai. Calley childishly claims that the reason he killed so many people is because the army never taught him that communists are human beings. His assessment is that he was there to kill ideology, not humans, and if only he had known that at the time, he would have objected.

Is that all we get about communism? It is a misunderstood term, epitomized by Calley's naivete? All criticism of communism is apparently refuted by Calley's misunderstanding of it, of his exaggeration of the effect it has on people. By the same token, the guide could just as well have explained that the NEA's use of the term "right-wing" encourages people to hate all conservatives, but that is not the proper slant for the NEA.

The values the NEA imposes on children are not restricted to the view that Communism is simply a benign, different, legitimate ideology, or that, for the last forty years, the entire defense policy of the United States has been based on the myth that communism is evil, with simple unilateral disarmament being the solution to the entire problem. Indeed, the NEA seems anxious to wreck America's capacity to defend itself, apparently so that the U.S. will more readily submit, if not to the Soviet Union, then to a one-world government.

NEA brochures routinely define "militarism" as an elitist, hierarchical ideology which values strength over human qualities and denies the equal worth of nations and individuals.

Here is how it answers "questions frequently raised about the arms race."[6]

21

Q: But aren't we risking our way of life if we allow the Russians to get ahead?

A: The $1 trillion defense budget that the President (Reagan) seeks for the next four years will do more to undermine our democratic values and standard of living than anything the Russians can do.

Q: But how can we trust the Russians? How can we be sure they won't cheat?

A: We can trust them as much as they can trust us. [7]

Here, the NEA is spreading the familar gospel of unilateral disarmament. The arguments show a complete ignorance of the Soviet track record for violating arms-control treaties, such as the chemical weapons ban and the treaties on nuclear testing. Indeed, because the Soviet Union is a closed society, we do not even know the full extent of the violations and, of course, neither do the Soviet citizens themselves. And while much is made of the U.S. satellite surveillance system, it stands to reason that if we did not know for years whether Israel or South Africa (our allies with open societies and a free press) had or did not have nuclear weapons, we certainly cannot be confident in our ability to gauge Soviet nuclear testing.

In addition, the NEA advances the curious and radical notion that building up one's defenses undermines one's security. This argument simply runs counter to reason. Never in the history of the world has weakness proved an effective rebuttal to strength. Indeed, it should be quite obvious that the opposite is true.

Of course, it is not too surprising the NEA does not find the Soviet Union a threat since it is advocating the imposition of a Soviet-style totalitarianism on future generations of children. In fact, as we have already seen, the NEA has been very busy in this regard.

Do we want this kind of indoctrination for our children? Don't they have the right to be fully informed in a history class about the nature and past history of the Soviet Union? Don't they have the right to choose what views they will hold on U.S. defense policy—based on solid, historically correct information—without having the NEA ramming its own wayward dogma down their throats? I believe they do.

Indoctrination is always an evil since it impinges upon freedom of thought. It is particularly insidious, however, when it is applied to children because their minds are not yet fully developed. To indoctrinate children is virtually to destroy their minds, to render them, often permanently, unable to think clearly and arrive at carefully weighed decisions.

A glowing example of the NEA's indoctrination program is the curriculum, "<u>Choices: A Unit in Conflict and Nuclear War</u>," which was funded jointly by the Union of Concerned Scientists, a radical left-wing organization, the NEA and their Massachusetts state affiliate. Although this booklet was supposedly only "made available" to teachers through its catalogue, it was reported in a Florida newspaper that the curriculum was sent as a pilot program to 48 junior high and high schools throughout the country. In fact, it made its way into the public high school where I taught.

In this 144 page booklet, which has some ten lessons on the dangers of nuclear war, we discover that nuclear weapons are themselves evil, especially when used to defend the United States. Soviet nuclear weapons, though bad, are not as evil as those of the United States, because, according to the curriculum, the Soviets do not harbor hostile intent.

<u>Choices</u> says the action-reaction cycle of the arms race is what most threatens world peace, and the only solution is a "nuclear freeze" or unilateral disarmament. The U.S. is portrayed as the instigator of every nuclear escalation, and the Soviet Union is seen as a society compelled to respond to the villainous U.S. military build-up. In other words, the Soviets merely react to acts of aggression by the United States.

"Better Red than dead," seems to be the message of <u>Choices</u>. Naturally, the booklet fails to show that under current U.S. defense policy, peace is being preserved. Nor is there any suggestion that our people could opt for being neither Red nor dead, or that even if we surrendered to the Soviets on NEA instructions, there is no guarantee that we would not be both Red <u>and</u> dead!

In order to frighten students, the NEA provides them with the most terrifying accounts of what a nuclear war would be like if it happened in their home towns. Vivid descriptions of mutilated bodies are used to argue, not by logic but by emotion, that surrendering to the Soviet Union is the only way to avoid this scenario—if we resist, we will all perish.

Albert Shanker, president of the American Federation of Teachers (AFT), the second largest teacher's union in America behind the NEA, and one of their more outspoken critics, says, teachers have a responsibility to be balanced and fair.

But fairness is not what we get from the NEA, particularly when it suggests that the reason for the Soviet invasions of Poland and Afghanistan was that these were "some unfriendly countries," as though the Poles and the Afghans were to be blamed for the hostility and provoked a Soviet invasion.

Similarly, the NEA argues that the United States' efforts to defend itself against existing Soviet terrorism simply provokes the Soviet Union into committing more barbarisms. The NEA apparently believes if the United States were to be passive, and refuse to resist, the Soviet leadership would become less totalitarian. We need not look back any further than the Carter Administration to see the error in this logic.

Even the *Washington Post,* which is generally considered to be very liberal in its editorial policy (and, indeed, its news policy), criticized the NEA for <u>Choices</u>, calling it "propaganda."

"This is not teaching in any normally accepted, or for that matter acceptable, sense. It is political indoctrination," said a *Washington Post* editorial. The educrats have very cleverly weaved their propaganda into classroom textbooks. Their message is anti-Judeo/Christian, anti-family, anti-traditional values, but pro-humanist and pro-socialist.

Led by the NEA, these educrats employ a double standard whenever anyone has the audacity to suggest there might possibly be some textbooks that should not be used in the public schools.

Almost on cue, the self-appointed spokesmen for our so-called educational establishment start screaming "censorship." For good measure, critics are labeled "racists," "Fascists," and "fanatics" by these same defenders of "freedom" who put out such literary masterpieces as "How to Deal With Name-Calling."

Such rantings and ravings are designed to intimidate or shame the critics into silence, and unfortunately, for the most part, it works. So the schools meet little resistance as they continue to use a variety of propaganda manuals, like the Choices curriculum as your children's textbooks.

There is an obvious double standard at work here because through the NEA's stranglehold on education they, in essence, control what goes into the textbooks. Content recommendations and selections are made by NEA-controlled teacher radicals (there is always a handful in any school district) who sit on the textbook selection committees. These people are the ultimate "censors," but they are very clever about the way they do it—slowly and subtly so the public will not catch on until the books are entrenched. What could have been done in one fell swoop by a communist dictator through government force is done gradually so that today in America virtually every textbook in use in the public schools that upholds, promotes or teaches basic and traditional values has been censored.

Take the following high school U.S. history text up for adoption in Texas in 1985. It:

—blames President Reagan for the entire increase in the national debt;

—stereotypes conservatives as hypocritical and anti-libertarian, and liberals as compassionate and progressive;

—claims that supply-side economics (free enterprise) discriminates against the poor;

—says "the formation of business corporations" harmed "ordinary working people;" and;

—blames the rise of South American dictatorships on U.S. capitalism.[8]

The educational elite's hostility to America's traditional values is further shown by a constant refusal to permit any voluntary religious activity on school property (even though the taxes of many religious people "bought" that property).

For example:

1) Stein vs. Oshinsky (1965): a U.S. Circuit Court upheld a school principal's order forbidding a kindergarten student from saying silent grace before his meals on his own initiative.

2) Stone vs. Graham (1980): the U.S. Supreme Court held that the posting of the Ten Commandments on classroom walls in public schools is unconstitutional. Forget how appropriate they are in a world history class seeing as they were the first written moral law code in the history of the world.

3) In Dade County, Florida: a federal court blocked the screening of historical films in a classroom. A film based on Jamestown was banned because settlers had erected a cross and a film on Valley Forge was banned because it showed George Washington kneeling in prayer.

As if this is not bad enough, the educats not only permit but encourage the dissemination of their own beliefs—collectivism, one-world government, and humanistic ethics—throughout the school system.

If you doubt me, go to your public school's library and note how few, if any, books there are on such subject matters as the pro-life movement, anti-homosexuality, American patriotism, creationist science, traditional monogamous family values, and so forth. I challenge you to find a children's book more recent than thirty years old that includes in the course of the story a family going to church on Sunday. Instead you will find textbooks expressing atheism and humanism on every subject imaginable. Here is a tiny sampling:

EVOLUTION: "many scientists believe that the apparent relationships are because simple organisms gradually developed into more complex organisms."[9]

SITUATION ETHICS: "There are exceptions in almost all moral laws, depending on the situation. What is wrong in one instance may be right in another. Most children learn that it is wrong to lie. But later they may learn that it's tactless, if not actually wrong, not to lie under certain circumstances."[10]

SEXUAL PERMISSIVENESS: "Delbert and Sally are living together while they are in college. They do not expect to marry . . . they feel that living together provides each with love, affection and support."[11]

COLLECTIVISM: "the Communist government provides many benefits for their workers . . . The governments also provide for health care, long vacations, and old age incomes. Personal incomes tend to be low . . . but expenses are low also. Most older people in Eastern Europe can meet their daily needs without much difficulty."[12]

ONE-WORLD GOVERNMENT OR GLOBALISM: "Many people think a stronger United Nations or a new international organization is needed if we and the other peoples of the world are to move safely into the 21st century. Only a stronger world body, they argue, can meet tomorrow's challenges."[13]

DEATH EDUCATION: "In one program in our little county (Palm Beach, Florida) first graders made their own coffins out of shoe boxes."

"When my daughter was twelve years old, she was given a questionnaire by her seventh grade health teacher without my knowledge or consent. She was asked: 'What reasons would motivate you to commit suicide?' Five reasons were listed from which she was to choose."[14]

These few examples show how the humanist philosophy is spreading its poison through our school system, both public and private (many private schools use the same texts as their public counterparts). For a moment, take a look at the footnotes for the above citations and see which courses seem to contain the more blatant examples of humanism: home economics, English literature, history, civics, geography, psychology and even science. Very few classes or school districts are exempt from humanism. You, as parents, must start from the premise that your child's classroom is not exempt. From there, you must determine to what extent it pervades your child's lessons.

Unfortunately, a careful study of the materials being presented in our public schools makes it clear that our classrooms have turned from centers of learning in which knowledge is imparted to youngsters to centers of humanistic indoctrination where the primary focus is the development of a new social order (socialism).

CHAPTER 3 FOOTNOTES

1. Mayhew and Edwards, The Dewey School, (New York, NY: D. Appleton-Century, 1936; Atherton Press 1965) page 436.

2. John Dewey, Ethical Principles Underlying Education, (Chicago, IL.: University of Chicago Press, 1903) page 12.

3. Samuel Blumenfeld, NEA: Trojan Horse of American Education (Boise, ID.: Paradigm Company, 1984) page 182.

4. Letter to Loyalty Review Board by Attorney General Clark, December 4, 1947. Copies made available by Dr. Paul Busiek.

5. "FBI Intelligence Division Report on: Soviet Active Measures Relating to the U.S. Peace Movement," Department of Justice, FBI, March 1983. Copy made available by Dr. Paul Busiek.

6. Blumenfeld, NEA: page 198.

7. Blumenfeld, NEA, page 199.

8. Our Land, Our Time, A History of the United States, 1985, published by Coronado.

9. Exploring Livings Things, Lardlaw, 1977, Grade 7, Life Science.

10. Inquiries in Sociology, Qllyn, 1972, High School Psychology.

11. Person to Person, Benait, 1981, Grades 6-8, Homemaking.

12. World Geography, Follett, 1980, High School Geography.

13. American Citizenship Program, Scholastic, 1977, High School Civics.

14. Phyllis Schlafly, Child Abuse in the Classroom (Alton, IL.: Pere Margurette Press, 1984) page 371.

CHAPTER 4

SOCIALISM: THE LEAP INTO DARKNESS

Life is a gift of God to man, but the means to sustain that life are not given by our Creator. Instead, man is put into a 'sink or swim' situation. Man must sustain his life by his own devices, and to do this, he must have knowledge.

The function of knowledge is the survival of the individual. Human beings must use their minds rationally to deal with the world that confronts them. But they must have both the intellectual and moral tools to deal with the vast and different situations they will face throughout their lives.

Knowledge is the key not only to mankind's survival but to adding any joy or prosperity with which to elevate himself above the level of an organism whose only concern is survival. It is when man moves past this mere survival instinct that he is able to burst forth and let his creative genius flow and produce the wonders we all take for granted—science, art, music, technology and medicine, to name a few.

The key to mankind's knowledge and flowering is his mind. It is only by thinking and acting upon those thoughts that man can know what will further his life and what will harm it. So, developing one's mind becomes one of the most important tasks facing the individual. This is the primary function of education—to assist man in developing his mind so that he will have the tools to survive in a world in which he must live and function.

The acquisition of knowledge, or the educating process, begins with the individual's birth and ends with his death. As mentioned earlier in this book, individuals learn, or become "educated" many places—in their homes, at work, at play, reading, watching movies or television; almost any human activity imaginable can be a learning experience.

Since no two individuals are the same, yet each must learn to function and survive in a world composed of fellow humans, none of whom think or act exactly as he does, a free social order offers the best opportunity for the individual to develop to his or her maximum ability.

Since a free social order rests on the premise that self-government is the basic government of human order, and that any weakening of or decline of self-government necessarily entails a decline in individual liberty and responsibility and the rise of tyranny and slavery, the need to be instructed in self-government becomes crucial. Self-government ultimately rests on individual responsibility, and the source of any action, responsible or otherwise, is thought. The individual is a minority of one and, as such, is the smallest, the most important minority, and should be, therefore, the most protected of all minorities.

If the life and property of the individual are protected, then the rights of all people are protected—blacks, Hispanics, women, farmers, factory workers and factory owners. Rights for minority groups, however, are a political concept and are usually used as a tool for collectivist social engineers to usurp power or steal wealth by violating the rights of the individual.

Since the individual benefits most from a free social order, his education, especially that learned from the public schools, is supposed to train his mind to cope with demands. Individualistic thinking, responsibility, and a love of liberty are the foundations of just such an educational system.

Unfortunately, today's education, riddled with the socialist philosophy of John Dewey, continually pushed by the NEA, is a disaster for American education and American society for the reason that it does not promote or focus on individualistic thinking.

There are only two choices for mankind: either human beings live

free with their individual liberties, or they live as slaves to big government and its regimentation over the lives of all.

For slavery of the latter type to survive in the United States, Americans must somehow be convinced that tyranny is better than liberty—
and for that to happen, the "convincing" must be handed out in small
increments, a classical case of poisoning by consuming small doses
over a long period of time.

So it is with promulgating a collectivist tyranny on a free society
like America—small doses over a long period of time. And what better
place to start than with small children whose minds are impressionable
when entering the public school system? What more captive audience
do the forces of tyranny have than our public school classrooms?

And that is precisely how John Dewey and his humanist idealogues
began imposing socialistic collectivism upon the American people.
According to Dewey's writings, man is a biological organism completely molded by his environment; and that environment is constantly
changing. Dewey argued that it was useless to teach children any moral
absolutes, such as those found in the Holy Bible, because there are
none.

Dewey rejected all fixed moral laws and eternal truths and principles. He insisted that truth was relative, that absolutes were not admis-
sible and that change was inevitable and desirable. Desirable that is,
if that change could be manipulated in favor of Dewey's philosophy
which encouraged rebellion against religion, capitalism and individualism.

This meant that schools had to be turned into centers for indoctrination of the young—innocuous looking classrooms could be used to
plant the seeds of destruction of our free social order into the innocent,
pliable young minds of America's schoolchildren.

Therefore, the purpose of teachers in Dewey's new system of education was as "social change agents" who would help to indoctrinate
children into the envisioned new social order. Although Dewey raised

a token protest against the term "indoctrinate," it was laughable in the face of his laudatory writings on the subject.

"There is an important difference," he said, "between education with respect to a new social order and indoctrination into settled convictions about that order. The first activity, in my judgment, is necessary."[1] In short, it is not indoctrination if it involves imposing socialism on society. The difference, apparently, is that in the first case, the "new social order" has yet to be created; in the latter case, socialism has become entrenched. So educationally speaking, any question as to whether one referred to it as "indoctrination" or not was moot.

The choice, as Dewey saw it, was either acceptance of his brand of socialism by means of persuasion, or having it forceably established by imposition of a dictatorship. In Dewey's words, "Social planning can be had only by means of approaching dictatorship unless education is socially planned."[2]

Dewey wanted a socialist America but he wanted it by means other than violent revolution. He wrote:

> The Communist Manifesto presented two alternatives: either the revolutionary change and transfer of power to the proletariat or the common ruin of the contending parties. Today, the civil war that would be adequate to effect transfer of power and a reconstruction of society at large, as understood by official communists, would seem to present but one possible consequence; the ruin of all parties and the destruction of civilized life. This fact enough alone is to lead us to consider the potentialities of the method of intelligence.[3]

Dewey's "method of intelligence" involved, of course, the public schools. He claimed that the obstacles to socialism were nasty, old ingrained habits caused by so-called "institutional relationships fixed in pre-scientific age." In other words, old-fashioned individuality and responsibility were among the obstacles to Dewey's socialist paradise.

These obstacles could be removed through education. Individualism had to adapt itself to the needs of collectivism, according to Dewey. He wrote:

> When knowledge is regarded as originating and developing within an individual, the ties which bind the mental life of one to that of his fellows are ignored and denied.
>
> When the social quality of individualized mental operations is denied, it becomes a problem to find connections which will unite an individual with his fellows. Moral individualism is set up by the conscious separation of different centers of life. It has its roots in the notion that the consciousness of each person is wholly private, a self-enclosed continent, intrinsically independent of the ideas, wishes, purposes of everybody else.[4]

If you have any lingering doubts about Dewey's hostility to individualism, then consider this statement: "The last stand of oligarchial and anti-social seclusion is perpetuation of this purely **individualistic** notion of intelligence."[5] (Emphasis added)

Just what would the People's Republic of the United States be like? In spite of NEA propaganda, socialism would be a return to the miserable dark ages of slavery. Life in socialist America would indeed be, to quote the philosopher Thomas Hobbes, "nasty, brutish and short."

Then, just what is the basis and appeal of socialism?

It has a noble-sounding, albeit naive, ethical premise: From each according to his ability; to each according to his need." It almost sounds downright Christian in its idealism—sharing, caring and loving your neighbor is the centerpiece of Christianity. No wonder it strikes a sympathetic chord in a culture having Judeo-Christian roots.

But do not be deceived— it is a <u>dangerous</u> illusion. Socialism is nothing more than the legalized plunder and destruction of society's productive citizens to the resulting misery of all. In a socialist society each individual's needs are secondary to the needs of the state.

Author George Reisman observed in his writings on the subject, "The essential fact to grasp about socialism . . . is that it is simply an act of destruction—it destroys private ownership and the profit motive, and that is essentially all it does. It has nothing to put in its place. Socialism, in other words, is not actually an alternative economic system to private ownership of the means of production. It is merely a negation of the system based on private ownership."[6] Reisman is not alone in his condemnation of the destructive nature of socialism. The great early 20th century economist Ludwig von Mises was well aware of it long before Resiman.

> Socialism is not in the least what it pretends to be. It is not the pioneer of a better and finer world, but the spoiler of what thousands of years of civilization have created. It does not build; it destroys. For destruction is the essence of it. It produces nothing, it only consumes what the social order based on private ownership in the means of production of what already exists.[7]

A look around the globe will demonstrate the reality concerning the destructive nature of socialism. Yet socialism's apologists will vainly protest that true socialism has not really been tried; or that where socialism has been tried, it has been mismanaged or taken over by corrupt men.

Socialism's outcome cannot be any other way, for it simply cannot work, despite the claims of its proponents. They maintain that justice, equality, or whatever else they dream up, requires socialism, and that it is nothing more than a replacement for capitalism and all its alleged inequities, with the state as producer and distributor for all society's goods and services.

Proponents' justifications are usually accompanied by assertions that such a system will distribute goods and services more fairly, more justly, or more equally—whatever buzzwords will gain the required sympathy.

Reality denies the sugar-coated terminology of socialism. Advocates of socialism do little more than to semantically sanitize the use of brute force. This public relations tactic is essential because freedom and property, both of which disappear in a socialist state, can only be taken from the individual in two ways: by consent or by force (or threat of force).

Consent derived from envy is socialism's road to victory, no matter how the heirs of John Dewey may deny it.

The John Dewey's of the world are like the serpent in the Garden of Eden; they want to tempt man into believing he can get something that does not belong to him—something for nothing. Socialism's proponents think private possessions are downright dangerous. They believe, and perhaps understandably so, that possessions have a seductive power: the more you have the more you want.

Having too many possessions may or may not harden our hearts, but the would-be socialist wants to instill a feeling of resentment against the person who has possessions, as well as a feeling of guilt in the man who owns them. Thus the property owner is psychologically assaulted from both sides, by resentment and envy on the one hand and a sense of guilt for his success on the other.

Of the two psychological forces buffeting the individual, the force of envy is the most destructive. Envy is often confused with jealousy and covetousness, which have to do with wanting the possessions and privileges of others. Envy is much worse and much more dangerous. Envy is the feeling that someone else's having something is to blame for the fact that you do not have it. The principle motive becomes thus not so much to take, but to destroy. The object becomes to cut the fellow down to the level, or below the level, of the one who is envious.

Helmut Schoeck's study of envy drives home its terrible social consequences. Envy is the root of socialism, he argues. We cannot understand socialism as strictly the product of covetousness which Schoeck calls jealousy—that is, it is not simply the desire of one group of voters to plunder by legislation a portion of another group's assets. Rather it is the desire to destroy those who are perceived to be better off, better looking, smarter, more privileged, or whatever.

Writes Schoeck:

> It is anguish to perceive the prosperity and advantages of others. Envy is emphatically an act of perception. As we shall see, there are no objective criteria for what it is that stimulates envy. And herein lies the error of political egalitarians who believe it is only necessary to eliminate once and for all certain inequalities to produce a harmonious society of equals devoid of envy. Anyone who has a propensity for envy, who is driven by that emotion, will always manage to find enviable qualities of possessions in others to arouse envy . . . One begrudges others their personal or material assets, being as a rule almost more intent on their acquisition. The professional thief is less tormented, less motivated by envy, than is the arsonist. Beneath the envious man's primarily destructive desire is the realization that in the long run it would be a very demanding responsibility were he to have the envied man's qualities or possessions, and that the best kind of world would be one in which neither he, the subject, nor object of his envy would have them.
>
> For instance, an envy-oriented politician regards a lower national income per capita as more tolerable than one that is higher for all and includes a number of wealthy men.[8]

And it is this envious, destructive mentality, nurturing itself on the nation that claims "wealth is the cause of my poverty"; that is the root appeal of socialism.

When we envy, we rejoice in the misfortune of others. We like to think, or justify our feelings, by rationalizing that they "deserve" to be brought down. The advocates of socialism feed on this feeling. Hitler, for example, was painfully successful in making German people envious of others, particularly the Jews.

So, as we have seen, envy is motivated towards destruction. Socialist policies are geared towards plunder and have nothing to do with capital accumulation or the growth of real wealth.

Envy is also a destructive influence on the foundations of society. If the cultural ethic is the destruction of anyone who owns something which others do not, the result is chaos. If you are fearful of your neighbor's envy, you will not produce. Success and productivity become dangerous, and the whole culture declines. George Gilder, noted economist, is right: "Rather than wealth causing poverty, it is far more true to say that what causes it is the widespread belief that wealth does."[9]

The policies of envy and guilt result in nothing less than class war—the socialist path to his paradise is strewn with the corpses of his victims.

Permeating the destructiveness of envy is violence. The socialist doctrine of economic equality, egged on by the cultivation of widespread envy throughout a society, requires the stealing of property and the denial of economic freedoms. The socialist does not humble himself, he envies. He does not work, he steals. His plea for "equality" is in reality a grasp for power.

The "public policy" programs calling for "structural change" by the socialist require policemen with very physical clout. It is clout consisting of lead bullets, steel bayonets, iron chains and concrete cells.

The socialist may claim he is only calling for voluntary equalization, but he lies. (Which should not surprise anyone. After all, he has demonstrated his willingness to steal. Why should lying pose any moral dilemma to him?) In the end, socialist equalization schemes can only be effected through violence, theft and prohibition of man's freedoms. The possessions of some are taken and "redistributed" to others. It is the force of law directed against the producers, and economic equality becomes nothing more than legalized inequality, with producers getting the short end of the stick.

This is not justice . . . , it is tyranny. It is legalized lawless-ness. Under these circumstances, the state does not claim to be stealing when it adopts socialist policies of plunder. Paul Johnson has well observed, "the destructive capacity of the individual, however vicious, is small; of the state, however well intentioned, almost limitless."[10]

Socialism is inseparable from violence. Regardless of all their professions of peaceful intent, socialists everywhere have had to resort to the use of violence to bring about their goals. Again, there is no alternative. By its very nature socialism empowers the state to regulate people's activities and confiscate people's property—and since most people are reluctant to relinquish what they have earned, violence is required.

Socialism is the trendy Utopianism of the modern age, and all Utopias eventually require violence. As Johnson aptly terms it, "the experience of the twentieth century shows emphatically that Utopianism is never far from gangsterism."[11]

In the first few months of 1918 the Cheka (Lenin's secret police) executed, according to its official figures, only twenty-two prisoners. In the second half of the year it carried out 6,000 executions, and in the whole of 1919 some 10,000. W.J. Chamberlain, the first historian of the revolution, who was an eye-witness, calculated that by the end of 1920 the Cheka had carried out over 50,000 death sentences.[12]

Remember, socialism and gangsterism go hand in hand. Keep this in mind as you consider Johnson's reminder to us that,

. . . the Tsar's secret police, the Okhrana, had numbered 15,000 which made it by far the largest body of its kind in the old world. By contrast, the Cheka, within three years of its establishment, had a strength of 250,000 full-time agents. Its activities were on a correspondingly ample scale.[13]

Examples of socialism's bloody legacy are there for all but the blind to see: Stalin slaughtering millions of peasants in his drive to collectivize agriculture; Mao Tse Tung's massacre of more than 60 million Chinese when he imposed the socialist paradise on China; and more recently we have the example of the socialist spear carrier Pol Pot exterminating half the population of Cambodia, saving only the children which he placed in indoctrination centers (schools) immediately.

Socialism's history is indeed bloody. It is responsible for the most appalling movements in the history of mankind. For those readers who are skeptical of this, I recommend two books: at least one of Alexander Solzhenitsyn's three Gulag Archipelago works and The Socialist Phenomenon by Igor Shafarevich (Harper and Rowe, 1980) should be required reading for anyone wanting to see what kind of society exists under socialism.

How do you feel about your children, America's children, being indoctrinated to socialist thought in our public schools? Do you want to entrust them to the tender mercies of an educational system that is controlled by the purveyors of socialism, and the violence which inevitably comes of it?

Remember, Dewey pursued socialism with a religious fervor, and so does the NEA. Socialism has basically become their new religion, only God has been banished and replaced by the state.

Although Dewey claimed to be a pragmatist and a disbeliever in absolutes, the unavoidable outcome of his thinking was the "absolutization" of the state, which becomes the source of morality and truth. Just as the state becomes Dewey's new religion, so do those attributes of a society—law, morality and justice—become whatever the state says they are. The masses might get justice according to Stalin, morality according to Mao, and law according to Pol Pot.

Socialism as a religion of man has no place for God. Bishop Fulton J. Sheen made the point almost thirty years ago when he told the U.S. Congress about the evil nature of Communism. He said:

There are several reasons why there is no place for God in

Communism. One is because of its concept of freedom. Suppose I correlate the problem of religion and the problem of freedom in answering your question, and let me begin with freedom and then go to religion.

A man is free on the inside because he has a soul that he can call his own. Wherever you have the spirit, you have the freedom. A pencil has no freedom, ice has no freedom to be warm, fire has no freedom to be cold. You begin to have freedom only when you have something immaterial or spiritual.

Now freedom must have some external guaranty of itself. The external guaranty of human freedom is called property. A man is free on the inside because he can call his soul his own; he is free on the outside because he can call something he has his own. Therefore private property is the economic guaranty of human freedom.

Suppose you now concoct a system in which you want to possess man totally. On what conditions can you erect a totalitarian system so that man belongs to you completely? One, you have got to deny spirit; two, you have got to deny property.

That is why the existence of God and private property are both denied simultaneously by Communism. If a man has no soul, he cannot allege that he has any relationship with anyone outside the state. If he has no property, he is dependant upon the state even for his physical existence. Therefore the denial of God and the denial of freedom are both conditions of slavery.[14]

Man will be the servant either of God or of the state. The purpose of God's law is to preserve man from any attempt of either the state or some other idol to become god over man, so that he might bring God's kingdom to society. The logical conclusion of state control over a man's property is the loss of man's liberty, and both result from a loss of faith. The state, to affirm domination over man, must seek to negate Christianity or other theistic-centered religion and private property.

The result is always slavery. Call it what you wish—humanism, socialism, Communism—it does not really matter, for they all necessarily follow upon one another and each results in the same thing—the absolute denial of spiritual and material freedom, hence slavery.

Here are some examples of how this wayward dogma is being presented to your children in the public schools:

ANTI-FREE ENTERPRISE:

"Conclude the activity by pointing out that this breakdown in public morality revealed the need for greater government supervision."[15]

"One of the cornerstones of most socialistic philosophies is the concept of individual freedom, especially the freeing of human beings from the burden of unnecessary and onerous labor in service of profit-makers."[16]

"Develop a skit based upon the need to redistribute land. The main characters should be wealthy land-owners, landless farmers, and government officials. Let each explain how the redistribution would affect them, and have each suggest the possibilities of solving the problem so that all will benefit."[17]

"The Communist governments provide many benefits for their workers . . . . The government also provides for health care, long vacations and old-age income. Personal income tends to be low . . . But expenses are also low. Most people in Eastern Europe can meet their daily needs without much difficulty."[18]

ONE-WORLD GOVERNMENT:

" . . . some people think that the countries of the world must come together under a world government . . . that only with a world government is there a chance of saving the earth for humankind."[19]

" . . . write a constitution for a world government . . . "[20]

"Many people think a stronger UN or a new international organization is needed if we and the other peoples of the world are to move safely into the 21st century. Only a stronger world body, they argue, can meet tomorrow's challenges."[21]

This is the "bright" future that is being preached to our children in the public schools. It is time to wake up parents, before it is too late to save your children from a mindset that will doom them and our society.

How can you know whether or not your schools are trying to turn your children into brainwashed socialists by indoctrinating them with humanist/socialist dogma?

Look at their textbooks and see if the following terms are used in a pro-socialist, anti-capitalist context (as described on the following page). If so, then rest assured your children are being indoctrinated into accepting socialism as the new earthly paradise.

TWENTY COMMON PHRASES MARKING SOCIALISM IN TEXTBOOKS

1) "EQUAL DISTRIBUTION"—to imply taking supply away by force from some in order to give it to somebody else.

2) "FAIR SHARE"—to mean that if you work hard and reap the rewards of your effort what you get is somehow not "fair" because your reward implies your gaining more than your fellow human beings.

3) "CAPITALISM CAUSES INEQUALITIES"—is a dead give-a-way; it implies that rewarding effort and hard work, the fuel of capitalism, is somehow immoral.

4) "POVERTY AND SOCIAL INJUSTICE"—buzzwords for the socialist's ideological premise that one's environment, not one's human mistakes, is the root cause of poverty and/or social injustice. This is an especially insidious concept because it leads one to the concept that one is not responsible for his or her own actions. Used frequently with another socialist buzzword: "social conscience," as opposed to personal conscience.

5) "EQUALIZE"—when used in its social context it means the leveling of all differences among people and the equal sharing of all property and material goods. It should not be used synonymously with their term "equality."

6) "SOCIAL RESPONSIBILITY"—in the socialist context, it means being free from self-responsibilities and is tied in with the concept of the state picking up the responsibilities abdicated by the individual.

7) EXPLOITATION OF THE POOR"—by corporations and business. Capitalism is portrayed as a method of exploiting the weak.

8) "FASCISM"—as synonymous with capitalism and big business.

9) "NEEDS OF MAN"—filled by outside forces such as society or the state.

10) "ACHIEVEMENT"—as though it were the profit-motivated rhetoric of the businessman that, according to the socialists, causes hang-ups and unhappiness.

11) "GOVERNMENT"—as a necessary force to control the people for their own good; socialists arrogantly assume only they know what is in everyone's best interest.

12) "INDIVIDUALISM"—as a destructive motive caused by selfishness; as something to be avoided by each person or prevented in others by force if necessary.

13) "MAN'S NATURE"—designed to be directed by "higher" causes, such as the socialist utopia instead of God.

14) "PRIDE"—as an undesirable state of vanity, egotism and conceit. Often replaced by socialists with the term "feel good about oneself."

15) "MORALITY"—as subjective, with variable, situational rules for serving "higher" causes, such as socialism

16) "THE PEOPLE"—interpreted as the "working class": the group the socialist claims to be working for. In actuality, this "class" is the object of the socialist's coercive, destructive policies.

17) "SELFLESSNESS"—as the ultimate state for man to strive for—i.e., the individual renounces all personal possessions.

18) "TECHNOLOGY"—according to the socialist, it is a major cause of today's problems and misery. It causes pollution, war and waste. It should be slowed, stopped, or eliminated so man can return to nature.

19) "MATERIALISTIC SOCIETY"— used derisively to refer to any thriving industrial-technological society. The socialist's scorn of the materialistic society is done in the same terms as hostility toward technology.

20) "VALUE"—as something relative that can never be defined in absolute terms. A changing entity that varies from person-to-person and culture-to-culture.

****The ultimate humanism, which is socialism, is being spread through education not only in America but throughout the world. Below is an example of the blatant socialist/communist indoctrination which was being taught by the Nicaraguan Sandinista's.

Keep in mind that NEA Resolution I-11 reads:

> The NEA urges the U.S. government to refrain from any U.S. plan for overt or covert action that would destabilize Nicaragua or would adversely affect that government's successful campaign against illiteracy.[22]

The example below is part of what the NEA refers to as their "successful illiteracy campaign" which union officials use as their excuse to support the Marxist regime over U.S. backed contras. These people knew exactly what they were doing.

You would not think simple mathematics, such as addition, subtraction and division, would lend itself to communist indoctrination. But, as you can see, you are wrong. Look at the grade school math curriculum used by the Sandinistas in Nicaragua's mandatory schools.

Examples of Nicaragua's literacy campaign that was endorsed by the NEA

MATEMATICA

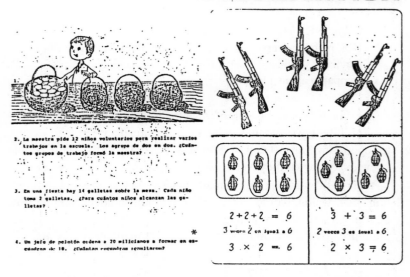

2. La maestra pide 12 niños voluntarios para realizar varios trabajos en la escuela. Los agrupa de dos en dos. ¿Cuántos grupos de trabajo formó la maestra?

3. En una fiesta hay 14 galletas sobre la mesa. Cada niño toma 2 galletas. ¿Para cuántos niños alcanzan las galletas?

4. Un jefe de pelotón ordena a 20 milicianos a formar en escuadras de 10. ¿Cuántas escuadras resultaron? *

$$2 + 2 + 2 = 6$$
3 veces 2 es igual a 6
$$3 \times 2 = 6$$

$$3 + 3 = 6$$
2 veces 3 es igual a 6
$$2 \times 3 = 6$$

* Translation: A platoon leader orders 20 militia men to form in platoons of 10. How many platoons were comprised?

CHAPTER 4 FOOTNOTES

1. John Dewey, Education and the Social Order, (New York: League for Industrial Democracy, 1936) page 10.

2. Dewey, Education, page 13.

3. John Dewey, Liberalism and Social Action, (New York: G.P. Putnam and Sons, 1935) page 84.

4. John Dewey, Democracy and Education, (New York, McMillan, 1916: Free Press Paperback Edition 1966) page 297.

5. Dewey, Liberalism, Op. cit., page 52.

6. George Reisman, The Government Against the Economy, (Ottawa, Illinois: Caroline House Publishers, Inc., 1979) page 151.

7. Ludwig von Mises, Socialism: An Economic and Sociological Analysis, (London, England: Jonathan Cape, 1951) page 458, f. pp. 76ff.

8. Helmut Schoeck, A Theory of Social Behavior, (New York, N.Y.: Harcourt Brace Iovanovich, 1966 and 1970) page 19.

9. George Gilder, Wealth and Poverty, (New York, N.Y.: Basic Books, 1981) page 99.

10. Johnson, Modern Times: The World From the Twenties to the Eighties, (New York, N.Y.: Harper and Row, 1983) page 14.

11. Johnson, Modern, page 708.

12. Johnson, Modern, page 70.

13. Johnson, Modern, page 68.

14. Committee on Un-American Activities, House of Representatives, 85th Congress, Washington, D.C.: G.P.O., 1958. The Ideological Conditions of Slavery, Staff Consultations with Rabbi S. Andhil Fineburg, Bishop Fulton J. Sheen, Dr. Daniel A. Poling, page 11. September 4, 1925; October 18, 1957.

15. A History of the U.S. From 1877, Holt, 1979, HS American History, TG-3, column 2, paragraph 4.

16. Sociology: The Study of Human Interaction, Random House, 1976, HS Sociology, SE-363.

17. "Skill Activities No. 1," Land and People, Scott Foresman, 1983, HS World Geography, SE-534, column 2.

18. World Geography, Follett, 1980, HS World Geography, SE-325, column 1, paragraph 1.

19. United States Government: The People Decide, Science Research Association, 1979, HS Civics, SE-451, column 1, paragraph 4, column 2, line 4.

20. American Citizenship: The Way We Govern, Adison-Wesley, 1979, HS Civics, SE-451, column 2, paragraph 2.

21. American Citizenship Program, Scholastic, 1977, HS Civics, SE-785.

22. NEA Handbook 1984-85, page 248.

CHAPTER 5

JOHN DEWEY'S BEST FRIEND— NEA'S SOCIALIST LOVE AFFAIR

The goal of socialist education has been evident since 1932, when the former chairman of the Communist Party U.S.A. (CPUSA) William Z. Foster predicted that someday all of America's schools will be grouped under a National Department of Education. It took almost a half a century before Jimmy Carter federalized education, thus creating Foster's "National Department of Education," renamed the "Department of Education" (DOE).

John Dewey's dream of socializing American education through the public school system has been greatly enhanced by the NEA. As mentioned frequently in this book, the NEA admits to being a political organization but piously denies it is a far-left group mascarading as a teacher's union which wants to impose socialism and internationalism on the American people.

But what does the evidence say? Let us look at statements from NEA union officials, past and present; let us examine some of the events the NEA has sponsored and attended; and let us hear what socialist and Communist groups have to say about the NEA.

Comrade Foster, wrote that he wanted the "cultural revolution" to be advanced under the auspices of a national department of education (DOE.) As we have seen, ironically, that is exactly the payoff price the NEA exacted from Jimmy Carter for their help in his election win in 1976.

Foster felt that the DOE should be cleaned of religious and patriotic articles which symbolized bourgeois ideology. In his DOE, students would be taught on the basis of the Marxist dialectic in order to familiarize them with new concepts of materialism, ethics and internationalism necessary for survival in his new Socialist society.

We know what Foster wanted for the DOE. What does the NEA want from it? An NEA publication entitled, *Today's Education*, printed an article in a 1976 issue called "A Declaration of Interdependence" by one-world proponent Henry Steele Commager which, more or less, laid it on the line. Among other things Commager said:

> Now we must join with others to bring forth a new world order . . . It is essential that mankind free itself from the limitations of national prejudice. [He means patriotism.]
>
> All people are part of one global community . . . We call upon all nations to strengthen and sustain the United Nations and its specialized agencies, and other institutions of world order, and to broaden the jurisdiction of the World Court. [1]

Some of this appears to be innocent enough, but not when you realize what the NEA surely knows. The United Nations has been dominated, if not completely controlled, by the Soviet Union and its satellites for years.

The NEA calls for the U.S. literally to surrender its independence to the eastern block held U.N. And it audaciously prints this article in the Bicentennial year of American Independence.

It is no wonder columnist Russell Evans views the NEA as the driving force behind this New World Order. They had already swindled a cabinet level Department of Education, which meant they now have complete control over education. In addition, he claims, that the Federal Reserve wants to control the currency, the Trilateral Commission wants to control the economy, the National Council of Churches wants to control religion and such globalism would crush our national sovereignty.

In 1908 the NEA passed a resolution which established high schools as poor man's colleges, rather than preparatory schools, which is what they were always intended to be.

Now none of us would deny that the poor as well as the rich should avail themselves of public education. But the NEA formulation is unmistakably socialist by pitting the rich against the poor.

In 1973, the NEA declared in its 15th Yearbook, Department of Superintendence:

> The present capitalistic and nationalistic school system has been supplanted in but one place—Russia—and that change was effected by revolution. Hence the verdict of history would seem to indicate that we are likely to have to depend upon revolution for social change of an important and far-reaching character. [2]

This socialist interpretation was extended into the 1960s, when an NEA publication, "The Root of Opposition to Federal Aid to Education," noted:

> Under the surface, in reality, it is an economic battle—the classic pattern of historic battles between the haves and the have nots, between those who control the wealth of the land and those who make up the masses. [3]

The brochure continued:

> It is not popular, or even polite, to describe it in these terms. We are all brainwashed from childhood to pretend that the United States has no classes or masses. We are all supposed to

be Americans, believing that capitalism and free enterprise came down to us on stone tablets from the mountain.[4]

Actually, the socialist ideologues of the NEA are completely ignorant of how the free market, free enterprise system works. If they knew, they would understand the economic fallacies inherent in socialism.

In speculating on the NEA's hostility to the free enterprise system, consider the presence of top NEA officials at several meetings and caucuses of socialist groups, such as the Socialist Caucus at the Democratic Party convention in 1980.

The Socialist Caucus was attended by some 250 people who passed a resolution that pledged "to move the Democratic Party beyond the limits of Keynesianism towards an economy that meets social needs through public control." As a prelude to the Socialist Caucus meeting, a convention rally was held at New York's Town Hall; speakers included union activists Caesar Chavez and Douglas Fraser, feminist leader Eleanor Smeal, and the NEA's executive director, Terry Herndon.

The socialistic and communistic tendencies of the NEA's hierarchy do not necessarily reflect the ideological bent of its members. From time to time, a disgruntled member will crawl out from under the NEA's propagandist swill to expose the union for what it really is—a militant, leftist labor union. This was evidenced some thirteen years ago when in early 1977, an NEA document entitled "A Working Economy for Americans" was made public by an NEA member who became frustrated with the NEA's leftist agenda. The NEA publication shows a shockingly blatant hostility towards freedom in the marketplace, economic incentive and capitalism-created jobs.

The NEA states that: "The private enterprise system is in need of change . . . It is long past time for the grabbing, greedy, self-interest which too often characterizes our society today to be replaced by a concern for the public interest. Yet this concern can be realized only through governmental mechanisms."[5]

The NEA's attack on free enterprise is only a part of its leftist crusade. It also routinely attacks patriotism, American defense policy, religion and traditional morality.

Atheist groups have been unable to ignore the wooing sounds coming from the NEA. The anti-religious magazine *The Humanist*, for example, printed in 1983 an article called "A New Religion for a New Age," by John Dunphy. He wrote:

> I am convinced that the battle for humankind's future must be waged and won in the public school classroom by teachers who correctly perceive their role as the proselytizers of a new faith; a religion of humanity that recognizes and respects what theologians call divinity in every human being.[6]

Notice the terms "new faith" and "religion of humanity" which denote that we are talking about humanist religion, the very humanism that is said to be a bogeyman of right-wingers and evangelists.

And what about Christianity? Dunphy believes it should perish in a class-conflict with humanism.

> The classrooms must and will become an arena of conflict between the old and the new—the rotting corpse of Christianity, together with all its adjacent misery, and the new faith of Humanism, resplendent in its promise of a world in which the never-realized Christian idea of "love thy neighbor" will finally be achieved.[7]

Quite simply, a large part of the NEA's final goal for America is a public school system in which Christian values are trampled on and eradicated, humanism reigns supreme, standards of excellence and character give way to standards of egalitarianism and minority rule, and patriotism and national pride are destroyed in favor of globalism and internationalism, where the U.S. bows down to the Soviet-rigged consensus in the United Nations.

Phil Kiesling wrote in the respected liberal publication *The Washington Monthly,* "If Marx and Engels were living in today's America, they would be writing the Education Manifesto. Millions of our citizens are being oppressed, not by the evils of the capitalist system, but by a public school system that is bad and getting worse."[8]

Does all of this mean the NEA is deliberately ruining the schools? Or that they want to see the public school system ruined? The truth is, the NEA could not care less about the state of public education—it is interested solely in power and political objectives. How convenient for the NEA that the effects of their various policies are a degradation of the school system. Because, then, as Kiesling notes, an atmosphere of frustration and repression is created out of which the NEA's goal of revolution may result.

A review of documents put out by the Communist Party U.S.A. (CPUSA) and related socialist and far-left groups shows that these people realize they have an ally in the NEA.

They also realize the way for communism to achieve power in the U.S. is not by working independently, outside the two-party apparatus, for change, but rather for communists to work within the Democratic Party. Since the NEA is also working entirely within the Democratic Party, this makes for real chumminess between education officials and far-left organizers.

Gus Hall, the infamous American Communist, wrote in *Political Affairs,* described as a "theoretical journal of the Communist Party USA," that the CPUSA should work with radical candidates in the Democratic Party in order to achieve its objectives.

The CPUSA had developed a coalition strategy which Hall phrases thus: " Communists should be careful not to appear to be in any way dividing, rather than uniting, those who are against the Reagan forces."[9]

Education was an important part of this anti-Reagan coalition. The NEA itself admits this over and over. It classified Reagan as "an enemy of education." That is because he refused to be pals with the kinds of people who are popular over at the NEA, namely Gus Hall and his comrades.

Interestingly, Hall sees his alliance with groups like the trade unions and the NEA as "a major opportunity to mobilize the whole party to speak to millions through radio, television, newspaper, speaking on college campuses, at rallies and press conferences, and by issuing our own electoral material."[10]

As an example of the success of coalitions containing communists and others in the Democratic Party, Hall proudly cites the march by 500,000 people in New York in June of 1982, which he calls "a milestone for the movement for peace and sanity in our time."[11]

Sanity aside—the peace Mr. Hall refers to is the peace of the grave because that will be the fate of every American's hopes and dreams if he or she succumbs to the lure of socialism.

The blatant support and consistent involvement of the NEA's top leaders in collaboration with socialist organizations, communist front groups and leftist ideologies serves to highlight its leftist bias.

One such case involved former President Reagan's certification of El Salvador as remaining eligible for U.S. military aid in their fight against communist guerrillas. This was done in compliance with a law passed by Congress requiring presidential certification every 180 days. According to the law, the Administration must determine that the government in question is making progress in human rights, in exercising control over its military, in developing its land reform program and in establishing a dialogue for the purpose of both ending civil war and of establishing a democratic electoral process.

Anticipating this decision by the Reagan Administration, the ultra-leftist, Marxist support group called the Committee in Solidarity with the People of El Salvador (CISPES), initiated a number of legislative and press actions in support of the armed Marxist terrorists in El Salvador. Other groups included in the CISPES coalition were the National Labor Committee in Support of Democracy and Human Rights in El Salvador (NLC-ES). Among those prominent leftists listed on the NLC-ES letterhead were Chavez, William Winpinsinger and, then-President of the NEA, Willard McGuire.

The NEA's love for socialism is well documented. For example, in 1982 they were actively involved in a Solidarity Day "Peace Demonstration" in New York City. Evidence now shows the Communist Party U.S.A. was actively involved in organizing and participating in the demonstration, although the news media, which have never really taken Communist activity in this country seriously, presented the occasion as a "rainbow coalition" of peace activists from all walks of life.

But here is Rap Lewis' comment in the official magazine of the CPUSA: "Solidarity Day gave the lie to the most expressed alibi of right-wing union leaders—that the rank and file would not respond to militant initiatives. As a result, the prestige of labor has grown and the influence of the right has declined."[12]

This Communist rhetoric is written in their own jargon, so we must decipher it. "Labor" refers to "committed Communists." The "right" refers to anyone who opposes Soviet foreign policy. "Peace" refers to what the U.S. arms build-up threatens, while the Soviet build-up is said to further peace. Then there is "militant initiatives," which is a common euphemism for Communists meaning "violent revolution."

Gus Hall, presidential candidate for CPUSA, also had some words of wisdom about the Solidarity Day demonstration:

> Our party's indispensable and unique contribution in the struggle for peace and detente' must be the exposure of the Big Lie. We must work more diligently, effectively and creatively in a planned way to break through the barriers of lies, distortions, myths and suppression.
>
> My personal experience on radio, TV, and college campuses

is that once we reach the people with the truth about the Soviet peace policies they respond favorably.[13]

The truth about Soviet peace policies? Here we see the unequivocal pro-Soviet bent of what is being said. It is not the bilateral arms build-up per se that is being opposed, but rather the U.S. arms build-up— strictly unilateral.

In view of this, it was interesting to see Mary Hatwood-Futrell, past-president of the NEA, among those marching in front of the so-called "peace coalition" on Solidarity Day. She stood proudly alongside other prominent leftists like: Donna Brazile, of the U.S. Student Association; Dorothy Height, president of the National Council of Negro Women; Randall Forsberg, founder of the Nuclear Freeze campaign; and Jesse Jackson, perennial presidential candidate who seeks to severely cut defense expenditures.

Immediately following the demonstration, an editorial by then-president Willard McGuire boasted, "In the spirit of solidarity NEA salutes a century of accomplishment . . .

"NEA is proud to be a professional organization. We are also proud to be part of the labor movement and are proud to have joined together with the AFL-CIO, the NAACP, and other national regional organizations—on September 19, Solidarity Day—in protest against the Reagan Administration's economic policies."[14]

And even still, some members of the media will deny the peace demonstration had any Communists.

Just how sympathetic the NEA is to Communism is clearly delineated in a line by a reporter for the Communist *Daily World*, who wrote concerning the 1981 NEA convention: "Nowhere in the basic documents of the NEA, in their resolutions or new business items, are there any anti-Soviet or anti-socialist positions . . . It seems unlikely that the path the NEA is now taking will be reversed."[15] And it has not.

Just how important a role does the NEA play in this Democratic Party-Communist Party coalition? Quoting directly from an article written in *Political Affairs* by Tim Wheeler, who is also a writer for *Daily World*, the CPUSA newspaper:

> The Communist Party candidates for President and Vice President will be a powerful voice in the elections, putting forward a genuine alternative to Reaganism, and will play a unifying role in the anti-Reagan movement. In the course of this struggle, the Communist Party will emerge as a stronger force fighting for the unity of the working class and all oppressed people of the United States, and for an end to exploitation and all the evils of war and racism, through a socialist government that will plan the social, political, and economic life of the nation for the benefit of all.[16]

Immediately following this is a description of the "New Coalition" that the communists will help build, after which is noted: The National Education Association had contributed office space in its headquarters building in Washington.

Excuse me? Did he say the NEA gave office space to a Communist Party coalition organized to help defeat Reagan and establish socialism/communism in the United States? The conclusion is unavoidable. They are either in cahoots with these subversives or are the biggest dupes in the history of politics.

Speaking of being duped: A series of teacher exchanges sponsored by the NEA is very illustrative of its attitude toward socialism/communism and the Soviet Union. Over the last decade, according to NEA literature, the organization has received several delegations from the government controlled, so called "teacher unions" of the Soviet Union.

Even the NEA's peers in the education establishment thought this a poor idea. The American Federation of Teachers (AFT) was quoted as saying, "The Communist governments consider it a great propaganda coup to have their phony 'unions' accepted around the world."[17]

The NEA, on the other hand, has praised these unions and presented their representatives to the education and press communities as legitimate representatives of teachers in the Soviet Union.

The AFT document continues:

> . . . in 1979, the NEA reciprocated by sending an official delegation to the Soviet Union to meet with their so-called "teacher unions." The NEA also attempted to sponsor an official delegation from the "Cuban Teachers' Union" in March of 1981, but visas were denied by the U.S. State Department.[18]

The Soviet News Agency, TASS, used the occasion for a massive propaganda victory telling its citizens the fact that free unions in America recognized unions in Russia meant that unions in Russia must be free. According to a TASS report, "the members of the U.S. NEA delegation were able to exchange opinions with their Soviet colleagues on problems of educating the rising generation . . . and to see for themselves the specific achievements of the Soviets in these fields."[19]

Once again, quoting from the AFT's document:

> The NEA has also opened up its own publication to an uncritical presentation of Soviet propaganda. The NEA national newspaper featured a centerfold interview with Tamara Yanushkovskaya, whom it described as the "USSR's Teacher Union President."
>
> The newspaper article—which was sent to the households of over a million teachers—gave Yanushkovskaya a free hand to set forth the usual propaganda about how well everyone in the USSR is doing and the great progress being made in the school system.
>
> It raised not a word of challenge when she claimed that "according to Soviet legislation, the demands of the trade unions must be met."
>
> The NEA article didn't even hint that Yanushkovskaya

wasn't a legitimate trade unionist. Nor did it point out, as so many Soviet exiles have testified, that the Soviet educational system forces political indoctrination upon children at the earliest ages, allows only one point of view, and encourages children to spy on each other and their parents.[20]

According to Soviet legislation, the demands of the trade unions must be met? Is that why free trade unionists in the Soviet Union are sent to jail or to mental institutions? Of course the demands of official unions are met, because they coincide with the official policy. Are they representative of the Soviet worker or the Soviet people? Of course not.

Vladimir Borisov, a Soviet dissident (exiled in June, 1980 after years of harassment—physical and mental— at the hands of the KGB) explained following his escape from the Soviet Union:

> . . . Russian workers are not free. Soviet unions are not free either. They are just branches of the Government. They work for the State and not for their members . . . By supporting the official trade unions, you give them the respectability they desperately need. By supporting these tools of the Soviet government, you betray the ordinary Russian working man, the very kind of people you claim to represent.[21]

By contrast, the AFT refuses to acknowledge the Soviet's phony unions or their counterparts in other communist countries. It has urged the NEA to cut off its ties with these bogus unions and stop receiving Soviet and Cuban officials.

But in this, the AFT is like the father who asks his daughter to stop dating the car thief. She cannot; her heart has been lost to him. So also the NEA refuses to stop receiving representatives from the Soviet Union and Cuba. Perhaps they represent the vision of the future for the NEA? Here are some examples that may support this.

At the NEA's national convention in Dallas in 1978, the NEA vocally supported the attempt of Hector Marroquin to remain in the U.S. Marroquin was a communist terrorist wanted in Mexico for crimes against the state. He was also a member of the Socialist Workers' Party, an arm of the Trotskyite communists.

When NEA vice-president Willard McGuire announced passage of a proposal calling for Marroquin's visa clearance, several hundred NEA officials applauded. Revolutionary communism does indeed have its adherents in the U.S. Marroquin confirmed this when he openly admitted he was being supported by Angela Davis (Gus Hall's running mate when he ran for President on the CPUSA ticket) and the Communist Party.

Many of the more heinous NEA activities were sponsored under the direction of NEA executive director Terry Herndon, who described himself as a left-wing Democrat. In 1979, Herndon had the NEA give its official endorsement to a TV series on the Soviet Union's role in World War II, called "The Unknown War." So biased and full of propaganda was this 'documentary' that even the *New York Times* cried foul.

The *Times* claimed the series distorted by omission, over-simplification and half truth. It said the film was soft-core propaganda rather than an honest attempt to arrive at historic truth. Nothing, according to the *Times* made this clearer than the fact that it was scheduled to be shown unaltered the following year on Soviet television.

Even Al Shanker, president of the liberal AFT, said 'The Unknown War' was a disgraceful pro-Soviet movie:

> The first program sets the stage by telling us that in the 1930s the quality of life in the Soviet Union was improving. There is no mention of the forced collectivization which resulted in the deaths of more than 10 million Ukranian and Russian peasants from 1931 to 1933, nothing of the purge trials, no awareness of the Gulag Archipelago. The series defends the Hitler-Stalin pact as a clever ploy to buy time to prepare for war—a theory

which does not conform to historical evidence available. The Soviet invasion of Poland in 1939 is whitewashed as a move to reclaim land seized by Poland eighteen years earlier. Lithuania, Latvia and Estonia go unmentioned.[22]

My own suspicion is that the NEA is friendly towards Soviet totalitarianism because it supposes that any opposition to them would stand in the way of the NEA goal of a collectivized world government. The NEA seems to want this above all else. It would do away with our own system at all costs; it wants a benign world order, if possible, but, if necessary they seem to be willing to take a Soviet-controlled totalitarian world order.

It is obvious the NEA lusts after socialism with all its heart and soul. The time has come for us to examine this destructive ideology that has spread such utter misery and destruction whenever it has been imposed on more unfortunate nations.

CHAPTER FIVE FOOTNOTES

1. Henry Steele Commager, "A Declaration of Interdependence," *Today's Education*, NEA, March/April 1976.

2. NEA 15th Annual Yearbook, National Education Association (Washington, D.C., 1973).

3. The Root of Opposition to Federal Aid to Education, NEA, 1967.

4. Root.

5. A Working Economy for Americans, NEA, 1977

6. John Dunphy, "A Religion for a New Age" *The Humanist*, January 1983: page 13.

7. Dunphy, page 13.

8. Phil Kiesling, "The Class War We Can't Afford to Lose," *Washington Monthly*, June, 1982 edition: page 28.

9. Robert Moir, *The Daily World*, June 25, 1981.

10. Moir.

11. Moir.

12. Moir.

13. Moir.

14. Gus Hall, *The Daily World*, June 25, 1981.

15. Robert Moir, *The Daily World*, July, 25, 1981.

16. Tim Wheeler, *Political Affairs*, Washington D.C. July, 1981.

17. The AFT VS. The NEA, Item #31, AFT publication, May, 1983: page 14.

18. AFT, page 14.

19. TASS news release, "Gross Discrimination," February 17, 1981.

20. AFT, page 15.

21. Vladimir Borisov, "An Open Letter to British Trade Unionists," *Free Trade Union News*, July, 1980, page 7.

22. AFT, page 17.

CHAPTER 6

EGALITARIANISM: SOCIAL POLICY OR SOCIAL DEMOLITION?

The next time you hear your child talking about equality, you should be on your guard, for he or she has probably been exposed to the deadly virus of egalitarianism. Pay close attention to them, and if you discover they are advocating a policy of leveling off all people to a status of equality in life, then indeed they have been exposed to the evils of egalitarian philosophy.

Most Americans unanimously accept the concept of equality. But their concepts differ considerably from the purveyors of egalitarianism in the education establishment.

Almost without exception, Americans demand political equality. Equal access of all Americans to partake in the political system raises no argument today. Likewise, Americans demand equality of access to opportunity to participate in the economic and cultural life of America. No wonder the term "equality" strikes such a responsive chord in the American soul.

Unfortunately for most Americans, the education establishment has a different concept of equality called "egalitarianism." But these people, led, once again, by the NEA, are clever in the way they explain their definition. They say it is nothing more than a social philosophy that advocates the leveling of social, political and economic inequalities.

That sounds nice, doesn't it? After all, who could be against social, political and economic equality? But remember, NEA union officials are masters of deception. Reality is much harsher, for what the advocates of egalitarianism neglect to tell you is the heavy handed manner of its imposition.

Once the fog of egalitarian rhetoric is pierced, we see that it is nothing more than a coercive policy of equalizing all mankind to conform to arbitrary, man-made canons of social justice. Stripped of all its fancy nonsense, it is simply a philosophy that works towards eliminating all individual and property rights through government force.

To most of us that sounds like socialism, even though many egalitarians would protest that, unlike socialism, private property would still exist in their ideal society. A closer examination of their philosophy, however, will lay that claim to rest.

Proponents of egalitarianism stress the equal sharing of all property and rights as the central point of their philosophy. But how does the equal sharing of all property give anyone a property right? It does not. If you or I are forced to share with someone else, then none of us having a "share" really owns any part of it. The government becomes the owner, we become the borrowers. This runs afoul of the leveling that is essential to so-called egalitarianism.

The only way to level property is to do away with private ownership. That is socialism. Egalitarianism then must stamp out diversity among individuals and groups, and can only succeed by the imposition of force: totalitarianism.

Why would egalitarianists need to resort to such drastic means? The answer is quite simple: Egalitarianism violates both the nature of man and the universe and can not work in practice, so man must be forced to accept it. Intellectually, it is just about as valid as the view the earth is flat. Like the flat-earth idea, egalitarianism should be tossed in the old intellectual trash heap before it does any more damage to mankind.

Egalitarianism starts to flounder intellectually over the term "equality." Just what is "equality"? If two people both weigh the same, they can be considered "equal" in weight. The only way any two people can be equal in the fullest sense is they must be identical in all their attributes. This is biologically impossible—even identical twins have their differences.

It was the philosopher Rothbard's contention that unless all men are created identically with respect to all attributes, the egalitarian ideal simply cannot be achieved.

Biology, therefore, throws a huge monkey wrench into egalitarian fantasies. This is borne out by biological research which emphasizes more and more the great range of individual diversity throughout the entire human organism.

Instead of equality, mankind is characterized by a high degree of diversity, attributes, differentiation and skills. In short, no two people are alike, thus, no two people are "equal" in the purest sense of the word.

The egalitarian, completely ignoring the reality of the world, instead considers all people—and therefore all groups—to be uniform and equal. Any differences must be due to abstract social and cultural pressures that tend to become media buzz words such as "oppression," "discrimination," "racism," and "sexism." The egalitarian feels that all the world is a clear slate that can be changed at the whim and wish of the human will that is directing the process. In other words, egalitarians claim the world can be changed by the mere wish or fulminations of human beings. The execution of this wish, however, requires a powerful state with a monstrous bureaucracy possessing far-reaching draconian powers over the individual life.

The 18th century champion of liberty and author of <u>Wealth of Nations</u>, Adam Smith, recognized the danger posed by what he called the man of the system—that is, the man who loves the omnipotent state.

> The man of the system is apt to be very wise in his own concert, and is often so enamored of the supposed beauty of his own ideal plan of government that he cannot suffer the smallest deviation from any part of it. He goes on to establish it com-

pletely and in all its parts, without any regard either to the great interests or to the strong prejudices which may oppose it; he seems to imagine that he can arrange the different members of a great society with as much ease as the hand arranges the different pieces upon a chess board; he does not consider that the pieces upon the chess board have no other principles of motion besides that which the hand impresses upon them, but that, in the great chess board of human society, every single piece has a principle of notion of its own, altogether different from that which the legislature might choose to impress upon it. [1]

Smith's comments were made in 1759, but they are just as valid today as they were over two hundred years ago. The egalitarians treat men as objects to be manipulated so as to construct a reality out of egalitarian fantasies.

Smith further blasts the arrogance and single-mindedness of the social engineer. His words fit today's NEA egalitarian proponents to a tee:

. . . But to insist upon establishing, and upon establishing all at once, and in spite of all opposition, everything which that idea may seem to require must often be the highest degree of arrogance. It is to erect his own judgment into the supreme standard of right and wrong. It is to fancy himself the only wise and worthy man in the commonwealth, and that his fellow citizens should accommodate themselves to him, and not he to them . . . [2]

This arrogance is compounded when egalitarians prey upon the guilt of those skeptical victims of their philosophy. The importance of this for the egalitarian cannot be stressed enough. If society can be made to feel guilty, for whatever reason—poverty, racism, sexism—people will be unwilling to withstand the efforts of an enslaving egalitarian state. A guilt ridden society is ripe for conquest.

Guilt promotes passivity and impotence and, as a result, it leads people to believe that state controls are the only solution to a nation's problems. The passive population becomes such that it practically welcomes intervention from the state, and the egalitarians are only too happy to comply.

And so the pliant masses, having been primed by years of egalitarian indoctrination in the public schools (as evidenced by your child's sudden concern and advocacy for various equalization schemes), wind up manipulated by their own feelings of envy, guilt and despair into surrendering control of their lives and going into the bondage and misery that an egalitarian state produces.

Simply stated, then: The utopian doctrine of egalitarianism requires the stealing of property from men and women (often under the guise of taxation) coupled with the denial of economic and personal freedom.

Despite protests to the contrary, the egalitarians' "peaceful intentions" amount to perpetrating their brand of utopianism through violent revolution to bring about their goals. It cannot be otherwise. The very nature of egalitarianism—that the state be empowered to regulate people's activities and confiscate property in the name of "equality"—demands violence.

The notion that imposition of egalitarianism requires violence has been voiced by many. The tens of millions butchered by Hitler, Stalin, Mao and Pol Pot, all in the name of an alleged equality to produce an egalitarian-socialist utopian society, should convince even the most dubious.

There remains one more gruesome event that is theoretically possible under egalitarianism which should show the ultimate nightmare in egalitarian thought.

Today, it is medically possible to take the organs of the dead and transplant them into living people, thus restoring them to health. Kidney, heart and corneal transplants immediately come to mind. Now, according to egalitarianism, this poses a social problem. Should we wait until a person's death to cut out his eyes, for example, when other men need them? According to the tenets of egalitarianism, should we not regard everybody's eyes as public property and devise a fair and equal method of distribution? Would it not be true to their wayward dogma to advocate taking out one of a living man's eyes and giving it to a blind man, so as to equalize both? The concept, gruesome as it may seem, nevertheless reflects egalitarianism to its philosophical core.

Moreover, egalitarianism is not a noble social experiment. It is a bloody, repressive tyranny and for it to be indoctrinated into our youth in the public schools is nothing short of criminal. The downtrodden of the Eastern block are overcoming their oppressors, now it is time for us to do the same.

CHAPTER 6 FOOTNOTES

1. Adam Smith, Wealth of Nations, (Canada: Random House, 1937) page 214.
2. Smith, Wealth, page 214.

CHAPTER 7

NEA—VOODOO EDUCATION

Imagine the educational bureaucracy in Washington, D.C., being controlled by persons with views and policies directly opposed to your own—in the areas of child-rearing, family decisions and religious beliefs. It sounds like waking up from a nightmare where America has been taken over by a totalitarian regime and the golden age of democracy has ended. The pathetic truth of the matter is that this has become a reality—it is happening today in the 1990s. One look at our public schools is proof enough.

The question most often posed is, when did parents and conscientious legislators relinquish control of their children to the educational gestapo?

We have already discussed the power of the NEA and their political payoff for helping to get Jimmy Carter elected—the Department of Education.

When this occurred, two major changes took place:

1) the state affiliates of the NEA lost most of their clout when the bulk of their power was transferred to the national headquarters in Washington, D.C. and,

2) the already overpopulated staff at the NEA's national office was expanded and began to play a more aggressive role in creating and implementing the NEA's liberal national policies. With the NEA's acquisition of a national Department of Education (DOE), it has made terrifying gains towards complete control of education and political ideology in America.

Gordon Drake of Christian Crusade believes the NEA has created a school system in which "our children are being indoctrinated for a new collectivist world government."[1] Or, as former DOE Secretary Terrell Bell puts it, a "global world concept."

Economist Milton Friedman put it best when he said public schools are the only bastion of socialism in a sea of free enterprise in America.

Where are the men and women of good conscience and common sense—parents and teachers—who should have been heard across this land long before now on this vital issue of who has control of the children? They are part of the giant groundswell of concerned citizens who are demanding accountability and change from the public school system.

Is there any existing proof, other than speculation, for such serious allegations against the NEA hierarchy? The supporting evidence is as close as your own community school and the NEA's own literature. Take the NEA's "Model United Nations" curriculum where high school seniors are taught that free enterprise is the cause of poverty in developing countries. Wouldn't the Founding Fathers love that one! What the children do not learn is what most of us accepted long ago— on most key global issues the United Nations distorts reality. Instead, these students learn it is the U.S. who distorts reality and even exacerbates global tensions.

In this widely used NEA-promoted curriculum, the United Nations is presented as the accurate reflection of global reality instead of the pro-Soviet forum whose primary function is to deprive the U.S. of freedom and democracy.

Consider the NEA's liberal proselytizing on nuclear war. Phyllis Schlafly says of the NEA's anti-nuke curriculum, Choices, "Choices portrays the U.S. as instigator of virtually every new arms race development. The U.S.'s 'action' caused the Soviet's 'reaction' in 1954 when America developed the first hydrogen bomb and the subsequent development of the Soviet's in 1955. In truth, the U.S. actually delayed the development of the H-bomb from the late 1940s on and

rushed production in 1954 when we learned the Soviet's were dangerously close to deploying their own."[2]

When the NEA was confronted on the use and dissemination of this
curriculum guide, they claimed to have only made the program available through their catalogue. In fact, the program was sent to at least
48 junior high schools as a pilot program and made its way into many
high schools throughout the nation.[3]

The NEA and its counterparts refuse to be responsible in the field
of curricula development. Instead, they choose to feed children's fears
by scaring them to death with a gloom and doom philosophy in the
guise of responsible curriculum.

Do parents prefer that their children be taught pacifism instead of
defense, and the false notion that the U.S. is as guilty as the Soviets
as a threat to world peace?

Of course not, and the NEA knows this, so they were not consulted.
The education establishment has always been certain it knows what is
best for our children, and assumes that we do not.

When the educrats teach our children a 'better Red than dead' philosophy, they obviously do not understand that 'where there is no vision, the people perish'; and, conversely, where there is a vision,
Americans must be prepared to sacrifice life. That is also why the lure
of peaceful co-existence is a dangerous socialist technique of subver-
sion. Consistently, the Soviet strategy has been to persuade non-so-
cialist leaders that co-existence with socialism is the only open course
to a free world.

We must view Gorbachev's *glastnost* and *perestroika* policies in the
context of the Soviet's bloody past and continual repression of their
own people. Many Americans have completely accepted Gorbachev's
policies as proof of long-term change in the Soviet Union and I pray
they are right. But, I am a student of history and one thing history
teaches you is how hard it is for a leopard to change its spots and how
only time is the true indicator of how sincere a country, it's leaders
and policies really are. In other words, if a person has been holding a

gun to your head for forty years with the trigger cocked and suddenly uncocks the trigger but leaves the gun at your head, that hardly removes the threat. When every country in the Soviet controlled Eastern bloc institutes democratic reforms which include free elections, open borders and private ownership of property, then, I will take Gorbachev completely serious.

How should a history teacher approach the teaching of the Soviet role in history? By telling the truth! Armed with the facts about the history of Russia, students can make informed, educated decisions, and opinions on the future of the Soviet Union and it's relationship with the United States.

It is no coincidence the NEA's ideology so closely parallels that of socialist philosophy. An NEA booklet for use in public schools by teachers in 1977 states:

> The private enterprise system is in need of change. It is long past time for the grabbing greedy, self-interest which too often characterizes our society today to be replaced by a concern for the public interest. Yet this concern can be realized only through governmental mechanisms.[4]

Givens then recommended "taking them over and operating them at full capacity as a unified national system in the interest of all people."[5].

That, my friends, is exactly how things are done in the socialist paradise: the Soviet Union. All rational people know how bleak and harsh life is there. Yet the NEA wants to import that misery and impose it on American society.

The NEA's disdain for America's free market economy is mild compared to that of certain other educational activists, such as John Boyles. In late 1977, in *Educators Newsletter* (a Washington based bulletin) Mr. Boyles, the editor, commending the collectivist nursery schools of Eastern Europe, further boasted, "There appears to be no alternative to acknowledging that we have created a way of living in which public employees will perform a significant fraction of functions traditionally left to families."[6]

He went on to remark that "Marx, and other theoreticians of social change—Lenin, Ghandi and Mao Tse-Tung—have all spoken of the necessity of destroying the traditional fabric of family life in order to accommodate the needs of society undergoing economic transformation."[7]

With seeming regret, Boyles noted that some teachers and administrators resist new custodial functions for the schools. They can not hold back the tide, he claims: "The day is therefore fast approaching when the schools will be acknowledged for what they are becoming, society's agreed upon vehicle for institutionalizing social change."[8]

He proceeded to outline some details of this cheerful prospect. In the school system of the future, all children will be automatically enrolled at birth, in an Infant and Child Health Program. At age two, they will become eligible to attend standard day-care programs. School age children will attend from nine to five daily, plus optional custodial care. (This was Daniel Ortega's system in Nicaragua, when I visited in 1987.) "Preventative medical care and immunization services will be provided at all schools as part of a comprehensive national health system."[9] Legislation introduced in the past few years has borne an alarming resemblance to that program. One example is teen health clinics, in which children are allowed to obtain free birth control devices.

Schools, meanwhile, will be integrated with other community services.

Curriculum and programs in schools will come more and more to reflect long-range planning goals of the Central Bureaucracy. Thus, if the Administration adopts "collective consciousness" as a national goal, there may well be a federally-mandated educational program . . . in every school in the nation.[10]

More of the let-us-love-Big Brother theme, is exhibited as America's schools become "part of a comprehensive human services system which fulfills many of the functions traditionally assumed by the family."[11]

It is hard to believe that such dangerous and radical legislation and ideology could occur today in our Constitutional Republic. After all, haven't Republicans held the White House for the last ten years with good prospects of holding it for at least another six more?

It is even harder to believe that much of this socialist dogma is being forced-fed to our children without parental knowledge or approval. But remember, twenty five years ago, it was next to impossible to believe that Congress could create such an incipient totalitarian structure as the Department of Education with so little concern voiced by the citizenry.

Our apathy and passivity towards danger have been repeatedly observed by one qualified to speak of such things, Russian dissident Alexander Solzhenitsyn. He refers to apathy as a disease of the will of a prosperous people. Must we become a terminal case before we comprehend what centralization of power in government does to that government and to the freedom of the people living under it?

Make no mistake about it, federalizing the control of education in the United States was a gigantic step in the direction of a socialist state. It was a drastic departure from our tradition and constitutional concepts of the role of the government in education. It deserves far more attention, far more concern, than it has yet received.

Under DOE authority, an essential cog of socialism—the centralized control of education—has been set in place. The federal education bureaucracy in Washington, D.C., now immeasurably strengthened, and well-funded, is in a position to dictate even more radical approaches in the area of early childhood education and development. It has proven capable of subverting rapidly—and in a variety of ways—

the constitutional and traditional American ideal that the family has the primary role and responsibility for child-rearing and development.

The pernicious effect of federal aid to education and early childhood development lies, not chiefly in the vast bureaucratic expenditures we have seen, but more significantly in the federal control which inevitably accompanies this funding.

That the federal education establishment led by the NEA has repeatedly voiced interest in using the schools for 'social change' adds to the reasons for concern over the content of federally funded programs. In fact, in 1973, the Office of Education (OE) awarded the Rand Corporation a large grant to evaluate some of OE's "change agent" programs. This study indicates the importance which the federal thrust in this direction has assumed.

Dr. James Koerner, in his book, <u>Who Controls American Education?</u>, says this about the schools and social change:

> In a series of actions over the last dozen years the federal government in all three branches has made clear its conviction that the lower levels of government are unable, for whatever reasons, to cope with the civil rights movement and a number of other urgent problems. Most of these federal actions involve American education in one way or another. The central government has apparently decided that education is to be one of the chief instruments for solving all sorts of social and economic problems.[12]

The education theorists, individuals who are often less concerned with what and how children learn than with what kind of Utopian worlds the schools can produce, spoke in the 1930s concerning the importance of educating the "total child." Giovanni Gentile, Benito Mussolini's Minister of Education, spoke of "humanizing" education and furthering "cooperation" through the schools.

Today the schools of Communist China promote the idea of subordinating the individual to the interests of the state.

All these ideas are based on the belief that by changing the children, one shapes the world. The similarity of these philosophies to our own federal aid program lies in the elimination of the original goal of the schools as places of instruction. Once the schools are viewed as tools for something other than this original purpose, instruction, then the schools are serving not the goals of education for the individual, but rather the process of social engineering for Utopian dreamers. This notion is dangerously similar to the social tenets espoused by Mao during his frightening Cultural Revolution.

The educator's intention to intrude into the mental and social problems of a child to the point of total usurpation of parental rights is further made clear by the 1969 Report of the Joint Commission on Mental Health and Children, which served under the auspices of the federal government. The report read in part:

> Schools must begin to provide adequately for the emotional and moral development as well as their development in thinking. The schools as the major socializing agency in the community, must assume a direct responsibility for the attitudes and values of child development. [13]

The child advocate, psychologist and social technician should all reach aggressively into the community by sending workers out to the children's homes, recreational facilities and schools, according to the Commission's report.

It was through the use of federal aid that those who view the school as an instrument for social change acquired a firm enough grip on local school districts and the content of education to realize some of these goals. The availability of federal funds for research grants has also stimulated an interest in social engineering in the schools, sometimes to the extent that it seems the educators are actually creating mental health and social problems in order that they may later apply for another grant to devise a plan for solving the problems they deliberately created.

In order to understand the devastating effect the DOE has had on the education of our children, it is important to probe into the motivating philosophy of those forces which feed at the government trough. These forces include the multitude of educrats employed at DOE and an army of educationalists and behavioral scientists who are grant recipients from DOE. The vested interests of the NEA are intertwined with the institutionalized vested interests of the other two groups.

With the NEA's reward of the DOE, they quickly became the self-proclaimed spokesman for the educational establishment.

In early 1977, Mr. Richard L. Harris, a school superintendent in Phoenix, Arizona, became so disturbed at the NEA's power drive the he made public a letter describing what the NEA means to do to America's economic structure. He enclosed with his letter a page of excerpts from the NEA document "A Working Economy for Americans." They included: "For the government offers the only real potential for controlling and guiding the corporate sector, one capable of controlling and channeling corporate activity so as to meet human needs; and the growing problems of our society . . . intensify the need for a government role in restructuring and regulating the economy."
14

In essence, educationists, led by the NEA, have assumed they are to decide what changes are needed in society and teachers are to accomplish these changes by acting as 'social change agents'.

Textbooks, audio-visual materials and curricula are being developed to implement the NEA's ideas and changes, in the majority of cases, without the inclusion of parents and citizens in the decision making process.

Whereas, we once naively believed the battle for the children was fought simply between the elitists and grassroots Americans, a new factor has come into play. Our schools have become the educrat's testing ground for an "Americanized Socialist system."

Have parents and teachers in the United States been duped by the "aesopian tactics" of socialist activists? Has Soviet-style control taken the place of local control as the backbone of American education? The facts speak for themselves.

The DOE was intended to be and is increasingly, a puppet, with the NEA pulling the strings. The appointment by President Reagan of conservative William Bennett to replace Secretary Terrell Bell slowed that process but with an entrenched liberal bureaucracy, even Secretary Bennett had a tough time getting control of his own department. The NEA has swung its full weight into the world arena of politics and has become the prime vehicle of the radical left to gain political control of government by defeating those who oppose their views. Mary Hatwood-Futrell, former NEA president, said in 1982:

> There's no alternative to political involvement. Instruction and professional development [of teachers] have been on the back burner to us, compared with political action.[15]

The NEA has proved their commitment to influencing electoral politics with their hefty donations (over $4,000,000 in 1988 alone) to liberal candidates and mobilization of their more militant members to lobby Congress and elect or defeat candidates of the Left's choice. As noted author, Sam Blumenfeld, reminds us, the NEA is organized nationally, statewide and locally. They run like the well-oiled political machine they are. Their primary objective is to defeat supporters of traditional American values and substitute socialist stalwarts in their places. Without proponents of traditional educational values in their way, the NEA will be completely successful in turning American education into anti-American indoctrination.

CHAPTER 7 FOOTNOTES

1. Christian Crusade newsletter, Gordon Drake, Editor, (Washington, D.C.: Spring 1977 edition,) page 2.

2. Choices: A Unit on Nuclear Conflict, (Washington, D.C.: NEA publication, 1983) page 44.

3. *West Palm Beach Post,* March 21, 1983.

4. A Working Economy for Americans, 1977, page 21.

5. Working, page 21.

6. Educator Newsletter, Ernest Boyer, Editor, (Washington, D.C.: December 1977) page 4.

7. Educator, page 4.

8. Educator, page 4.

9. Educator, page 5.

10. Educator, page 5.

11. Educator, page 5.

12. Dr. James Koerner, Who Controls American Education?, (Beacon Press, 1968) page 168.

13. Report of the Joint Commission on Mental Health and Children, 1969, (Washington, D.C.: U.S. Government Printing Office).

14. Working, page 21-23.

15. *Los Angeles Times,* interview of Ms. Futrell, July, 1982.

CHAPTER 8

SECULAR HUMANISM: GIMMICKERY AND QUACKERY IN THE CLASSROOM

J acque Barzun once wrote a book called, <u>Teacher In America</u>, which was critical of the sorry state of the public education system in this country. In fact, he came down very hard on the public school system, terming them a "marsh land" where learning has been reduced to a competition between violence and ignorance.

The humanist's chickens have come home to roost with a vengeance. A lot of what Barzun was referring to is the direct result of the humanistic attitudes towards the schools. They treat them as nothing more than laboratories in which the unsuspecting children are reduced to human lab animals being subjected to the current social experiment that is fashionable among NEA educrats.

Of course, the NEA would never admit this, especially to parents. Instead they treat every latest education fad as a "progressive" new method of education. Clever devils, are they not—<u>who</u> can protest progress? Unfortunately, we have seen thirty years of their progress and it simply does not work. Give the devil his due—they will not admit it does not work, but they are always willing to try something new.

So-called progressive education is really the story of lunatic schemes, endless pseudo-reform, so-called breakthroughs—each introduced with much fanfare and kept afloat by media hype before quietly sinking into the sunset. New Math, Bilingual Ed, Open Classrooms, Head Start—and the worse it gets, the more they come up with. It would be almost laughable were it not for the frequency their lunacy is translated into government programs calculated to further separate man from his wallet. If you can swallow one or two ridiculous premises, you will find everything they say or do totally justified.

Let us take a careful and critical look at one such extreme example. They are debating what to call it—black English, "Ebonics" or "Ebony English" but the bottom line is that some linguists got together and came up with the bright idea of teaching black slang as "a language inherently as sound as standard English" so that by using bilingual education techniques, they could eventually teach black children standard English.

This brainstorm, initiated by Orlando Taylor, dean of Howard University's Communication Department passed the California state legislature on two different occasions. Governor George Deukmejian had the good sense to veto the proposed legislation both times.

If the whole thing sounds mindless, that is because the mind has nothing to do with it. Forget that this insanity would cost taxpayers millions of dollars.

It has nothing to do with the continuing poor performance among black children even though 1988 test scores showed black children had improved marginally on reading and writing skills. Some "experts" seem to think the reason black children continue to lag behind their white counterparts in academic achievement goes back to the vernacular, or dialect, that much of the black urban community speaks. So, instead of stigmatizing black children by giving them the idea their English is substandard, or telling them they have to stop saying things like "he be goin' to school," it was decided that black English would be incorporated into the school curriculum with the expectation that the children will then be more receptive to learning standard English.

Wonder of wonders! After twenty years of censoring Stephen Foster songs, banning the showing of Amos 'N Andy," and working to re-move "racist imagery" from <u>Huckleberry Finn</u>, out of deference to the black self-image, we are now told the way to improve the reading skills of both blacks and whites (there is no mention of white children being excluded from the program) is to have the youngsters tutored in "Ebonics," or Ebony English.

As we shall see, the liberals' logic is impervious to argument, and their arguments are impervious to facts—Fact Number One being a 1985 Public Opinion survey which showed that 77 percent of black Americans <u>rejected</u> the notion that minorities should be given prefer-ential treatment; 82 percent thought that if a young black person works hard enough he or she can usually get ahead in this country, despite existing problems like prejudice and past discrimination; and nearly half felt that black leaders (whom the liberal media chooses to ac-knowledge as such because they make their living attacking the exist-ing power structure) speak only for a minority of blacks in the United States.[1]

Fact Two: The biggest source of resistance to the black English pro-gram has been none other than middle-class blacks, who believe the program contributes to stereotyping; in other words, those who have overcome it are irritated that a vernacular associated with ignorance is being highlighted in their children's classrooms.

Fact Three: Even if there were a basis for comparison between lim-ited or non-English speaking foreign children and American blacks (as the liberals maintain), that cannot possibly explain how Italians, Dutch, Persians, and, more recently, Vietnamese children—who also go home to non-English speaking families—have managed to over-come their language deficiencies while black children's have suppos-edly remained the same all this time.

Liberal arguments in favor of the black English program are simi-larly flawed. Argument One: Because black dialect transcends geo-graphical state boundaries, and because blacks often shift between standard English in professional settings and black English in social settings, the black child, regardless of his family's economic status, is made more vulnerable to learning problems.

If this were true, then the Vietnamese child would be similarly hand-icapped—along with the Italians and Greeks and Armenians. If the argument were valid, then every child whose family uses slang in the social setting would be at risk educationally. It would mean Texans like me, who typically mouth such gems as "When do ya reckon y'all will be up this way a'gin?" would all spend their lives doing janitorial duty.

The only sensible way to handle the problem of substandard English is to teach the black child that slang is substandard English—anybody's slang. Then you teach him that slang is generally not the language of the business or professional setting and that it is not expected in more formal social settings either. You teach him standard English, by means of exercises and grammar drills. Critics can argue they are boring but boring or not, that is how proper English becomes "internalized," or made a usable part of one's knowledge.

Argument Two: If black children feel their own language is inferior, they just will not say anything to us. You have to consider their self-perception.

What kind of self-perception are these children going to have when they can not get a professional job? When people they would have liked to have as friends run the other direction because of the way they speak?

The way to handle the problem of black perception is to find black role models they can really look up to—professionals who have left their dialect and other cultural challenges behind and have gone on to become successful in their fields. There is a wealth of these professionals around today, and black children need someone other than Prince and Sheena to serve as models of success. If money is to be spent, get these professional black people out to these schools speaking, counseling and talking to the youngsters. If buses are to be used, bus these children for a few days each term into professional settings where successful black people are working so they can see just what they, too, can achieve. Too many black children have the impression that unless they are in sports, the entertainment field or drugs, they can never succeed financially.

Argument Three: You have to take a child in school just the way he is, not the way you would like him to be. Therefore, you must accommodate black dialect—especially in places where a full 10 percent of the students are speaking this non-standard English when they first enter school.

Show me a four-year-old who speaks "standard English," black or white or polka dot. Should we come up with a special program to accommodate baby talk, too? Or how about special courses to eradicate "Valley girl" speech, with its frequent repetition "for sure, for sure."

The problem is slang. Most white children, at some point in time, come around to the idea that there is good reason to abandon their slang. With television, movies and popular magazines, most children figure out when slang is being used and when it is not. The difference is that too many black children are not motivated to drop their slang.

This is not a question of race—black versus white. It is a question of proper versus improper grammar. And who decides what is proper? The body politic.

Of course the liberals are simply worried they will eventually lose their ability to pit racial and economic groups against each other. Lord help us if we should all begin to mingle naturally. Minorities need to realize that their true enemies are these liberals who wear their sensitivity on their sleeve as they pass and promote programs which do more to keep minorities in bondage than Simon Legree ever hoped to do. A recent example of how politicians exploit minorities, blacks in particular, as pawns in their political machinations, was the Bork nomination to the Supreme Court in which Senator Ted Kennedy intentionally and grossly misrepresented Judge Bork's record on civil rights in order to enrage minorities and enlist them in the cause against the nomination.

But let us continue on with our look of at the havoc which has been wreaked on our public education system by giving the liberals a free hand over the past twenty years. A brief history of "progressive education" will put the problem in better perspective.

Motivating techniques have always been popular with the liberals, the NEA in particular. Some bright ideas for motivating students include rock music in math classes, spicy role-playing experiments, and even a mock kidnapping. "Experts" have long since told teachers that grades are "dehumanizing," lecturing "passe," tests "traumatizing and stigmatizing," homework "undermining to family life," red, pencil markings "impersonal," and competition "damaging to the learner." If not for the disastrous consequences these have had, one would be tempted to laugh at the absurdity of the logic involved here.

In the 1940s and 1950s a "good school" used progressive methods based on student interests and activity projects. After the Soviets launched Sputnik in 1957, a "good school" was defined as one with high academic standards and special programs for gifted children, especially in the areas of math, science and foreign languages. By the late 1960s, the once high standards started to fall, and the "good school" became one where student participation and choice were emphasized. Since the mid- 1970s, parents and other brave souls started demanding that the educational pendulum swing back towards basics, standards and a coherent curriculum—away from the free-wheeling experimentation of the 1960s and 1970s.

Why all the faddism? Why the constant shift from rigorous standards in one decade to spontaneity and student interests in the next?

Our educational faddism stems from a deeply ingrained conviction among the liberal elite of the education establishment that the best way to reform society is to reform the schools. Abraham Lincoln once said, Whoever controls the philosophy of the schools, controls the political philosophy of the following generations.

Liberal meddling has shown that awareness of a social problem typically leads to the creation of a new school program, usually funded by the federal government! For example, to curb the rate of high traffic fatalities, driver education curricula were devised; to curb the rising rate of divorce, new courses on "Family Life" and "Single Living" were implemented; demands for racial integration were met with forced busing. So, American education has been the victim of programs aimed at societal change, which of course depends upon he social, political and economic climate of the country.

The educrats insist our schools be relevant to the needs of our society. A major problem is that those needs are determined by those same educrats which makes them predictably liberal. This has provoked intense struggles between groups with different views—parents and concerned citizens, in particular. Granted, there has been a certain amount of tension generated within the ranks of the education profession itself. The 20th century has seen the development of a new class of education policy makers and theoreticians who were not primarily classroom teachers.

As the profession became more involved in its role as social change agent, its leaders looked for more ways in which they could make significant contributions to solving social problems, paying no heed to the destruction of the nation's moral fiber in the process. Unlike the classroom teacher, who had little time or reason to wonder whether the study of history or literature would change society, the growing number of elitists in the education establishment's ranks—schools of education for would be teachers, city and state education departments, and professional associations and unions—interminably debated how to change the schools in order to serve society and to better address their own hidden agenda.

There has always been heated debate within the ranks on how schools should meet this societal responsibility. Historically, the debate has raged between the progressive educators of the John Dewey school and the traditionalists. The progressives argue that professional educators must be the ones to determine how to fit the individual to society and design their course offerings accordingly; traditionalists, on the other hand, contend that the only way to reform society is by making individuals more learned.

The traditionalist idea—that the central purpose of education is to increase students' intellectual powers—dominated American schools until the thirties. The Depression was significant because it allowed Dewey's progressive/socialist philosophy to make significant inroads into the education profession. When the Depression hit, it destroyed the job market for adolescents, thus swelling the enrollment in high schools. Many young people who would have gone on to work, stayed in schools instead. This abundance of students in our nation's school due to the economic situation was the perfect vehicle for dissatisfied liberals who wanted to change the academic structure.

The progressive philosophy, which argues that a school is a minia-ture society that defines what the larger society should be, encourages broadening the curriculum for a new brand of student. Thus, under the influence of progressivism, many schools introduced vocational and personal service courses at the expense of academic offerings.

After World War II, this kind of progressivism became known as "life adjustment education," and the liberals became the major force in American education. Principals boasted that their programs ad-justed students to the demands of real life, freeing them from dry ac-ademic studies. The new curricula centered around vocation, leisure activities, health, personal concerns and community problems. Exam-ples included "Developing An Effective Personality" or "Personal Im-provement," where junior high students learned what color of nail pol-ish to wear and how to improve their appearance.

Do not get me wrong. I am a proponent of vocational education for the simple fact that I do not believe that college is for every student. (Not because every student does not have the ability but because every student does not have the commitment and maturity to stick to a course of study for four years.) I believe vocational education is best served by requiring vocational education students to pursue an academic track simultaneously with their vocational schedule. What good does it do if someone can fix your hair or your air conditioner but they can not write well enough to make out an invoice or count well enough to make change?

Since the public never fully understood why these innovations were introduced in the first place, and why parents were not included in the decision-making, some communities became embroiled in heated political controversies. As a consequence, many parents began withdrawing their children from a public education system that had become unresponsive.

By the early 1950s, "life adjustment education" had been introduced in many school districts across the nation, and it became the target of ridicule by scores of critics, including laymen and informed parents. They charged not only that life adjustment education was conformist and anti-intellectual, but that it was also undemocratic because it provided academic studies only to college-bound students. Our schools were failing to equip youngsters with intellectual power, feeding them instead a poor diet of vocational training and watered down academics. Robert Hutchins, Chancellor of the University of Chicago, charged that the schools were integrating their program because students have so many needs. Perhaps the greatest idea that America has given the world, Hutchins said, is the idea of education for all. The world is entitled to know whether this idea means that everybody can be educated, or only that everybody must go to school.

Although progressive educators defended their programs and charged that the critics were reactionaries (out of touch with the modern world), the launch of Sputnik finished the debate, at least for the moment. Almost overnight, the nation became obsessed with the failure of the schools. School boards hastily installed new programs in math, science and foreign languages.

The post-Sputnik effect was almost immediate. Enrollments in foreign language classes rose and more teachers were trained in the areas of science, math and foreign languages. Schools modernized their labs and courses of study were rewritten substantially to reflect recent advances in scientific knowledge.

By the time the new curricula were ready for use in the classroom in the mid 1960s, however, the furor over Sputnik had abated. The calls for academic excellence had faded away, drowned out by the rising tide of social conflict in the cities and the disorders on college campuses.

The contemporary climate of social unrest, racial tension, and anti-war protest produced a new wave of critics and reformers, who—keeping with the liberal tradition of "saving" society by changing the schools—pointed their fingers of blame at the schools for all the social ills. According to the typical analysis, society was in deep trouble because the schools were too authoritarian in their insistence on standards of academic performance, dress codes, and behavior, and in addition, schools were branded as responsible for perpetuating institutionalized racism.

The federal government responded to the mood of federal crises with another pork barrel type approach. This time, they enacted a major school aid program whose primary beneficiaries were poor children. The liberals contended that this would not alter the fundamental structure of either education or society. What was needed, they said, was more freedom and spontaneity, which would surely produce higher motivation and therefore, better learning. In the universities students demanded courses that were relevant to political and social issues of the day.

During the late 1960s and early 1970s schools swung again towards progressivism. Many elementary schools adopted "open classrooms," which usually meant that the walls between classes were knocked down, and that students could exercise considerable 'freedom and choice' about what to do or not to do each day—much like the Montessori approach which was based on educational principles of the 20th century Italian educator by the same name. (The Montessori approach stresses the development of the child's own urge for creation and accomplishment and is directed towards kindergarten and pre-school children.) At the high school level, graduation requirements were lowered (to make it more equitable and fair) and enrollment fell in the basics such as math, English, science, history and foreign languages.

Alternative schools were established for students with special interests. Traditional subjects gave way to independent study, student-designed courses and topical electives.

The subjects affected most were English and social studies. Typically, these courses gave way to a plethora of electives. English was replaced with courses on the mass media, pop culture and popular fiction. Writing, once a part of every student's daily regimen, became a special course. History was splintered into mini-courses on black history, feminist history and literature, or "rap" sessions about values. Textbooks were rewritten to reflect these changes.

By the mid-1970s, academic indicators once more began to reveal a steady, nationwide down turn. SAT scores dropped drastically and in direct relation to increases in federal funding. Absenteeism and violence simultaneously showed a drastic rise.

Studies consistently found that during the 1970s high school students took more nonacademic courses and fewer of the advanced courses necessary for college preparation.

As evidence accumulated that the schools were slipping as academic institutions, public confidence plummeted. Parents called for back-to-basics curricula, demanded the restoration of academic standards and a return to discipline. Gallup polls consistently showed the public's greatest educational concern was the lack of discipline in the schools.

As usual, the schools, guided by the liberal education elite, followed society's shifting mood. One of the first things to go was New Math, a prominent post-Sputnik curriculum reform, which most students and many teachers and parents found to be incomprehensible. Schools that had torn down their walls for "Open Classrooms," rebuilt them. Alternative schools survived but their numbers shrank and their purpose became more clearly defined. By 1978, nearly 40 states had adopted minimum competency tests to ascertain whether students had learned enough to be promoted or to graduate.

Perhaps the biggest and most notorious of fads for the 1980s has been the structuring of curriculum around a teaching philosophy known as "secular humanism" or "humanism." Humanism is referred to by humanists as a "faith" and a "religion." *The Humanist,* the official magazine for the American Humanist Association, carried an article by Professor Gerald Larue of the University of Southern California entitled, "<u>The Way of Ethical Humanism: A Religion to Meet the Psychological Needs of Our Time</u>." In it he explained the humanist philosophy regarding religion:

> In humanism there is no supernaturalistic, paternalistic deity who has revealed his will for humans and who has made clear that there are punishments for disobedience to that will and rewards for obedience . . . We have no belief in an afterlife—no resurrection, no immorality, no reincarnation, no heaven, no hell, nor anything in between . . . There are no sacred scriptures, no salvation or deliverance from the reactions of a demanding father-god, no need to beg forgiveness for human error, no need for a god to require the killing of his own as an appeasing sacrifice for human sin. Our religion is based upon the best we know about our cosmos, our world and ourselves.[2]

Humanism was declared by the U.S. Supreme Court to be, in fact, a religion.[3] So much for separation of church and state. This religion does not need or have Sunday schools, instead it relies on public schools, Monday through Friday.

Critics will say the term simply means humaneness or humanitarianism and what is wrong with that? For starters, it is just not true and we do not have to look any further, again, than the humanist's own publication to establish that fact.

> . . . the battle for mankind's future must be waged and won in the public school classroom by teachers who correctly per-

in the public school classroom by teachers who correctly perceive their role as the proselytizer of a new faith; a religion of humanity . . . utilizing a classroom instead of a pulpit to convey humanist values in whatever subject they teach, . . . [4]

What is humanism? In a nutshell, it:

—Denies the deity of God, the inspiration of the Bible, and the divinity of Jesus Christ.
—Denies the existence of the soul, life after death, salvation and heaven, damnation and hell.
—Denies the Biblical account of creation.
—Believes that there are no absolutes, no right, no wrong—that moral values are self-determined and situational. Do your own thing, "as long as it does not harm anyone else."
—Believes in removal of distinctive roles of male and female.
—Believes in sexual freedom between consenting individuals, regardless of age, including premarital sex, male and female homosexuality, and incest.
—Believes in the right to abortion, euthanasia (mercy killing), and suicide.
—Believes in equal distribution of America's wealth to reduce poverty and bring about equality.
—Believes in control of the environment, control of energy and its limitations.
—Believes in removal of American patriotism and the free enterprise system, disarmament, and the creation of a one-world socialistic government.[5]

You may wonder how could the complex issues of "humanism" possibly be indoctrinated into your child in elementary or high school? Certainly not by accident! Under Lenin and Stalin, Pavlov developed the technique of conditioning dogs to bring about desired results, and from this crude beginning, Humanistic psychologists, and behavioral scientists successfully developed techniques which can gradually change your child's conscience, personality, values and behavior.

"An extensively used technique is Values Clarification (see Chapter 9) which can be used to convince the child that he has the right to develop his own personal values, free from parental influence and authority, free from religious influences. It can further convince the child that there are no absolutes, no right, no wrong. The child is told that whatever value he chooses is right for him as long as he uses their methodology."[6]

"Other humanistic strategies for behavioral change are role playing, whereby the child acts out emotional situations such as conflicts with parents, also magic circles, value appraisal scales, questionnaires, diaries, journals, public interviews, etc. Survival games and open ended situations of 'What would you do if . . . ?' develop situation ethics, to say the least."[7]

"Whatever the strategy, the objective is basically the same—to get your child to reveal his very heart, soul and mind, and even his subconscious thoughts before his peers and teachers. In turn the peer group openly discusses his personal feelings and values and challenges him to defend his values and how he arrived at them. (Peers who challenge seldom accept values resulting from parental and religious influence). A child's only defense for some values may be that the parents that he loves hold the same values. Thus, both the child's and parents' values are subjected to open criticism from peers when his values differ from theirs. Skilled 'change agents' (teachers) can manipulate discussions to create peer pressure for conformity to non-Christian standards. They have been known to intimidate slow conformers."[8]

When I say that this philosophy is pervasive in our public schools, I am not exaggerating. Below are examples of humanism in school textbooks. The quotes are necessarily brief but their content amplifies the views presented in this chapter. Please feel free to examine the texts in a more lengthy and detailed fashion to see the full extent of humanistic indoctrination.

HUMANISM IN TEXTBOOKS:

EVOLUTION: " . . . Infants can grasp an object such as a finger, so strongly that they can be lifted into the air. We suspect this reflex is left over from an earlier stage in human evolution, when babies had to cling to their ape-like mothers' coats while mothers were climbing or searching for food."[9]

" . . . between 5 and 2 million years ago, [we saw] the appearance of human beings."[10]

SELF AUTHORITY (INDIVIDUAL AUTONOMY): "It is not always wrong to challenge rules. Questioning—and even rebelling against—some rules is part of growing up . . . "[11]

"The place, the opportunity and their bodies all say 'Go!' How far this couple goes must be their own decision."[12]

" . . . Your decision about using marijuana is important to you. You should be the one to make it . . . "[13]

"Think of a situation that would probably result in a difference of opinion between yourself and your parents. How would you defend your position? With what arguments would your parents counter? Write a dialogue between your parents and yourself."[14]

SITUATION ETHICS: " . . . There are exceptions to almost all moral laws, depending on the situation. What is wrong in one instance may be right in another. Most children learn that it's wrong to lie. But later they may learn that it's tactless, if not actually wrong, not to lie under certain circumstances . . . "[15]

" . . . (1) It is important to work hard . . . (4) You should tell the truth at all times . . . (14) Stealing is bad . . . " "Let each pupil decide for himself how he feels about each. Emphasize that this is not a test, and there are no 'right' or 'wrong' answers . . . "[16]

DISTORTED REALISM: "Each instructor uses 'sex terms' differently. Write down all the terms referring to body parts and elimination and pronounce them in private, a little louder than necessary, or at a volume level suited to the classroom."[17]

" . . . Swearing is often called street language. You've probably felt the urge to use daring words . . . Experimenting with swearing is often a stage in maturing for both boys and girls . . . "[18]

SEXUAL PERMISSIVENESS: "Adolescent petting is an important opportunity to learn about sexual responses and to gratify sexual and emotional desires without a more serious commitment."[19]

"Have students write a one-sentence statement on "Why sex urges can be fun for an adolescent."[20]

"A person with variant sexual interests is not necessarily bad, sick, or mentally ill . . . "[21]

DEATH EDUCATION: "What would you like to have written on your tombstone? Give your answer in 20 words or less."[22]

"The thought of death sometimes occurs in a sexual context . . . in that the event of orgasm, like the event of dying, involves a surrender to the involuntary and the unknown."[23]

Secular humanism stands alone as the single most destructive force in public education. Its doctrine is not only non-academic, which is what schools are supposed to be, but it serves to undermine any values that the child may have brought from home. It leaves the child confused, rebellious, resentful and morally bankrupt.

What has been the effect of this history of educational fads? For one thing, no single educational innovation has been universally adopted. Clearly discernible, however, is that as federal intervention increased, school track records have plummeted.

If the past is any guide we can expect the liberals to continue on the idea that the current interest in excellence will last only as long as there is a general perception that society's welfare depends on the educators' ability to indoctrinate children to the liberal's global concept of world government. They will argue that this alone will ensure our ability to compete successfully in the international marketplace of goods and ideas. If we experience an internal crises of confidence comparable to the Depression or the late 1960s, then we might expect a return to the kind of educational progressivism that stresses self and community rather than competition and achievement.

Whatever the state of politics and society, America's schools need an anchor. And we need an informed constituency of concerned parents and citizens who will take charge and refocus the debate—not on what is best for the vested interest of the professional education establishment, but on what is best for our children, the free market, and the United States.

Educational progressivism no doubt will once again candy coat its same old appeal to parents, this time promising to improve their child's learning by increasing their intrinsic motivation. They will promise to teach them how to be scientists and engineers, if you will just sign off on the federal government supplying school districts with computers—which many believe to be just another fad.

This time we can not afford to be smooth-talked. We have witnessed fadism and it does not work. We must insist on less government intervention, a return to parental control of the schools and extrinsic motivation. External disciplines such as grades and course requirements are necessary. In any event, it is clear that parents must not abdicate their roles and responsibilities to the NEA-progressive education elite.

CHAPTER 8 FOOTNOTES

1. *Public Opinion*, August/September 1985, "Who Speaks For Black America?" by Linda S. Lichter, page 41.

2. *The Humanist,* September 1984, published by the American Humanist Association, page 5.

3. Torcaso vs. Watkins 367 US 488 (1961) and U.S. vs. Seeger 380 US 163 (1964)

4. *The Humanist*, American Humanist Association, January/February 1983 edition, page 6.

5. Humanist Manifestos I and II. Prometheus Books, Buffalo, NY, The Aspen Institute for Humanistic Studies, Freemen Digest, Provo, Utah.

6. Lottie Beth Hobbes, Is Humanism Molesting Your Child, Pro Family Forum, (Dallas, TX.: 1983) page 3.

7. Hobbes, Is, page 3.

8. Hobbes, Is, page 3.

9. Understanding Psychology, Random House, 1977, HS Psychology, SE-168, lines 1-3.

10. Land and People: A World Geography, Scott-Foresman, 1982, HS World Geography, paragraph 3, SE-77.

11. Health and Safety For You, McGraw Hill, Webster Division, 1980, HS Health, SE-56, paragraph 6.

12. Masculinity and Femininity, Houghton-Mifflin, 1976, Grades 7-12, Sex Education, SE-21.

13. Good Health For You, Laidlaw, 1983, Grade 5 Health, SE-178, Column 2, paragraph 2, lines 8-12.

14. Rebels, Ginn 360, 1969, Grade 8 Basal Reader, SE-85, last paragraph.

15. Inquiries In Sociology, Allyn & Bacon, 1978, HS Psychology, SE-45, column 2, paragraph 1, lines 5-11.

16. LESSON 3: Values and Culture . . . What Are Values?, Man and Society, Silver Burdett, 1972, Grade 5, Social Studies, SE 10-11.

17. Married Life, Bennett, 1976, HS Homemaking, TDG-8, Col. 2.

18. Me: Understanding Myself and Others, Bennett, 1982, Grades 6-8 Homemaking, SE-201, column 1, paragraph 5, lines 1-2, 5-7.

19. Life and Health, Random House, 1980, Grades 9-10 Health, SE-161 picture caption.

20. Activity C, Finding My Way, Bennett, 1979, Grades 6-12 Homemaking, TG-10, Column 1.

21. Finding, SE-218, column 1, paragraph 4, lines 1-3.

22. Let's Talk About Health, Cebco Standard Publishers, 1980, HS Health & Safety, SE-31, column 2, lines 7-10.

23. Life and Health, Random House, 1976, Grades 9-10 Health, SE-486, column 2, paragraph 1.

HOW PARENTS CAN EVALUATE CURRICULA

**Here is a checklist to help parents evaluate elementary and secondary school materials. The "it" in these questions can be a curriculum, textbook, computer courseware, film, teacher's manual, workbook, or mimeographed papers used in classrooms.

1) Is it anti-parent? Does it lead the child to believe that parents are ignorant, old-fashioned or out of touch with the modern world?

2) Does it suggest that the child not tell his parents what he is taught in class? Does it instruct the child not to take home the textbook or questionnaire or other school materials?

3) Does it encourage the child to seek advice from organizations or adults other than the parents (such as Planned Parenthood, a teen health clinic or the ACLU)?

4) Does it present information which depresses the child, leads him to a negative view of himself, his country, or his future? Does it produce fear and despair in the child, instead of faith in his family and country, and hope in the future?

5) Is it preoccupied with death and tragedy? Does it encourage the child to dwell on unhappy or tragic events, or to foster and retain bad feelings such as hate, anger, and revenge? Does it require the child to write morbid exercises, such as his own epitaph or a description of the last death in the child's family?

6) Is it anti-parent and anti-religion by leading the child to reject the moral standards and values he has been taught in home and in church? Does it lead the child to believe that there are no absolute moral standards, but that the morality of an act depends on the situation?

7) Does it present courses about sex, suicide, alcohol, or illegal drugs in such a way as to encourage experimentation? Does it desensitize the child to the use of gutter language?

8) Does it use pre- and post-testing to measure attitudinal change?

9) Is it anti-religion? Does it lead the child to believe that religion

is unimportant or out-of-date? Does it censor out all knowledge of the importance and influence of religion in American history?

10) Does it affirmatively teach the ideology of secular humanism or that all religions are equally valid? Does it have a constant questioning of values, standards and authority and teach that all moral decisions and lifestyles are equally to be respected?

11) Does it attack the child's religious faith by ridiculing the belief that God created the earth? Does it spend class time on such anti-religious elements as the occult, witchcraft, or astrology?

12) Does it force the child to make choices in hypothetical situations which require him to decide that it is all right to lie, cheat, steal, kill, have sex outside of marriage, have an abortion, or commit suicide? Does it pose hypothetical dilemmas which upset the child's moral values taught in the home, and induce him to seek the approval of his peers?

13) Does it spend precious class time on lessons, exercises and questions about feelings and attitudes, rather than teaching knowledge, facts and basic skills?

14) Does it force the child to play psychological games in class such as survival games, Magic Circle or Dungeons and Dragons?

15) Does it force the child to answer questionnaires or surveys about the child's personal or family attitudes, feelings, behavior, customs, or political and religious preferences, all of which invade the family's privacy and are none of the school's business?

16) Does it force the child to engage (or be exposed to) role-playing of socio-political situations or unhappy personal problems caused by divorce, premarital sex, pregnancy or venereal diseases?

17) Does it force the child to write a journal or diary (or even compositions) which require him to reveal private family information or to relive and remember unhappy events and feelings?

18) Does it require classroom discussion of personal and private matters which embarrass the child in front of his peers?

19) Does it force the child to confront adult problems which are too complex and unsuitable for his tender years, such as nuclear war?

20) Does it describe America as an unjust society (unfair to economic or racial groups or to women) rather than telling the truth that America has given more freedom and opportunity to more people than any nation in the history of the world?

21) Does it blur traditional concepts of gender identity and force the child to accept the radical notion of a gender-free society in which there are no differences in attitudes and occupations between men and women? Does it include role reversals by showing women in hard physical labor jobs and men as house-husbands?

22) Does it debunk the American private enterprise system and lead the child to believe that socialism is better? Does it make the child feel guilty about our high standard of living? Does it lead the child to believe that government spending programs are the formula for economic prosperity, rather than hard work and perseverance?

23) Does it propagandize for domestic spending programs, while attacking defense spending and economy in government? Does it lead the child to believe that disarmament rather than defense can prevent a future war?

24) Does it debunk or censor out our nation's heroes such as George Washington and Abraham Lincoln, but spend much time studying controversial contemporary figures?

25) Does it downgrade patriotism and lead the child to believe that other nations have better systems, or that some type of global one-world government or United Nation's control would be superior to ours in solving world problems? Does it use UNESCO developed curricula to promote acceptance of a one-world government?

CHAPTER 9

VALUES EDUCATION: PSYCHO-THERAPY IN THE CLASSROOM

The teacher said she was hoping to inspire some good discussion, but when it was announced over the intercom at Jamestown High School that the Soviets had bombed n American ship in the Baltic Sea and the President was about to address a joint session of Congress, what they got was stunned silence, tears and one student who went into shock.

The teachers were puzzled and the administrators bewildered; they claimed to be totally unprepared for the reaction. The experiment was cancelled.

You would think with all the education psychology courses teachers are forced to endure in college, someone would have remembered a similar incident in 1938—the War of the Worlds broadcast—which sent thousands of panic-stricken citizens into the streets. But no one thought of that, and this wound up being just one more example of what the education establishment likes to call "innovative lesson planning" and "meaningful learning experiences."

The teaching methodology described above is known as "values clarification or values education." It is a humanistic indoctrination technique designed to destroy a child's personal code of morals that has been transmitted to him through religious traditions and his upbringing. It's purpose is to insure the child is taught to develop a set of ethical standards based on the assumption that there are no absolute values—no clearly designated rights and wrongs.

Where did this educational quackery begin and how did it get into our public schools? Professor Richard Baer, Jr., writing for *The Wall Street Journal* says:

> Back in the mid-1960s, social scientists Louis E. Raths, Merrill Harmin and Sidney B. Simon developed the teaching method known as Values Clarification, advertising it as an ideal way to deal with values without taking sides or indoctrinating students in one particular value position . . . . To tell a student that stealing is wrong or that kindness and loyalty are good values, would be, according to Values Clarification, to manipulate and coerce a student. Teachers should help students discover and clarify their own personal values instead of trying to force **someone else's** (emphasis added) values on them.[1]

Excuse me? But are we to understand that parents are expected to send their children to the public schools, bear the cost for their education through mandatory taxes, and then submit to a systematic undermining of their values, which they are teaching to their children at home? Yes, that is the gist of it.

Mr. Baer sheds more light on this by explaining who the culprits are and how they have succeeded in their plans:

> Spread by teacher workshops, paid for in part by state and federal tax dollars, Values Clarification caught on quickly in the early 1970s and became popular with many teachers and administrators. It's use in public school sex-education classes and by local Planned Parenthood groups was particularly noteworthy, for whether intended or not, adolescents were in effect given the message that parents, the school or society had no right to tell them what standards should guide sexual behavior. Whether premarital sex was right or wrong, for instance, ado-

lescents would discover for themselves as they were helped to clarify their personal values.[2]

The humanist-collectivist value systems purport to free man from responsibility for his actions, but with disastrous consequences. The gospel according to humanism is that delinquency (child or adult) is not evidence of sin, nor does unseemly conduct indicate any desire to do evil; rather, it is all part of the learning experience. Thus, behavior is developmental, according to humanist philosophy.

Values clarification, then, is the humanist attempt to change the moral concepts of children. They do this by cleverly proclaiming that they want the children to have maximum choice, or autonomy, in choosing the values they will live by. Of course, such an approach greatly massages the ego of the students, who do not know any better.

The biggest problem confronting the humanists is that they cannot get their hands on the children until (at five or six years old) they are forced into the school system. However, once the child begins his perilous journey through the schools, the humanists begin their brainwashing. In order to instill this new morality, through the process of values clarification, they must first break down the value system that children bring to school—the one instilled by their parents, church and society at large.

The key to values clarification is to question everything—including your parents and your church. No one, including your parents, is to be assumed to have the truth. Their "truth" is not necessarily your "truth." The child is told he must "clarify" his values to ascertain what his truth is, to find out what is "right" for him.

The humanist begins from the sickening premise that the American family structure produces mentally ill children. Allow me to quote Dr. Pierce of Harvard University lecturing teachers in Colorado:

> Every child in America who enters school at the age of five is mentally ill, because he comes to school with allegiance toward our elected officials, toward our founding fathers, toward

our institutions, toward the preservation of this form of government . . . [3]

Where do our friends at the NEA fit into this? As usual, they are at the forefront of the controversy. That the NEA is solidly committed to the brainwashing techniques of values clarification is evidenced by its sponsorship of the National Training Laboratory in Group Development in Bethel, Maine. This brainwashing center had been founded and run by a German social psychologist, Kurt Lervin. Lervin was the intellectual godfather of the psychology of the collective, having invented "sensitivity training" and "group dynamics." He eventually was attracted by the possibilities of applying these approaches to education. Here is a quote from the National Training Laboratories which, by the way, are funded with federal tax-dollars:

> Although they (the children) appear to behave appropriately and seem normal by most cultural standards, they may actually be in need of mental health care. In order to help them **change**, adapt and conform to the planned society in which there will be no conflict of attitudes or beliefs.[4]

Lervin perceived the group as crucial to human behavior. This was so because "the group to which an individual belongs is the ground for his perceptions, his feelings and his actions . . . It is the ground of the social group that gives to the individual his figured character."[5]

Lervin, being a dedicated humanist, was quite concerned with social change but found a particularly troublesome stumbling block—the independent thinker. He discovered that his brainwashing did not work that well on individuals who relied on their own independent judgment. The way to change was again through group dynamics.

Alfred Marrov, an associate and disciple of Lervin's agreed:

> To effect any sort of change in the goals or outlooks of a group, a change in its equilibrium is necessary. To try to do this by appealing to members individually is seldom effective . . . . Thus the behavior of the whole group may be more easily

changed than that of a single member. This willingness to stick together (cohesiveness) is an essential characteristic of any group. Indeed, without it, it is doubtful that a group could be said to exist at all.

What renders a group cohesive is . . . how dynamically interdependent they are. Out of reciprocal dependence for the achievement of goals there arises a readiness to share chores and challenges, and even to reconcile personality clashes.[6]

The NEA/humanist technique is diabolically clever: manipulate the group to manipulate the individual—use group or peer pressure on the stubborn individual. And what better place to use group manipulation tricks than on a "group" or classroom full of trusting, innocent children. And, what better way to implement this methodology than by encouraging unsuspecting teachers to use pre-designed curriculum guides. Give the devil his due, the NEA elitists are not stupid. As long as these mind manipulators couch their techniques in lofty sounding academic jargon, which is designed to fool both the rank and file teacher and the parent, they can proceed relatively unimpeded. Their brainwashing methods are passed off, therefore, as strategies to improve the child's ability to "think for himself."

Such soothing reassurances were designed to lull the unsuspecting parent to sleep while educators gradually altered the child's values, behavior, conscience and personality.

One of the bedrock tenets of humanism incorporated in values clarification is the concept that there is no predetermined set of values. Instead, values are merely situational decisions, if they exist at all.

That such utterances are pure nonsense is obvious. It is just as wrong today to murder, steal, or cheat as it was before humanism came on the scene, and will continue to be long after it has been assigned to history's trash heap. Attitudes against murder, stealing or lying are time-tested rules (which even criminals acknowledge within their own ranks). They have existed in almost every human society for as long as recorded human history. To arrogantly preach that such values do not exist is to publicly proclaim one's stupidity.

Nevertheless, based upon the lie of the non-existence of absolute values, the NEA/humanists use values clarification as a teaching technique to brainwash your children. The key component of its method is to convince the child that he has the "right" to develop his own personal values and morality—"to do his own thing." This new-found morality is of course free from such authorities as the church, society or parents. The only authority is oneself. In other words, the child is answerable to nothing higher than his own greed.

Unfortunately, these classroom methods of indoctrination have taken a frightening toll on our children which is not too surprising. After all, a child looks to adults for guidance and advice. As such, the child has an innate trust of what grownups tell him.

But imagine the confusion that confronts the child when his parents teach him one set of values and his teacher, another authority figure, teaches values that may be diametrically opposed to whatever the youngster is hearing at home. Keep in mind we are not talking about college students here; we are talking about small children who do not have the ability to deal with such wide disparities. Not only does this confuse the child, but it sets up a deep inner conflict. Who is right, the child wonders? And who should I try to please, my parents or my teacher? These questions are not answered when a teacher expounds the philosophy of situational ethics and tells the child in essence, "nobody is right or wrong; whatever you decide to do in a given situation is right for you." The child knows that in the final analysis he has to please the authority figures around him. His teacher will let his parents know if he does not "behave," whatever that means; his parents will be angry if he comes home and begins doing things of which they do not approve. It is a catch-22 situation for the child. Instead of clearing up confusion or easing tensions, the school is guilty of heaping more doubt on an already befuddled student.

Here is an example of the values clarification approach used in the book, <u>Values Clarification: A Handbook of Practical Strategies for Teachers and Students</u> by Simon, Howe, and Kirschenbaum. This teacher's guide was an outgrowth of the thinking of John Dewey, which the authors freely admit.

Valuing, according to the book is composed of seven sub-processes:

1. Prize and cherish the value. (The child has now become a law unto himself. The values are his and his alone.)

2. Publicly affirm the value. (This reinforces the new value more firmly into the child's subconscious.)

3. Choose from alternatives. (By choosing from alternatives one rejects the absolute of the Judeo-Christian ethic and chooses one of his own.)

4. Choose after considering the consequences. (By rejecting the Judeo-Christian ethic and the individual's accountability to God, then the individual can do whatever he wants with impunity.)

5. Choose the value freely. (This means free from religious or parental dictates or "repressive" concepts of morality.)

6. Act on the value. (If you decide to do your own thing then you must act on it. For example, is you decide homosexuality is all right, then you must act upon that decision.)

7. Act upon the value with a pattern, consistency and repetition. (The child has now chosen a new lifestyle. His values are no longer the same as his parents. He now intends to live by his <u>own</u> new system.)

Using values clarification, it is clear that America's public school classrooms have become a battleground where the NEA/humanists are waging intense psychological warfare against all traditional values.

Is there anything good to be said about values clarification? It does emphasize the worth of man in the collective sense, human potential, world beauty and the worth of human society. It is a reasonable statement to say that humanists are determined to use reason and science to improve the condition of all men—and that can legitimately be construed as highly moral. The point is, however, that when you remove the flowery rhetoric you expose the stark truth. These things by themselves are not enough and a situational approach to morality, which is really just self-indulgence, will not bring happiness in the end. Self-indulgence has doomed every civilization that has ever tried it.

How is the humanistic philosophy of moral relativism and situation ethics translated into school curriculum or teaching strategies in the classroom? Let us look at excerpts from the official transcript of proceedings before the Department of Education on the Hatch Amendment. These are real parents revealing the very real problem of values clarification in their own schools:

The importance of "relevance" in today's education was exemplified by this passage in an 8th grade English textbook: "Write a suicide note." The following is the example given in the text. "I am finally going to do it. Unemployment drives me crazy. Inflation makes me angry. The cost of living turns my stomach. Big business raises the cost of candy and gum. Teachers expect too much. School takes away my freedom. I can't communicate with my parents. My parents don't understand me. I have said my goodbyes. I fought a good fight but I have met defeat."

That depressing advice was supposed to be "relevant." It was taken from an "activity" approach to Basic English, Part 2, published by the New England School Development Council in Newton, Massachusetts.[7]

When my daughter was 12 years old, she was given a questionnaire by her 7th grade Health teacher without my knowledge or consent. She was asked many personal questions including being required to give her views about life after death. She was asked, "What reasons would motivate you to commit suicide?" Five reasons were listed from which she was expected to choose.

She was given a list of ten ways of dying, including violent death, and asked to list them in order of "most to least preferred." She was asked what should be done to her if she was terminally ill. Two of the five choices offered her by the framers of this questionnaire were mercy killing.[8]

Children are keeping diaries which teachers read daily and comment on. Teachers are being asked to use this holistic approach under the misconception that diaries are kept to check grammar and punctuation. A mother called me to complain about her daughter's diary. The child had written that she was angry with her mother and that she wanted to kill her. The teacher responded in red ink to this child's remarks in the diary, saying, "Don't kill her, just punch her out."[9]

This question was included for group discussion in 3rd grade: "How many of you ever wanted to beat up your parents?"[10]

A survival game which my 7th grade son participated in required him to eliminate five out of ten whom they did not have room for on the spaceship.[11]

In one program in our county, little first graders made their own coffins out of shoeboxes.[12]

How many of you have ever lied? How many of you seem to be lying more than you used to? How many of you think it's okay to lie if it makes someone feel good?

Then they go on to say, "If Granny sends you a dress you don't like, what do you tell her?" And they go on to say why it is okay to lie if it makes somebody feel good.

The last statement in this exercise is: "Finish the following statement: I would lie if_____.[13]

Here is another technique or strategy that is typical of the survival activities used in the values education process. The students are expected to compare, evaluate and make a value judgment on the lives of the survivors so as to determine which ones are more fit than the others to live. It goes something like this:

The teacher has the students sit close together in one corner of the classroom on the floor. She turns out the lights and pulls down all the shades. She puts a lighted candle in the center of the group. Then she explains the situation.

The class, on an outing to some nearby caves, has been trapped hundreds of feet below the ground by a cave-in. There is a narrow passageway leading up and out of the cavern where they are trapped. Night is coming fast and there is no one around for miles to help. They decide they will form a single file line and try to work their way out of the cave. But at any moment there might be another rock slide. The ones nearest to the front of the line will have the best chances for survival. Each member of the class will give his reasons for why he should be at the head of the line. After hearing each other's reasons they will vote thereby determining the order by which they will file out.

This game leaves room for many unanswered questions in a child's mind and could be very destructive to the self-esteem of those not placed near the beginning of the line. And besides that, the activity itself takes an entire class period or two, time that should be used in furthering academic learning.

And as to the question of infringement on the privacy of the family, according to the University of Wisconsin's Alan Lockwood, "a substantial proportion of the contents and methods of values clarification constitutes a threat to the privacy rights of students and their families." . . . the method permits students to say, 'I pass' when the teacher asks them to complete such open ended sentences as 'If I had 24 hours to live . . . ,' 'Secretly I wish . . . ' or 'My parents are usually . . . ' But many of these 'projective techniques' are designed in such a fashion . . . that students often will realize too late that they have divulged more about themselves and their families than they wish or feel is appropriate in a public setting. Moreover, the method itself incorporates pressure toward self-disclosure."[14]

As a schoolteacher, I can assure you that most teachers are unaware of the effects of such exercises on their students. They tend to view these teaching strategies more as non-boring diversionary tactics and, in that sense, they are right. For instance, death has always held a fascination for man and children are no exception, but children do not have the emotional and mental maturity to deal with it.

Many parents become frustrated because, when they have attempted to find out what is going on in their child's classroom, they have had the school door literally shut in their faces. It has become increasingly more difficult for the average parent to find out precisely what is being taught in the classroom.

Despite the Hatch Amendment of 1986, consent forms are virtually non-existent. Those consent forms which are sent home are often so vague and generalized that parents do not understand the implications. In most areas, parents sign an all-purpose permission slip at the beginning of the year which includes permission for speech therapy (if needed), fluoride treatments, participation in field trips, and guidance counseling. The assumption that counseling would be given on a one-to-one, as needed basis proves false as many parents find that their children were involved in classroom group therapy, whether they needed it or not.

When these parents asked to see the classroom materials used in this exercise, almost without fail, they were met with stony silence, denials that any written material had been used or they were simply told they could not see the materials. Let us face it, parents are denied access to curricula taught to their children because they would be appalled at how their children are spending their school day. I still contend that any teacher who has nothing to hide, will gladly show parents everything they use in a classroom.

Parents have been left back in school, not because they have failed to learn the assigned classwork, but because they have learned it too well. We have a tradition of trust in America's public school system. Every parent wants the best for his child and that includes the best education. So when the education experts claim that "values clarification" is the new and improved method of learning, parents are hesitant to disagree. It is not until they see the results of these high sounding theories that they overcome their age-old trust and voice their anger.

Parents must insist that their children not participate in counseling or any course that uses values clarification. They will probably be met with stiff resistance. Teachers and administrators have historically fought the decision to remove a child from this sort of harmful environment. Parents become demoralized when they realize that just because resistance has been overcome, the battle is not necessarily won. Often the student is required to go to the class while attendance is taken and then he must get up and walk out. He then sits at a desk in the hall outside the classroom, or goes to the library, alone and embarrassed at being singled out. This is peer pressure at its worst.

Remember, even though you have the legal right (by virtue of the Hatch Amendment) to stop this from happening to your child, removal from certain classes is not enough to ensure he is not subjected to psychological abuse. As values clarification becomes more widely embraced by the experts, it is being written into all course curricula, although history and English are still the prime targets of the humanists.

This all sounds rather bleak, but what are your options? Just give your children up to the humanists? Obviously, we cannot do that. We have to fight and for most of us, because of financial limitations, that means we are bound to fight it out in the public school arena. Your main job must be to find out how and to what degree it is being used on your child.

Parents can spot values clarification in the curriculum by asking their children some easy, straight-forward questions. Does your teacher have you place yourself in a role-playing situation? Do you keep a journal or a diary at school? Do you ever discuss death, personal or family affairs, political preferences or religion? Are you ever asked to question your parents, your religion or other figures of authority?

Ask your children's teachers if they ever use curriculum developed by Planned Parenthood, SIECUS, Aspen Institute, the NEA or other questionable sources for their supplemental material. Work to eliminate the federal role in education. Education is not a federal issue and the federal government has no business usurping parent's rights in the name of equality.

But, most importantly, parents and taxpayers must decide whether or not they want their children surrounded by the NEA's planned confusion. If not, get involved. Demand the removal of these teaching methodologies and materials from the classroom or take your children to a more objective setting.

From the courtesy of the Mel Gablers in Longview, Texas, I have reprinted, in Chapter 18, an excellent guide which shows you how to spot values clarification in your local schools and how to effectively fight it. This brave couple has been on the front line for years and the thoroughness of their work proves it.

At the end of this chapter I have included a copy of the Hatch Amendment; a guide on how to apply it to your own situation; a model letter you can have placed in your child's permanent file which should help to protect him; and, "Model State Legislation" which you could send to your state legislator and ask him to introduce as an amendment to the state education code. By the way, the language in this model piece would also be appropriate in a school district's education code.

A serious problem this country faces is the inability of parents to admit it is happening in their school. This "it can't happen here" attitude is not only wrong, since I do not know of one school district in America that has not incorporated secular humanism into the school day in one form or another. This denial actually helps the social engineers to get away with their destructive attack on your traditional values.

Another problem we face is that most teachers will plead innocent to any social engineering, not because they are not doing it, because they never make the connection that the "non-boring, diversionary" assignments they use are actually part of what we have been discussing. You must remember that the secular humanist philosophy is spread throughout the curriculum and textbooks so that children, parents and, yes, even teachers, only see bits and pieces of it. Although there are plenty of teachers out there who know exactly what they are doing, there are more who never realize they are simply bit actors in a large scale production. This may sound like a weak explanation but when you have gone through four years of education courses where your enlightened professors taught you it is your responsibility as an educator to socialize children as well as give them their fundamental education, it is easier to swallow than most of us would like to admit. For example, how many teachers who play survival games or show survival films ever make the connection that what they are doing, in effect, is de-sensitizing children to death? How many of them ever stop to realize the ramifications of such an act—easier acceptance of euthanasia and abortion.

When you approach the school principal and teachers, I would suggest you do it in a non-combative way. Always take the moral high ground. It is rightfully yours to stand on in such a confrontation. Simply make the school aware of your rights as a parent and your intentions to be very involved with your child's education—even to the point of watch-dogging the school. You will be surprised what a 'chilling effect' that knowledge has on teachers.

In closing this chapter, let me remind parents of a few things. First, isn't it about time for some righteous indignation? The fact is, it is past time!

The public schools are just that—the public's schools. Your children are not wards of the state, they belong to you. You have the primary responsibility for their education and you do not relinquish those rights when you put them on a school bus in the morning.

Teachers and school administrators are public servants—not public masters. That means they work for you—the public. You have every right to question what goes on in your child's school. Your tax dollars (more than half of them) go to support that school system, pay salaries and buy textbooks and curriculum materials.

If the school refuses to let you see the materials because they are 'state owned' and are not to be removed from the school premises, remind them <u>you are the state</u>! Then offer to go to the library and review them so they never have to leave school grounds. If they still refuse to let you view them, go directly to the school board. From there, continue upwards—the mayor, state legislators, governors, congressmen, senators and the Department of Education where you can file a violation of the Hatch Amendment against your school district if it comes to that.

Also, never underestimate the power of the pen. It should not be too difficult to find a sympathetic reporter (or just one who sees a good story) to whom you can relay your tale of woe. You will be pleasantly surprised how accommodating school administrators can become when threatened with a little bad publicity.

In other words, parents must boldly seize what is rightfully theirs. They must control the education of their own children and break the NEA's stranglehold on public education. The stakes are too high not to fight—the stakes are our children.

CHAPTER 9 FOOTNOTES

1. Richard A. Baer, "Parents, Schools and Values Clarification" *The Wall Street Journal*, April 12, 1982: page 14.

2. Baer, page 14.

3. Clova Wood, Behind the Scenes of Education (P.O. Box 460916, Garland, Texas, 1986) page 3.

4. Wood, Behind, page 5.

5. Kurt Lervin, Resolving Social Conflicts edited by Gertrude W. Lervin (New York, NY: Harper and Rowe, 1948,) pp. VII.

6. Alfred J. Marrov, The Practical Theorist: The Life and Work of Kurt Lervin, (New York, NY: Basic Books, 1969) page 169.

7. Phyllis Schlafly, Child Abuse in the Classroom, (Eagle Forum, Alton, IL: March 13-27, 1984) page 308, testimony of Anne Pfizenmaier.

8. Schlafly, Child, page 371, testimony of Gail T. Bjork.

9. Schlafly, Child, page 113, testimony of Marcy Meenan.

10. Schlafly, Child, page 57, testimony of Joanne Lisac.

11. Schlafly, Child, page 406, testimony of Snookie Dellinger.

12. Schlafly, Child, page 368, testimony of Doris D'Antoni.

13. Schlafly, Child, page 332, testimony of Robert Duarte.

14. "Parents, Schools and Values Clarification," *The Wall Street Journal*, April 12, 1982, page 14.

MODEL STATE LEGISLATION
for introduction into
(STATE) EDUCATION CODE
OUTLAWING VALUES CLARIFICATION

**Adopted from Section 60650, Article 4 of the California Education Code, April 30, 1977.

"No test, questionnaire, survey or examination containing any questions about the pupil's personal beliefs or practices in sex, family life, politics, morality and religion, or any questions about his parents' or guardians' beliefs and practices in sex, family life, politics, morality and religion, shall be administered to any pupil in kindergarten or Grade 1 through 12, inclusive, unless the parent or guardian of the pupil is notified in writing that such test, questionnaire, survey or examination is to be administered and the parent or guardian of the pupil gives written permission for the pupil to take such test, questionnaire, survey or examination in advance."

SUGGESTIONS FOR APPLYING THE HATCH AMENDMENT REGULATIONS

The Hatch Amendment Regulations will not remove the materials from the classroom, only your child. This law gives the parents a foothold to complain about methods, questionnaires, objectionable films and materials. If you believe your child is being subjected to psychological treatment or psychiatric or psychological testing through the use of questionnaires, teaching methodology, games, etc., you may asked to have your child removed from the setting and insist the school follow the law by obtaining written permission before using the method in the classroom. A closer look at the wording of the Hatch Amendment will give you a better understanding of what it covers.

Educators will usually rebut the wording "research and experimental" by saying the game or activity is not being used for these reasons. Under 98.3(b), the explanation for those terms is: "any program or project that is designed to explore or develop new or unproven teaching methods or techniques." If the teaching technique has been proven, ask to see the report. An example of this is a program called "Leap," designed for talented and gifted children. Upon examination of the project, it was clear to see it was designed to invade the psyche. Under the Hatch Amendment, this cannot be done without prior written permission from the parent.

Educators tend to argue the word "testing" when confronted. The law defines "testing," pertaining to psychiatric or psychological testing, as an activity or method used to elicit information about attitudes, habits, traits, or opinions, beliefs or feelings not pertaining to academic instruction, and "treatment" is defined as an activity that accomplishes the same.

These definitions narrow the field for educators' use of the games, questionnaires, computer programs and other activities to achieve the results listed above. Once you have determined which methods or activities are in violation, follow the proper procedures for filing a formal complaint. Start with the teacher, principal, superintendent, and finally the school board. Document your records by keeping copies of all correspondence, take notes during phone calls (add dates and time) and always take a witness with you to any meeting when possible.

If the school is guilty of violating the Hatch regulations, the government can remove federal funding from the program in question or the school. Many teachers when approached by parents will state that the program in question is not financed with federal funds, therefore, it does not fall within the pervue of the Hatch Amendment. Keep in mind, if the teacher went to an in-service training to learn about the program, this qualifies the program as being federally funded. It is easier for a parent to make a case that every activity during a school day is in some way linked to federal funding than it is for an educator to make the opposite argument.

If the school chooses to challenge your position, file a complaint. Good media coverage can often turn the tide. Contact your local newspaper immediately and inform them of the situation. You may be instrumental in alerting other parents about methods being used on their children thus, gaining their support.

WARNING:

DO NOT sign requests for psychological testing (or any testing) that you do not understand. These permission slips are usually sent home at the beginning of the year and include request for parental permission for the school to give vision and hearing tests. Watch what you sign and, if you do not understand any part of it, do not sign it at all. Make your own permission slip for inclusion in your child's files telling the school exactly what you are giving permission for them to do. By signing something which is all inclusive, you may find out later that you have signed away your very rights to your child.

**Courtesy of Maryland Coalition of Concerned Parents on Privacy Rights in the Public Schools.

MODEL PARENT'S RIGHTS LETTER

**This letter, courtesy of Eagle Forum, should be rewritten by you with a copy sent directly to the president of your local school board and another copy to the principal of your child's school. Tell him/her that you wish this to be included as part of your child's official school folder.

Date_____

School Board President/Principal

Address

City/State/Zip

Dear_____:

I am the parent of_____who attends
_____School. Under U.S. legislation and court decisions, parents have the primary responsibility for their children's education, and pupils have certain rights which the school may not deny. Parents have the right to assurance that their children's beliefs and values are not undermined by the schools. Pupils have the right to have and to hold their values and moral standards without direct or indirect manipulation by the schools through curricula, textbooks, audio-visual materials or supplementary assignments.

Accordingly, I hereby request that my child be involved in NO school activities listed below unless I have first reviewed all the relevant materials and have given my written consent for their use:

Psychological and psychiatric examinations, tests or surveys that are designed to elicit information about attitudes, habits, traits, opinions, beliefs, or feelings of an individual or group;

Psychological and psychiatric treatment that is designed to affect behavioral, emotional or attitudinal characteristics of an individual or group;

Values clarification, use of moral dilemmas, discussion of religious or moral standards, role-playing or open ended discussions of situations involving moral issues, and survival games including life/death decision exercises;

Death education including abortion, euthanasia, suicide, use of violence, and discussions of death and dying;

Curricula pertaining to alcohol and drugs;

Action in nuclear war, nuclear policy and nuclear classroom games;

Nationalistic, one-world government or globalism curricula;

Discussions and testing on inter-personal relationships, discussion of attitudes towards parents and parenting;

Discussions on human sexuality, including premarital sex, extramarital sex, contraception, abortion, homosexuality, group sex and marriages, prostitution, incest, masturbation, bestiality, divorce, population control, role playing, sex behavior and attitudes of student and family;

Pornography and any materials containing profanity and/or sexual explicitness;

Fantasy techniques; hypnotic techniques, imagery and suggestology;

Evolution, including the idea that man has developed from previous or lower types of livings things;

Discussions of witchcraft, occultism, the supernatural and Eastern mysticism;

Political affiliations and beliefs of students and family; personal religious beliefs and practices; and appraisals of other individuals with whom the child has family relationships;

No discussions of privileged and analogous relationships, such as those of lawyers, physicians and ministers; including the student's role in family activities and finances;

Academic personality tests, questionnaires on personal and family life and attitudes;

Biography assignments; log books, personal journals and diaries;

Techniques in self-revelation; sensitivity training, group encounter sessions, talk-ins, magic circles, self-evaluation and auto-criticism; strategies designed for self-disclosure;

Sociograms, sociodramas, blindfold walks and isolation techniques;

The purpose of this letter is to preserve my child's rights under the Protection of Pupil Rights Amendment (the Hatch Amendment) to the General Education Provisions Act, and under its regulations as published in the Federal Register of September 6, 1984 which became effective November 12, 1984. These regulations provide a procedure for filing complaints at the local level, and then with the U.S. Department of Education. If a voluntary remedy fails, federal funds are withdrawn from those in violation of the law. I respectfully ask you to send me a substantive response to this letter, attaching a copy of your policy statement on procedures for parental permission requirements, to notify all my child's teachers, and to keep a copy of this letter in my child's permanent file. Thank you for your cooperation.

Signature

HATCH AMENDMENT

PROTECTION OF PUPIL RIGHTS

20 U.S. Code 1232h

Inspection of parents or guardians of instructional material:

(a) All instructional materials, including teacher's manuals, films, tapes or other supplementary instructional material which will be used in connection with any research or experimentation program or project shall be available for inspection by the parents or guardians of the children engaged in such program or project. For the purpose of this section "research or experimentation program or project" means any program or project in any applicable program designed to explore or develop new or unproven teaching methods and techniques.

Psychiatric or psychological examinations, testing or treatment:

(b) No student shall be required, as part of any applicable program, to submit to psychiatric examination, testing or treatment, in which the primary purpose is to reveal information concerning:

1) political affiliations;

2) mental and psychological problems potentially embarrassing to the student or his family;

3) sex behavior and attitudes;

4) illegal, anti-social, self-incriminating and demeaning behavior;

5) critical appraisals of other individuals with whom respondents have close family relationships;

6) legally recognized, privileged and analogous relationships, such as those of lawyers, physicians and ministers.

7) income (other than that required by law to determine eligibility for participation in a program or for receiving financial assistance

under such program), without the prior consent of the student (if the student is an adult or an emancipated minor), or in the case of unemancipated minor, without the prior written consent of the parent.

SEX EDUCATION: A DEVALUATION OF LOVE

For years experts of various sorts, including the self-styled "sex-perts" of the NEA have been telling us that the only way to solve the problem of adolescent pregnancy is to implement a program of sex education in the public schools.

"About 80 percent of public-school children in major U.S. cities now take some kind of sex-education course . . . . Only Maryland, New Jersey and Washington, D.C., **require** (emphasis added) the subject in all schools."[1]

Now, after more than a decade of sex education courses, we are told by the Allen Guttmacher Institute (research arm of Planned Parenthood Federation of America) that our country leads nearly every developed nation in teenage pregnancy, abortion and childbearing because, even after all we have done in the area of sex instruction and the liberalization of sex-related policies, it still is not enough!

We are to understand that the lowest rate of teenage pregnancy, abortion and childbearing are found among societies which have free abortion services and readily available contraceptives for teenagers as well as cradle-to-grave sex education courses. And if that is not enough, the Guttmacher researchers explain that it is our "high religiosity," our intolerance of sexual permissiveness which is really to blame for the teenage birth and pregnancy rate.

The Guttmacher report is a classic case of the expression "statistics can be made to say anything," since it omits vast quantities of data, ignores the research of dissenting experts in the field, and carefully weaves a hodgepodge of numerical computations with Guttmacher's own preconceived determinations and passes it all off as incontrovertible evidence.

Let us look at some of the statistics. From 1971-79, there was a 50 percent increase in premarital sex among all teenagers and an 80 percent increase among white teenage girls. Illegitimate births went up 90 percent among all teenage girls.

Professor Jaqueline Kasun of Humboldt State University in California has looked at the statistics in that state and found that for every additional $1 million spent on teenage pregnancy prevention, teen pregnancies increased by 2000. California's experience bears out that the universal rule "if you subsidize something you will get more of it" applies to teenage sex as well.

The Washington Post reports, "Teenage pregnancy costs the federal government almost $20 billion a year, according to a study by the Center for Population Options."[2]

Guttmacher's report was too busy glorifying Sweden as the Mecca of sexual tolerance to mention a petition, signed in March of 1964, in which 140 eminent Swedish doctors, expressed their concern over sexual hysteria in the young there. Sex education became compulsory in Sweden in 1954, and it was not long before its disastrous effects started showing up. From 1959 to 1964 the gonorrhea rate climbed 75 percent and 52 percent of these cases occurred among young people. Between 1963 and 1974 divorces tripled in Sweden; during the same period the marriage rate dropped 66 percent.

By 1976 one baby in three in Sweden was illegitimate despite the aborting of half of all teenage pregnancies.

But nothing deters the sexperts from their basic thesis: saturate youngsters as early as possible with explicit sexual instruction and they will turn into young adults who are, in the words of an NEA brochure to parents, "comfortable with their sexuality" and, thus, "sexually responsible."

What are the effects of such teaching? A young mother of three children testified before the Hatch Committee hearings in 1984. This is what she had to say:

> As a result of the indoctrination that I received as a student, I began abusing drugs and became sexually promiscuous. As a result, I became pregnant twice, and twice aborted my babies, the effects of which are still evident with me today.
>
> I was applauded by my teachers for my decision to abort and encouraged to share my experiences with my peers. When I was a senior in high school I was living with my boyfriend. Because of this I was invited to speak to the Marriage Class at my school, and I discussed the personal and intimate details of that situation.
>
> It was only after I had nearly ruined my life that I began to reconsider what I had been taught in the public schools.[3]

One aspect of the sexperts' crusade is that they encourage sexuality among teenagers by making contraceptives readily available to school children, often without the knowledge of the parents and school officials themselves. This is done via the newest sex-related public school money waster, the teen health clinic. But parents are beginning to fight back as *TIME* magazine reports:

> The feistiest combatants are fighting against not school curriculums but school clinics. These health facilities are attached to or near public schools around the country, and they are spreading rapidly. Most are funded with a mix of private and public money. All offer across-the-board medical care. Some 28 percent dispense contraceptives. 52 percent prescribe them, and the rest make referrals to family-planning agencies.[4]

This is exactly what happened in New York City as *The Washington Post* reported on December 20, 1986: "Another storm erupted in

New York City this fall when some school board members and parents discovered that contraceptives were being dispensed at several school-based clinics without specific parental consent."[5]

New York City is not alone as another *Post* story proves:

> Jina Washington got a note from her teacher, left her fifth-period class at Pinkston High School and stepped over to the health clinic. An hour later, she walked out with birth control pills . . . Jina is 14 . . . . when a child becomes sexually active—even if that child is only in the ninth grade—the clinic (West Dallas Youth Clinic provides birth control pills, diaphragms, foam and condoms.[6]

Because of the increased number of teenagers enticed by the notion that contraceptive sex is synonymous with responsible sex and influenced by both adult and peer pressure to engage in sex, the net result is an increase in sexual activity, unplanned pregnancies, abortions and illegitimate births. This happens despite the use of contraceptives or abortion by people affected by these sex education programs.

"A six-volume 1984 analysis by Mathtech, Inc., of nine programs around the country came to the conclusion after a seven year investigation that sex-ed courses had almost no effect on contraceptive use, views about premarital sex, or such social skills as assertiveness and self-understanding."[7]

But there is even more disturbing proof: " . . . two studies by Utah researchers named Stan Weed and Joseph Olsen. Their major finding is that during a period when the number of teens using family-planning clinics rose from 300,000 to 1.5 million, the teen pregnancy rate actually increased 19 percent. Births were down, they said, but only because of abortion."[8]

In other words teen-age births are down but teen-age pregnancies are up. Teen clinics are successful in teaching teens how to avoid giving birth but woefully lacking in teaching them how not to get pregnant.

"Another study tends to back the Weed-Olsen view. Deborah Anne Dawson, as a doctoral student at John Hopkins University, found that two-thirds of girls between 15 and 19 have had some instruction about birth control and pregnancy, with only 16 percent lacking any such education at all. Her conclusion: teaching about birth control and pregnancy has no significant effect on the pregnancy rate among teens, presumably because teenagers are more emotional than rational about sex and its risks."[9]

In spite of sex education, which is supposed to warn teens of the pitfalls of sex, the 20 percent of teenagers who used birth control drugs or devices in 1976 accounted for 23.5 percent of the unintended pregnancies among all teenagers. It appears that young adults using contraceptives were 21.6 percent more likely to become accidentally pregnant than those who didn't use contraceptives.

Do the sexperts know that their programs will be damaging to young people? I think they do.

American Life Lobby News reported in May of 1986 that Oregon students were rewarded for returning clinic forms granting parental permission for "treatment and services" from the Roosevelt High School Teen Health Center by offering a drawing for albums, Trailblazer tickets and gift certificates.

Such hype for a teen clinic is the kind of appeal that former Education Secretary, William Bennett, called "an abdication of moral authority."

Of course, the real reason Guttmacher and his cohorts insist on their position, despite dissension from well-known authorities, is that they begin with the premise that there is nothing wrong with promiscuous sex and intend to preserve that viewpoint. So they ignore experts like Weed, Olsen, Dr. William McGrath or Dr. Melvin Anchell, whose premise is less fashionable: that promiscuous sex is not good for people, especially youngsters.

In Anchell's book, Sex and Insanity, he documents the information that Guttmacher's people do not want to look at: the adverse effects of pornography and sex education on normal sexual development.

Armed with the hard evidence of actual case studies and first-hand investigative experience, Anchell affirms what most of us have always intuitively known: that human sexuality is not just about physical gratification or reproduction, that the most important components of sexuality are crucial to the development of civilization.

Dr. Anchell, as well as others, explain from a medical standpoint exactly how premature sex education, and particularly the kind of mass instruction that is public school fare, actually impedes normal sexual development; how it bypasses the "latency" stage of development when sexual energies are typically converted into affection. But the Guttmacher staff does not wish to confuse anyone with the facts. They want parents to permit them to catapult their children into a world of "authoritative sexual knowledge" for which youngsters are not ready, and present them with literature and sexual paraphernalia which only will only serve as sexual stimulants rather than instruction.

Dr. McGrath writes:

> There is a phase of personality development called the latency period, during which the healthy child is not interested in sex. This interval from about the age of five until adolescence serves a very important biological purpose. It affords a child an opportunity to develop his own resources, his beginning physical and mental strength.
>
> Premature interest in sex is unnatural and will arrest or distort the development of the personality. Sex education should not be foisted on children; it should not begin in the grade schools.
>
> Anyone who would deliberately arouse the child's curiosity or stimulate his unready mind to troubled sexual preoccupations ought to have a millstone tied around his neck and be cast into the sea.[10]

Unfortunately, many of the so-called sex-ed texts and teaching materials look like they came from the pages of pornographic rags like *Hustler* or *Penthouse*.

I have included samples (at the end of this chapter) of some of these sex education materials for use in the public schools, but only after debating long and hard as to their appropriateness. On the one hand, they are so grossly disgusting as to be embarrassing to me and my readers. On the other hand, it is obvious that many parents are not aware of what is being shown to their children under the guise of sex education. For those people, I have included a "milder" example so they can see for themselves.

As the example shows, these are not designed to educate children about the dangers, responsibilities or sacredness of sex. Instead they encourage experimentation, legitimize abnormal behavior and, even encourage, under the mask of promoting "alternative lifestyles," homosexuality.

I have also (through the courtesy of Eagle Forum) included at the end of the chapter a step-by-step guide on how to evaluate pre-existing sex education curriculum in your child's school.

The problem of AIDS has added a new urgency to the old debate of sex-ed in the public classroom. Surgeon General Koop did a grave injustice to the Reagan administration (who had already made public their views against sex education) when he made his controversial comment, "There is now no doubt that we need sex education in schools and that it must include information on heterosexual and homosexual relationships . . . at the lowest possible grade (he later identified as Grade 3) . . . because of the deadly health hazard we have to be as explicit as necessary to get the message across."[11]

What did the American public have to say about Koop's strategy of teaching eight year olds about homosexual, or for that matter heterosexual, sex? In a *TIME* poll, only 23 percent of Americans agreed with him. Even professional educators were opposed.

We must be careful not to let the homosexual community, with its powerful lobbying force in Washington, D.C., heighten public hysteria and then use it in the public schools in a misguided effort to legitimize their sick lifestyle through early indoctrination of our children.

Really think about this for a moment. How would you feel if your eight year old was versed in the art of anal sex by your local school? That is not an exaggeration. How else do you teach a child about "safe sex" and not catching AIDS unless you first inform him just how you get it? Frankly, I would not want my eighteen year old in the awkward position of having a teacher being "as explicit as necessary" in order to explain AIDS, much less my elementary age child.

Did we, as parents, bring our children into the world in order for the NEA and Planned Parenthood to use our schools to turn them into perverts? The question answers itself—a resounding no! Yet, that is precisely what they will do if they succeed in ramming smut, under the guise of sex education, into the permanent curriculum of our public schools. Remember, two states and our nation's capitol have already mandated sex-ed which simply means that whether or not you as a parent feel you could do the job more responsibly at home, they have taken that decision away from you. The only option disgruntled parents have been left with is private education or home schooling.

Remember NEA Resolution B-23 of their 1984-85 Handbook which reads,

> The Association recognizes that sensitive sex education can be a positive force in promoting physical, mental and social health and that the public school must assume an increasingly important role in providing the instruction. Teachers must be qualified to teach in this area and must be legally protected from censorship and lawsuits.[12]

Legally protected from whom? You guessed it—from parents!

One would at least expect experts to know that children do not see things the way adults do; to understand that a child's view is very different from an adult's. But no, the sexual liberators wait until they see young teenage girls actually competing to see who can get pregnant first—as they did where I taught—before it occurs to them that maybe the kiddies were misinterpreting the message.

Meanwhile, the purveyors of pornography and cheap thrills, including the manufacturers of sex education paraphernalia, are making millions at the expense of our children. As a matter of fact, the NEA found it necessary in its 99th legislative agenda to call for an <u>exemption from pornography laws for its teachers</u> with respect to sex education classes.

That parents are poor sex educators and that sexual training ought to be taught beginning in the primary grades by "trained personnel" was an idea introduced in the 1960s by a quasi-governmental agency known as Sex Information and Education Council of the United States or SIECUS, headed by former Public Health Service employee, Mary Calderone, who marshalled forces and literally inundated school systems, government, the medical profession, and parents with pro sex-ed propaganda. Poorly organized and non-funded parent and teacher groups found themselves out-maneuvered by the Calderone-SIECUS missionaries, whose ideas were radical, even by 1980 standards.

SIECUS is a very strange breed of cat which, although it does not directly develop specific sex-ed programs or write textbooks, nevertheless has tremendous influence on sex education in America. It is a "think-tank" on sex. As such, it develops general philosophies, guidelines, and training concepts. People connected with SIECUS serve as advisors for other organizations, including the NEA. This enables them to spread their bizarre views on sex and sex education by means of other respectable organizations. To give you an idea of where they are coming from, founder and executive director Mary S. Calderone's latest book is <u>Fear of Eroticism and Its Human Implications</u>, which treats sex as sport—spectator and otherwise.

Mary Calderone was named Humanist of the Year in 1974 by the American Humanist Association. Apparently, Calderone's ultra-liberal views on sex run in the family because her husband owns burlesque theaters, including one which, in 1969, scheduled a show that was so grossly lewd and obscene the local district attorney would not allow it to be shown.

Who are some of the other people whose views are being transmitted to our children through sex education courses in the public schools?

Another more familar SIECUS board member is William Masters of the Masters-Johnson (so-called) sex therapists. This team studies human sexuality, although one cannot help wondering if "study" is the proper term.

Their famous and controversial report on human sexuality was based on data gathered on approximately 700 male and female subjects, who were hired to perform every imaginable sex act while Masters, Johnson and their colleagues, watched, took notes, and photographed the copulating subjects.

One of Masters' bright ideas to help "fix" his patients who were trying to overcome their sexual inadequacies is for the couple to check in for two weeks of study at his hotel-clinic at $2500 per couple. During the day the couples receive instruction and at night they practice what they learn during the day.

According to *Newsweek*, "not all patients who come to the foundation are married. To accommodate unmarried men, Masters and Johnson have introduced another unique concept in sexual therapy—the partner surrogate. They are single women who have been shown how to be sexually responsive—the surrogate participates in the physical aspects of the treatment program in the same manner as the wife would . . . "13

In other words, Masters uses prostitutes, but calls them "partner surrogates," which is supposed to sound scientific.

Now someone's sexual practices or orientation are his own business, but the tragic thing is that a young person's views can become firmly entrenched as a result of the sex ed programs that are being taught in our public schools. No wonder children are coming up with all sorts of emotional and physiological problems after exposure to this type of trash posturing as scientific knowledge.

In any case, the Guttmacher Institute's own reported statistics can hardly be considered an advertisement for the program. And although the report does not state how many of this nation's unwed teenage parents, either male or female, have had the blessing of sex education courses, chances are that most of them went through such a program. So, the reasons why the program has failed to produce the promised results should be obvious:

1. Sex education courses depersonalize a very personal subject. The courses desensitize young learners and encourage public expressions of private emotions and intimacies. Normal people do not perform sexually before an audience and are embarrassed at intrusions into their private sex lives.

2. Classroom sex educators cannot possibly know whether a particular child is "ready" for explicit sexual information. Only the parent, who is closest to the child, can know that. Children develop at different rates—your ten year old might be mature enough for this type of information at that age but your twelve year old still might not be ready for it.

3. Premature sexual instruction can cause irreparable harm to youngsters who are not ready for it; that is, children who are in the latency stage of development.

4. Instruction that ignores the compassion and affection elements of sexual relations reduces human love to the animal level. Since it is human beings and not animals which have the capacity to feel compassion, it follows that human sexuality involves more than physical gratification and reproduction. Since compassion and affection are also prerequisites of a civilized society, and the backbone of civilized society is the nuclear family unit, sex educators do a disservice by devaluing family life when they leave compassion, affection, love and marriage out of discussions about sex.

Lastly, and most important, sex education courses presume to take the issue out of the hands of parents and place it into the hands of the government, the NEA, Planned Parenthood and SIECUS. Perhaps many parents do feel "inadequate" teaching their children the facts of life, as the NEA suggests in its pamphlets to parents. Personally, I suspect those days have long been over. But just who is the NEA or the state government to tell parents they cannot do the jobs themselves if they want to? And sending a permission slip home with instructions to sign it or not sign it is only another method of intimidating parents into submission.

The bottom line is that mature love, and even the family itself, is being devalued in today's sex education courses. Neither the Guttmacher statistics nor the NEA pamphlets address that issue. It is well established that love and the nuclear family unit are the foundations upon which progress is built. Sexual liberators would take away from the family the very responsibilities which give it cohesion—thus spawning the very irresponsibility they claim to seek to avoid.

Are we as parents and taxpayers ready to throw in the towel on our children? Are we willing to accept that our children are nothing more than animals who have no dignity, no self-control over their sexual desires? Charles Krauthammer, syndicated columnist for *The Washington Post* wrote an article a while back which he entitled, "Teen-Age Sex: The Battle Is Lost." He went on to further acquiesce to the liberals on the issue of teen health clinics when he said, "Yes, birth control clinics are a kind of surrender. But at Little Big Horn surrender is the only sound strategy."[14]

The solution for parents is never to give up but, instead, to insist on their rights and stop allowing themselves to be manipulated. Polls show that the majority of Americans are comfortable with sex education being taught—on a non-mandatory basis—in the public schools. Although I personally would not allow my child to be in such a class, I certainly have no problem with parents who do. It is their right as parents to choose what is best for their children. It is only when they discover how this responsibility is being abused by the public schools that they become morally outraged. If parents will demand to be a part of the whole process from beginning to end, we may begin to see responsible sex education programs in the schools.

And parents are beginning to get <u>very</u> involved. They want the subject to be taught in the context of traditional values as a 1986 *TIMES* poll shows. I quote, "If most people want schools to teach children about sex, they also want teachers to be preachers. 70 percent say sex education programs should try to teach moral values—what students should or should not do sexually; moreover, 58 percent do not think it is possible to teach sex-related issues without discussing moral values."[15]

In the late 1980s we began to see parents take command of the situation by insisting on responsible curriculum:

> One (parent) group has confronted value-free teaching by devising and marketing a model curriculum that states traditional conservative values throughout. Teen-Aid Inc., with headquarters in Spokane and 25 affiliates in the U.S. and Canada, urges youngsters to "resist the tide" of a sex-saturated culture. The program tries to sharpen the "refusal skills" of students and sends summaries of lessons home to parents. Students are told to be careful about what clothes they wear on dates, and not to drink or take drugs while on a date.[16]

As these parents understand, not only do they have the right to the option of placing their children in or out of sex-ed classes, they should have the final say in what will be taught, what year sex education classes will begin, if they begin, how long a time period will be needed and exactly what will be taught—street sex or traditional values. The battle rages on and we are entering a crucial time where as psychiatrist Thomas Szasz, author of <u>Sex by Prescription</u>, says pressures on the public schools are bound to mount. "A covert struggle is going on to see who will control the free schools and mold the minds of other people's children."[17]

Just what do we expect of the public school system? What functions do we want them to perform for us? Do we want them to keep private records, function as psychoanalysts and professional babysitters who will teach our children everything from how to brush their teeth to driving, cooking, CPR and how to use contraceptives?

If not, and I sincerely hope not, parents **must** re-define what they want and expect from the public schools and demand that educators stay within the boundaries which the taxpayers in a local community have drawn. We must, as a nation, set our priorities straight and clarify our educational expectations.

Think about it.

CHAPTER 10 FOOTNOTES

1. John Leo, "Sex and Schools," *TIME,* November 24, 1986: page 55.

2. Dan Morgan, "Cost of Teenage Pregnancy," *The Washington Post,* October 24, 1989: page A23.

3. U.S. Department of Education hearings on Hatch Amendment, March 13-27, 1984, page 163, Testimony of Kay Fradeneck.

4. Hearings, page 57.

5. Sandra R. Gregg, "Birth Control Debate Stalls School Health Service Plans," *The Washington Post,* December 20, 1986: page A1.

6. Marc Fisher, "Confronting Teen-Age Sexuality," *The Washington Post,* April 14, 1987: page A1.

7. John Leo, "Sex and Schools," *TIME,* November 24, 1986: page 56.

8. Leo, page 58.

9. Leo, page 59.

10. Homer Duncan, "Humanistic Sex Education In the Public Schools" Missionary Crusader Publications, 1987: page 12.

11. Leo, *TIME,* page 54.

12. NEA Handbook, 1984-85 edition, Resolution B-23.

13. "Masters and Johnson," *NEWSWEEK,* May 4, 1970: page 90ff.

14. Charles Krauthammer, "Teen-Age Sex: The Battle Is Lost," *The Washington Post,* December 5, 1986: page A12.

15. "Sex and Schools," *TIME,* November 24, 1986: page 58.

16. *TIME,* page 57.

17. *TIME,* page 63.

SEX EDUCATION CHECK LIST

1. Does it omit all references to moral standards of right and wrong, teaching only animal-level sex?

2. Does it urge boys and girls to seek help from or consult only or primarily public agencies rather than their parents or religious advisers?

3. Does it require discussion and instruction to take place in sex-integrated (coed) classes rather than separate classes for boys and girls?

4. Does it require boys and girls to discuss private parts and sexual behavior openly in the classroom, with explicit vocabulary, thereby destroying their natural modesty, privacy, and psychological defenses (especially of the girls) against immoral sex?

5. Does it omit mentioning chastity as a method (the only absolute method) of preventing teenage pregnancies and VD?

6. Does it try to eliminate all guilt for sin?

7. Does it assume that all boys and girls are engaging in immoral sex, thereby encouraging them to accept promiscuous sexual acts as normal?

8. Does it omit mention of the spiritual, psychological, emotional, and physical benefits of premarital chastity, marital fidelity, and traditional family life?

9. Does it omit mention of the spiritual, psychological, emotional, and physical penalties and risks of fornication, adultery and promiscuity?

10. Does it require boys and girls to engage in role playing (pretending one is pregnant, pretending one has to admit having VD, pretending to use various types of contraceptives), thereby encouraging peer pressure to be exerted on the side of fornication rather than chastity?

11. Does it fail to stress marriage as the most moral, most fulfilling, and/or most socially acceptable method of enjoying sexual activity?

12. Does it encourage boys and girls not to tell their parents about the sex-ed curriculum, or about their sexual behavior or problems?

13. Does it present abortion as an acceptable method of birth control?

14. Does it use materials and references from the pro-abortion Planned Parenthood?

15. Does it present homosexual behavior as normal and acceptable?

16. Does it omit mention of the incurable types of VD which today affect millions of Americans? Does it falsely imply that all VD can be cured by treatment?

17. Does it give respectability to VD by listing famous people who had it?

18. Does it omit mention of the danger of cervical cancer in females from early promiscuity?

19. Does it use a vocabulary which disguises immorality? For example, "sexually active" to mean fornication, "sexual partners" to mean sex in or out of marriage, "fetus" to mean baby, "termination of pregnancy" to mean killing a preborn baby.

20. Does it require boys and girls to draw or trace on paper intimate parts of the male and female bodies?

21. Does it ask unnecessary questions which cause boys and girls to doubt their parents' religious and social values ("Is there a need for a wedding ceremony, religious or civil?")?

22. Does it force advanced concepts and vocabulary upon five to eight year old children too young to understand or be interested? (For example, selection of mate, Caesarean, pregnancy prevention, population control, ovulation, VD, sperm, ovum.)

23. Does it constantly propagandize for limiting the size of families by teaching that having more children means that each gets fewer economic benefit?

24. Can the sex-ed curriculum reasonably be described as a "how to do it" course in sexual acts (instruction which obviously encourages individual experimentation)?

**Courtesy of Eagle Forum, The Phyllis Schlafly Report, Vol. 14, No. 7, Section 1, February 1981.

Proposed "Block" sex education curriculum in New Jersey Public Schools

Draw the world's largest penis.

CHAPTER 11

BILINGUAL EDUCATION— SEGREGATION BY LANGUAGE

A little over a decade ago, an education crusade was mounted by the educational establishment to cope with the problem of people fleeing socialist tyranny to come to the United States. Most were unable to speak English.

Thus, the concept of bilingual education, which purported to teach these new arrivals and their children English so they could be absorbed successfully into the American culture. Bilingual education insists that a child should learn to read and think first in his native language.

According to the untiring social engineers at the NEA, the purpose of a bilingual education program was to give these non-English speaking newcomers special help in their studies until they could overcome the language barrier.

Ten years and $1.6 billion dollars later, what has this special help accomplished? Outside of beginning an entirely new education industry to train language specialists and concoct "bilingual education" materials, not much. Thousands of children are now able to go their entire school years without hearing so much as a single question directed towards them in English. This is education that is supposed to get these children through the language barrier and acculturation process?

What began as a transitional program designed to bridge a gap between cultures and eliminate alienation and stigmatization has wound up being a failed program which accomplishes precisely the opposite.

There have been cases, in Miami, for example, where a child has gone through the public school system for the entire twelve years without ever being required to speak any English. There is often no pretense made about the program being "transitional" towards anything.

"In those (larger) cities, large Hispanic populations have produced bilingual education programs that make it possible for a student to finish 12 years of school entirely in Spanish. And many do."[1] Even more remarkable is the fact that, "There are cases in Texas . . . non-English speaking Asian immigrant children are sitting in bilingual education classes where Spanish is being taught."[2]

"Furthermore, say the critics, although bilingual programs are supposed to be easing children away from the everyday use of, say, Spanish, and into English, they are in fact impeding the child's progress in his new language by reducing the urgency of his learning it. The unintended effect, to is to condemn the child to linguistic isolation in a cultural ghetto, leaving him woefully unprepared for either the commercial opportunities or the civic responsibilities of his new society."[3]

The result has been large-scale ethnic segregation by language, which in its insidious way, is just as destructive as discrimination. This is most aptly demonstrated by the plight of Hispanic Americans.

One fifth of all Hispanics over the age of 25 are categorized as functionally illiterate as compared with 10 percent of blacks and 3 percent of whites. The major reason for this is the language barrier—not understanding English.

So, we have millions of voting age, naturalized citizens who are cut off from the major sources of information and are at the mercy of those who can speak Spanish. They cling to those who speak their tongue and shut themselves off from the process of acculturation. More importantly, untold numbers of potential employees are cut off from the job market because of poor or non-existent English reading, writing and speaking skills. This, in effect, cuts them off from participating in the American dream of free enterprise and capitalism.

"Bilingual programs should serve as a bridge to full participation in the American mainstream. They should never segregate non-English speaking students in a way that will make it harder, not easier, for them to succeed in life."[4]

Unfortunately, these people's contact with America is limited to their bilingual spokesmen who act as go-betweens. By teaching their children in their native language, instead of English, the community is further kept in a state of dependency upon those bilingual spokesmen.

These foreign and alienated communities represent a nice, pliable voting block. They are naturalized citizens and eligible to participate in the American electoral process. But, being unable to absorb the information flying about the airwaves and print media, they, out of necessity, get their information from self-appointed leaders. Therefore, they are ripe for plucking by any bilingual demagogue who comes down the pike. They are ripe for exploitation.

One wonders if the NEA educrats' zeal for bilingual education is because it opens up the market for more and more teachers who are potential union supporters whether they want to be or not, depending on whether they live in a right to work state. It also does not seem to matter to the NEA that these teachers are not necessarily required to know the English language: "The Education Department . . . decreed that bilingual education teachers did not need to know English."[5] Coupled with their dream of turning America into a socialist's paradise, might not the NEA be deliberately working to fragmentize our society into separate, unassimilated groups? If these groups are kept separate and told only what the NEA wants them to know, they become a dangerously misinformed political force. If so, bilingual education is a cruel hoax perpetuated by those who have the gall to claim to be the champions of education and civil rights in the United States.

It goes without saying, that if any group—Hispanic, Vietnamese,

Laotian, Polish or whomever—is ever to complete the process blending into American society with a good chance for a successful future, the people must learn the language and skills of America. There is simply no way around that basic fact.

"In *Lau v. Nichols* . . . . the Supreme Court ruled for the first time that sink-or-swim (total immersion into the English language) violated the Civil Rights Act, which prohibits discrimination by racial or national origin in any program receiving federal financial help.

"The court did not mandate bilingual education; it simply mandated that students receive some special help. But when the Department of H.E.W.'s Office of Education convened a panel to draw up guidelines for federal enforcement of the *Lau* ruling, the panel members decided . . . that the government's preferred approach was the controversial and politically loaded practice of dual language teaching in the schools."[6]

Bilingual education was given a big boost by the U.S. Supreme Court (the newest of all unelected legislative bodies) when in 1974 in *Lau v. Nichols* they also ruled that Chinese-speaking students were entitled by law to instruction in a language they could understand.

Like vultures hovering over their prey, the NEA leadership pounced on this opportunity presented by the Supreme Court. The Office of Civil Rights, a division of the then Department of Health, Education and Welfare, was the bureaucracy which was to implement the Court's decision. It did so by issuing those innocuous sounding but deadly "informal" guidelines to bind more than 400 school districts nationwide. By 1980, these "informal" guidelines were requiring, not requesting, that school systems which have a group of 20 or more students sharing a foreign language must offer a full curriculum in their native language—not English. Bilingual programs were now, via bureaucratic decree, the law of the land. As usual, when bureaucrats meddle into things, chaos results. The bilingual education decrees were no different.

The new regulations, naturally, meant the necessity of hiring teachers who speak a foreign language. Just as one would expect, there were not enough to go around. So, teachers were trained and retrained, at taxpayer's expense, to speak a foreign tongue. As a stop-gap measure, bilingual individuals who were not even real teachers were brought in to provide interim teaching services. And the chaos was expedited by threatening the local school districts with a cut off in federal funds unless they complied.

It quickly became apparent that this bureaucratic scheme was turning into an educational nightmare. Reasonable people would expect a change to be in order. However, no one has ever accused bureaucrats of being reasonable.

The bureaucrats, never admitting defeat or mistakes, refused to change the program. Instead, they caved into special interest pressure groups such as the NEA, who adores any education program that wastes taxpayer's money. And, make no mistake about it, bilingual education has and continues to waste vast sums of our tax dollars. The NEA, of course, has a hidden agenda when it comes to bilingual education: keeping the masses malleable. How better than implementing public policy designed (perhaps unwittingly) to ensure that the poor, uneducated ethnic constituency remains poor and uneducated. Language has been the glue that provides cohesiveness and allows a minority group to be identified as a minority. If this is to continue then their language must be preserved at all costs. If they were to assimilate, the NEA would lose a political power base.

A *Time* magazine article said, "There are at least four ways for schools to teach students who speak another language at home:

> 1) Total immersion in English, which relies on the proven ability of children to master new languages. . . .
>
> 2) Short-term bilingual education, which may offer a full curriculum but is directed toward moving students into English language classes as rapidly as possible . . . .

3) Dual curriculum, which permits students to spend several years making the transition . . . .

4) Language and cultural maintenance, which seeks to enhance students' mastery of their first language while also teaching them English . . . .[7]

A Department of Education (DOE) review of the matter found that of all methods of teaching bilingual students English and mathematics, only some form of English really worked. In other words, the same method which was used with the German, Italian, and Greek immigrants to this country in the 1900s was the only one with any merit. Amazingly, these people had no problem mastering the acculturation process even when they had older family members in their household who spoke only in their native tongues. It probably helped that they were never patronized by government bureaucrats.

It has been said, "It is a classic story of good intentions going badly wrong. It began in the heady liberal 60s of civil-rights reform. Mexican American children were seen to be disadvantaged in English-speaking classes. So, in 1968, Congress voted $7.5 million for an experimental program of bilingual education. It left the method of removing the disadvantage to the discretion of the schools. So far, not so bad. The intention was clear: It was to help the children to assimilate by learning English.

"Big Brother was soon flexing his muscles. In 1974-78, Congress took away school discretion. Federal dollars were henceforth available only if the school taught in the child's native language, be it Jicarilla Apache or Passamaquoddy."[8]

Iris Rothberg wrote in the *Harvard Education Review* : "Research findings have shown that bilingual programs are neither better or worse than other instructional methods."[9] If so, then Rothberg was indirectly blasting the whole U.S. educational system because both the bilingual education program and the public school system in general were cranking out illiterates.

By then, however, the NEA educrats and their ideological soulmates had switched tactics in the defense of their programs. They simply ignored the disastrous results and started a campaign to characterize critics of bilingual education as racist and oppressive. Not only that, they slyly hinted that their critics might be just a little conceited for daring to put the English language first. So, the nature of the argument was changed and once again the public was on the defensive playing within the framework the NEA had laid out.

Having successfully framed the debate, the NEA made sure that rather than deliberating over the best way to teach children, the battleground became "the meaning and value of a child's native language"— whether a youngster will know who he is and feel good about himself and his culture.

Meanwhile, guess what method was found over and over again to be the best method for teaching children a foreign language? That is right, total immersion in the language, from "Good morning, how are you today?" to "See you tomorrow." Of course, Berlitz could have told us that twenty years ago.

Even Al Shanker, head of the AFT, is reasonable enough to see the folly in the bilingual education: "Bilingual education can be a useful educational tool, helping some students who speak no English at all to keep up with their schoolwork while rapidly learning English—a transitional program that seeks to place the student in the regular program as soon as possible. But it is not right for every other-language student in every school district—and it certainly shouldn't be mandated from Washington.

"Where bilingual education becomes a *political* tool, used by militant ethnic groups to reinforce separatism, children may never get into the mainstream. Their futures are being risked—and so is a country which depends on the use of one common language, English, to continuously create a nation of Americans out of people from many lands."[10]

Proponents of expensive programs seem to have an inborn ability to rest their cases on two sides of an argument at the same time. The NEA is no different.

When asked why bilingual education classes should be offered, they cited our multi-cultural, melting pot society. But when the classes failed to meet expectations, and people began to question the merits of continuing them, it was explained by these same proponents, that, well, sociologists had largely disavowed the melting-pot idea as not representative of our society. Instead, it was more a "mosaic," or "salad bowl," society, they said, with the distinctiveness of each element intact.

Thus a new minority was born—the linguistic minority—and a new political football game as well.

Realistically, the debate should center around the problems—not just in large southwestern cities like San Antonio, Miami, San Diego and Los Angeles, but in places like Chicago and New York, too. They are also plagued annually with an abundance of functionally illiterate (in English) young people. These young adults who attempt to enter the American work force are unwittingly hindered by an education that has been partly, if not completely, conducted in a foreign language.

The newcomers do not usually face discrimination on account of their race, as the liberals would have us believe but, rather, because of their educational deficiencies. The majority of them are only qualified for no more than low-level work due to their weak language skills.

Hispanics, for example, are well known for being industrious and hard-working employees, so why, then, does higher level employment so frequently elude them? It is because they have been too severely handicapped to deal with technical language requirements, which are needed in positions of responsibility. If they are going to live and earn a living in this country, they must be able to understand written instructions, fill out reports, read blueprints, do mathematical calculations, and other skills that first-line supervisors and foremen, among others, need. Compassion and emotionalism have nothing to do with it—unless you want to ask how a person can possibly "feel good about himself" if he cannot get a decent job.

"A few companies such as Zenith, Motorola, Bell & Howell, Hart, Schaffner & Marx and Bell Telephone Systems have devised courses of their own to repair some of these shortcomings and enable their Hispanic employees to compete in the business world."[11]

Ask yourself, and the proponents of bilingual education, while you are at it: How could I be as successful as I am if suddenly, I had to do what I do now in a country such as France, and could not speak a word of the French language? The answer is obvious, one would be at a serious disadvantage until he or she gained proficiency in the language.

Why should it be any different here?

It is a proven fact that children have the ability to master new languages readily. It is not true, as the NEA and other self-styled experts have indicated, that too much English, or any other language, disorients young people. Indeed, it would seem that under the 1964 Civil Rights Act, interpreted by the Supreme Court in the pivotal *Lau v. Nichols* case, it could well be argued that a violation of civil rights exists when no instruction in English is provided.

Once again, the Big Brother mentality of the liberal education establishment has overridden the good, common-sense thinking of the American public. We know, of course, as the melting pot of the world, we must maintain a healthy respect for the cultures and languages of all our citizens. Typically, we have always done so. But we also know that if our Hispanic element, and other newcomers, are ever to successfully complete the acculturation process and blend into American society with a reasonable opportunity for a successful future, young people must learn the language and skills of this country.

"A decade later, with half a million children enrolled in what their schools describe as bilingual programs, much of the whole enterprise has dismayed both its longtime critics and some of the people who most ardently believe in bilingual education. National Hispanic high school dropout rates . . . are as high as ever: just under 40 percent . . .

Teachers from San Francisco to Providence can be heard complaining that bilingual classes hold students back or keep them away from English. A U.S. Department of Education study, published in 1983 . . . found 'no consistent evidence' that dual-language instruction improved students' academic progress."[12]

It has been said that bilingual education may not be entirely responsible for the employment problems of foreign born young people, but research indicates it certainly has not been a remedy, either. If the majority of Americans agree with this view, then why do we continue to let the liberals force bilingualism on our school children? Especially when all of us, including the proponents of bilingualism, know it does not work. "Indeed, some of them (supporters of bilingual education) acknowledge that they view bilingual programs as a source of jobs for Hispanic administrators, teachers and aides. In cities with large minority enrollments, says a Chicago school principal . . . , "those of us who consider bilingual education ineffective are afraid that if we say so we will lose our jobs."[13]

This brings up a thornier issue concerning a deliberate fragmentation of our society into separate, unassimilated groups for political purposes. In the case of the so-called linguistic minority, this is particularly insidious.

For example, there are fifteen million or more Hispanics in this country—all potential voters. This is a political power base that is ripe for exploitation, particularly if these individuals are cut off from the available sources of information. It would not be the first time that contrived illiteracy has been used to preserve political power. Indeed, too much of the public policy today ensures that the poor and uneducated remain poor and uneducated. Since what binds the linguistic minority together is language rather than color, race or sex, the assimilation process must be hindered in order to maintain the status quo.

Former California Senator S.I. Hiyakawa is right when he points to the danger of bilingual education being used as a tool to encourage separatism in the United States. The future of not only the children involved, but the country itself, is at risk, because our nation depends upon its capacity to create one nation of Americans from a culturally dissimilar framework.

This is not to imply, of course, that there is no purpose in studying or in being fluent in languages other than English. Indeed, as the Europeans know, to be truly educated, such knowledge might rightly be considered indispensable.

The point here is that in this country we conduct our business and, for that matter, our entertainment and practically all our political debate in English. For that reason, young people who expect to remain here must be able to think in English and not be forever going through a series of mental translations to get the gist of what is going on.

Look at the many ethnic groups of European origin which immigrated to the United States between 1870 and the 1920s—the Italians, Germans, Chinese and others. They, too, formed their own communities at the beginning and the native language in those communities often prevailed; yet, despite the lack of bilingual programs, the children of these immigrants had no problem with English or the acculturation process that today's Hispanics, for instance, are facing. Nor did these youngsters lose their culture; instead, they gained one. Moreover, most immigrants will tell you that language barriers can be overcome fairly quickly and easily, and without loss of cultural heritage.

And they did not make a claim for special treatment such as bilingual education. It is interesting to note that even in the Spanish population in this country the rank and file are not making that claim either. The push comes from Hispanic political leaders and others who think they can use this constituency to their political advantage.

Any "special" instruction, then, should be short-term, integrated into the regular classroom setting, and above all, never mandated from On High at the federal level. What happened with bilingual education is typical of what happens every time you have the federal bureaucracy setting policy in what should be a local matter. Clearly it is ridiculous to imagine that the linguistic-cultural problems of Puerto Ricans in

New York are identical to those faced by Hispanics in Texas or Asian immigrants in San Francisco. The Vietnamese refugees have proven beyond a doubt that each wave of newcomers to our shores deals differently with the acculturation process, and local communities must be permitted to use whatever methods best meet their needs.

A blueprint for disaster is to have federal policy influencing state and local education laws to the point where school districts cannot function and, what is worse, wind up having to depend upon federal dollars to meet the regulations.

Moreover, even the most well intentioned educational programs conceived at the federal level have little chance of being successful by the time they filter down to the local level. A poorly conceived program, such as bilingual education, has no chance at all.

It was Theodore Roosevelt who said, "We have room for but one language here, and that is the English language, for we intend to see that the crucible turns our people out as Americans and not as dwellers in a polyglot boarding house."[14]

What should parents do who face the question of placing their child in a bilingual education program? First, go to the school and check out the course of study. How much of the school day and instruction are devoted to mastering the English language? How much of the school day is devoted to school work in the child's native tongue? How well is your child developing in his mastery of the English language? If you do not think he is doing very well and are dissatisfied with the program you have reviewed at your child's school, I suggest you take him out of it immediately and "mainstream" the child, putting him directly into all-English classes. Remember, ultimately you must make the value judgment on whether or not it is in your child's best interest to be in or continue a bilingual education program.

CHAPTER 11 FOOTNOTES

1. Mariah E. deForest, "How Hispanic Education Fails," *Chicago Tribune*, October 17, 1983: Section 1 page 11.

2. Carol Inherst, "Bennett Speech Renews Bilingual Teaching Row," *The Washington Times*, September 26, 1985: page 1A.

3. William Swanson, "The American Way." *TWA Ambassador*, March 1986: page 62.

4. President Ronald Reagan, speaking to the AFT, July 5, 1983.

5. George Archibald, "Hayakawa calls bilingualism a threat to American unity," *The Washington Times*, March 13, 1985: page A2.

6. Cynthia Gorney, "Bilingual Education's Dilemmas Persist," *Washington Post*, July 7, 1985: page A12.

7. Wm. A. Henry III, "Against A Confusion of Tongues," *TIME*, June 13, 1983: pages 30-31.

8. Harold Evans, "Melting Pot—Or Salad Bowl?" *U.S. News & World Report*, March 31, 1986: page 76.

9. Iris Rothberg, "Bilingual Education," *Harvard Education Review*, 1982 edition.

10. Al Shanker, "Schools Still Pressed to go Bilingual: Where We Stand," *New York Times*, April 10, 1983: page E9.

11. Mariah E. deForest, "How Hispanic Education Fails," *Chicago Tribune*, October 17, 1983: Section 1 page 11.

12. "Bilingual Programs Dismay Advocates As Well as Critics," *Washington Post*, July 8, 1985: page A8.

13. Henry, Against, page 30.

14. Henry, Against, page 31.

BRIEF SUMMARIES OF MISLEADING BILINGUAL EDUCATION STUDIES CITED TO SUPPORT STATE PLANS

The author would like to stress that this is an abbreviated version of a thorough and impressive analyses of bilingual education programs prepared by **U.S. English entitled **"Brief Summaries of Misleading Studies Cited to Support the New York State Bilingual Education Plan."** U.S. English, with over 350,000 members is the leading bilingual education reform group in America. They generously agreed to let their work be reprinted [which has been done in part] in this chapter. Copies of the complete study are available by contacting U.S. English at (202) 833-0100 or 818 Connecticut Avenue, NW #200, Washington, D.C., 20006.

HAKUTA, Kenji (1986) <u>Mirror of Language: The Debate on Bilingualism</u>. New York: Basic Books, Inc.

Reviewing studies that attempt to demonstrate the superiority of bilingual education, Hakuta admits that there are many faults and weaknesses in these studies:

> There is a sober truth that even the ardent advocate of bilingual education would not deny. Evaluation studies of the effectiveness of bilingual education in improving either English or math scores have not been overwhelmingly in favor of bilingual education . . . . An awkward tension blankets the lack of empirical demonstration of the success of bilingual education programs. <u>Someone promised bacon, but it's not there</u> (p. 219).

Nevertheless, Hakuta not only supports bilingual education, but urges a completely bi-cultural education for all children in order to create a linguistically and culturally pluralistic society. His commitment to a multicultural, multilingual society is logically opposed to assimilation and integration of language minorities, and he laments the "shift in mother tongue toward English in the United States" (pp. 229-230).

CUMMINS, J. (1980) "The Entry and Exit Fallacy in Bilingual Education." NABE Journal, Vol. IV, No. 3, Spring 1980.

Cummins offers a theory to justify long term native language instruction, claiming that it is essential for minority group students to first develop academic skills in their native language. He argues that they cannot develop essential academic skills in English because of ambivalence and hostility toward the majority (English speaking), cultural group and insecurity about their own language and culture. However, if academic ability is first developed in the native (minority) language, he claims it can later be "transferred" to the majority language.

The only evidence offered to support his "transference" theory is the result of studies in which "majority" English-speaking children were immersed (sink or swim) in "minority" French language schools in Canada. Nevertheless, they later proved to be high achievers in the majority language. He cites this as evidence that "Cognitive Academic Language Proficiency" (essential academic skills) is transferable from one language to another.

Cummins admits that the evidence cited, development of academic abilities in a "foreign" language in an "immersion" setting, would appear to contradict his strong support for native language instruction.

WILLIG, Ann C. (1985) "A Meta-Analysis of Selected Studies on the Effectiveness of Bilingual Education." Review of Educational Research, Fall 1985. Vol. 55, No. 3, pp. 269-317.

Selecting certain studies from a previous analysis (Baker & deKanter, 1981-83) that produced negative conclusions about bilingual education, Willig applies "meta-analysis" and reaches positive conclusions. However, Willig admits that the literature being analyzed is based on research that is "inadequate in design."

PEAL, E. & LAMBERT, W.E. (1962) The Relation of Bilingualism to Intelligence. Psychological Monographs, Vol. 76, no. 27, whole No. 546.

The authors note that in 23 previous studies on the relationship between bilingualism and intelligence, only two found favorable effects for bilingualism. The other studies found negative effects, citing "mental confusion" and "language handicaps" caused by "interference" between languages. They redefine these negative aspects as having positive qualities: "mental diversity," "flexibility," which they conclude can be regarded as enhanced mental ability, intelligence.

LEYBA, C.F. (1978) Longitudinal Study, Title VII Bilingual Program, Santa Fe Public Schools, Santa Fe, New Mexico. Los Angeles: National Dissemination and Assessment Center.

Lebya compared achievement over four years in English and math scores between a group of students in a Title VII bilingual program and a "control group" who apparently received no special treatment. He begins by criticizing the A.I.R. nationwide study (Danoff et al 1977-78) because it failed to include Santa Fe's allegedly "successful" bilingual program and because it was critical of bilingual programs in general.

Lebya then reports results from Santa Fe that appear to refute the A.I.R. study's conclusions by demonstrating that Title VII students " . . . showed over time increasing capability in English language skills, [and] . . . in the majority of cases outperformed the non-Title VII students in Reading and Mathematics."

However, others such as Powers and Rossman (1983), Rossell and Ross (1986), and Baker (1988) have questioned how Lebya could call the bilingual program successful when only 13 out of 90 comparison tests yielded any significant differences in favor of the bilingual program. There was too little significant evidence upon which to base a conclusion of any kind.

CHAPTER 12

DISCIPLINE: A NATIONAL DISGRACE

P robably the best piece of advice I ever received in teacher training college concerned discipline. One of my education professors taking note of my young years and youthful appearance, warned me "not to smile until after Christmas." He went on to explain that it is easier to let up on your students after the rules have been set than to start out slack and expect them to take you seriously later.

During my years as a public school teacher, I saw many of my colleagues besieged by rowdy, belligerent students whom they thought they could pacify by being their "buddies." As they soon learned, students are not interested in being "buddies" with their teachers. It confuses them and immediately sends out the signal that the teacher is going to be easy—a real pushover. Some teachers never learned and I watched their pathetic attempts to befriend their students fail, year after year.

Then, of course, there were those teachers who wised up, but usually too late. One thing is for sure, when you start out tough by setting the guidelines and climate for your classroom, you have the luxury later in the year of letting up—after they know who the boss is. The children still remember just how serious you can become and view your infrequent sociability as a treat. Ideally, that is the way it should be.

When you start out lax on discipline and try to get tough later, you are as good as dead. The students will not take you seriously and the best you can do is wait for next year, new students and hope you learned your lesson.

I still smile when I remember timid students announcing to me, after Christmas, "We thought you were so mean!" And, I still give silent thanks to my old education professor for his advice.

None of this needs to be a big mystery to teachers. In fact, it is actually quite basic. Children need, want and respect discipline.

A teacher is not doing her students or her student's parents (who expect an instructor to make the children behave so they can learn) a favor by playing social worker.

Today, discipline plays an even more important factor in education than it has historically. Teacher morale is low and they spend more of their time trying to maintain order in the classroom taking away valuable time for teaching.

For the first time in years, teachers have to contemplate the fact that when they walk out their front door in the morning, they might not be returning. This new reality affects parents and students as well. The majority of students in large public schools today literally fear for their safety.

For example, what would your comfort level be if you picked up the newspaper and read: "Four students have been recommended for expulsion and one teacher in the wake of a violent, racially motivated outburst at Minor High School in Birmingham, Alabama. The school's principal and a student were stabbed."[1]

Or, "A seventeen year old boy was shot to death last week, apparently accidentally, by another student who had brought a gun to school."[2]

In Washington, D.C., drive by murders during school lunch hours are the order of the day. In Los Angeles, teachers are so afraid of the gang-related youth violence in the public schools that the school district actually has a hard time placing teachers in these areas. Teachers who need to work, who want to work, but are too afraid to go to work. Sounds like a Geraldo Rivera show.

Let us look at just how serious the situation has become. In 1978 the National Institute of Education (NIE) released a survey on school violence. Many researchers believe that the conditions described in the report have actually worsened.

—In a typical month, about 2.4 million secondary school students had something stolen, and about 282,000 students reported being attacked.

—An average of 21 percent of all secondary students stated that they avoided restrooms and were afraid of being hurt or bothered at school.

—800,000 students reported staying home from school because they were afraid.

—In a month's time, 120,000 teachers had something stolen at school, 60,000 were forcibly robbed, and 5,200 were physically attacked.

—12 percent of the teachers hesitated to confront misbehaving students because of fear, and almost half of them have been subjected to verbal abuse.[3]

The situation is out of control. In this chapter, we will examine how we got into this mess, who is to blame, and what can be done to remedy the situation and bring order back to our public schools.

Once again we must lay much of the blame at the feet of the NEA union. Not only is the idea of discipline anathema to the NEA, but in some cases the union positively encourages lawless and hooliganish behavior, implying that to do so signals moral compassion. This is especially the case when young blacks commit crimes: they are simply expressing distaste for a society which has kept them down.

When Senator Birch Bayh held Senate Judiciary Hearings on violence and vandalism in the schools, the president of the NEA testified that youth alienation came from "hostilities in Southeast Asia" and "Watergate." The real cause of violence in our schools, the NEA spokesman said was "the country's reliance on military force" and "the increased use of violence in our society."[4]

I have never met a student who cut classes and broke windows because of Watergate; maybe you have. The point is: the NEA seeks to exempt delinquents and criminals of all responsibility for their actions. Schools who attempt to discipline students are said to be guilty of "outmoded disciplinary and educational practices." They are labeled "institutionally inflexible in meeting individual student needs."[5]

An NEA review of textbooks included a study of a Harper and Rowe children's novel about a 14-year-old Puerto Rican "street punk" who steals and whose father beats people. The study praised the kid for being a "hustler with morals"—he had "hustled a full meal from a sympathetic waitress but left her a large tip, explaining, 'I'm broke for restaurants, not people.'" This is the NEA's idea of high morality.

More astonishing, the NEA asks readers to admire the child's father, who is "in Attica for having assaulted a policeman during a Puerto Rican independence day rally 'which suggests that he has a sense of self-respect and self-determination.'" Please!

No wonder we find statements in an NEA brochure on discipline like the following:

> Punishment and reward belong in an autocratic social system. With the greater realization of democracy as a way of life, parents can no longer assume the role of autocratic authority. Today our whole social structure has changed. Our power over young people is sharply diminished, and they know it whether we do or not.[6]

It is one thing to say that discipline is not an effective way to control young people—this is a false but acceptable statement—but quite another to say that vandalism and violence are desirable expressions of social maturity on the parts of children and their elders.

The NEA's tactic in fighting discipline is always to focus on a minority of cases where excessive discipline has been used and to imply that these cases are representative of most parents and of most children.

For example, in a similar case the NEA reasoned from the fact that some children get marijuana, even though it is illegal, to the conclusion that it is desirable to legalize marijuana because anybody who wants it can get it readily anyway. They even went so far as, in their 1982-83 Handbook, to include a legislative agenda item for the 98th Congress which stated: " . . . Private possession and use of small quantities of marijuana should not carry criminal penalties."[7] They dropped this from their legislative agenda only when the public outcry became too much to handle.

Think a minute about their warped logic: It is desirable to legalize marijuana because anybody who wants it can get it easily. For one thing, that just is not true. Laws serve as moral statements. Some things are illegal even though they cannot be effectively enforced because they make an assertion about how society views certain actions. Adultery laws in earlier years are a good example.

There is a certain sense of irony in the NEA's attitude towards violence and discipline in our schools. On the one hand they support Marxist strong-arm tactics used by Daniel Ortega. NEA resolution 1-4 on U.S. involvement in Nicaragua states: "The NEA urges the U.S. government to refrain from any U.S. plan for overt or covert action that would destabilize Nicaragua or would adversely effect that government's successful campaign against illiteracy."[8] Yet, they welcome the intrusion of the U.S. federal government into the affairs of the public schools.

You hear a lot of empty rhetoric coming out of the NEA's national offices concerning their crusade against discipline. But let us look at the result of the NEA's crusade because the NEA's own statistics paint a gruesome picture: in 1979 they reported 120,000 physical attacks on teachers by students.

The public is much more aware of the problems than the NEA seems to be. A Gallup poll shows the American public thinks that lack of discipline is the public school's single biggest problem. 54 percent of those polled said that lack of respect for authority was the most common problem.[9]

Now where do you think children lost their respect for authority? You guessed it—in the public schools. Respect for authority was lost because of all the experimental fadism of the 1960s and 1970s. The educational quackery we dove head first into during those two decades drove the education profession to abandon the teaching of responsibility.

The problem of abandoning responsibility is best seen in light of the NEA's attitude toward morality. The NEA apparently does not believe that traditional morals have any place in the public schools. Instead, teachers have been expected (and trained) to be "reasonable and fair" to the students, rather than stern and demanding.

This was a blunder of immense consequences. It was the wrong message to send to children; such nonsense as, 'You are not responsible for your actions. Life is tough. I know that and understand why you did not finish your term paper on time—do not worry about it, you can have an extension.'

In other words: Do not worry about failure; it is not your fault because you are a victim of society; or, you really blew that test, but do not worry, you can retake it. On and on, ad nauseum.

Teachers were neither to teach nor be disciplinarians; they were expected to be social workers and psychologists instead. As a result, discipline was discarded in our public schools.

As pointed out earlier, this whole scenario tends to confuse children. They come from homes (most of them) where their parents are disciplinarians, and they expect the same at school. Human nature being what it is, teachers must expect students to try and get away with as much as possible. But the anything-goes attitude of the NEA was an unworkable philosophy of child management and produced only chaos.

All the signs pointed to its unworkability: students were copulating in school. Illegal drugs were available. Alcohol was being consumed in dangerous quantities. Foul language was pervasive. By making our schools "value free," by encouraging the "if it feels good, do it" attitude, adults have done nothing short of creating and fueling the problem. Children need guidelines, boundaries and a sense of direction. They do not feel good when they are pandered to by unenthusiastic people without any sense of discipline and order; they feel good about themselves when they operate under certain rules and certain restraints. They feel good about themselves when they accomplish something, when they learn something, when they acquire skills and participate with others in serious, structured activity.

Learning responsibility helps them to learn how to function as adults. Self-discipline helps them to learn how to rein in their naturally selfish emotions and passions. In short, it helps them develop a responsible mind.

Our public schools must once again be responsible for forcing youngsters to practice self-discipline and assume responsibility for themselves.

Saying something we all know—namely that we have a disciplinary problem in our schools—is one thing. What to do about it is another.

An article in *Today's Education,* sums up a very good remedy:

> What is needed within the limits of what the schools can provide is very simple: Tough, demanding teachers and school officials, with authority to put pressure on students and who will kick kid's behinds, metaphorically speaking, until they do their homework, do lots of it, do it accurately, do it on time, do it in correct English, and take criticism with civility.[10]

I think most people would agree that a child's behavior in school from time to time makes it necessary that his behind not only be kicked metaphorically but also physically. In short, most people believe that corporal punishment has a legitimate place in the public schools; but, again, not as a federally mandated decree from faceless bureaucrats in Washington, D.C.

In the early 1970s the public schools became a battle ground for proxy wars against America's Vietnam policies and the youth counterculture, in general. For the first time, challenges to dress codes (including hair length for boys) gave rise to a substantial volume of litigation in the courts. Students alleged that dress codes denied their individual rights to personal liberty, privacy and free expression. School officials argued that dress codes were necessary to ensure the orderly operation of the schools; promoted the limited goal of inculcating conformity to social customs of dress and grooming; and taught respect for authority. The court rulings, which were usually in favor of the students against the school officials, limited the discretion of school districts to handle disciplinary problems.[11]

Adoption of corporal punishment, if adopted at all and under what circumstances it is to be imposed, should be left entirely up to an elected school board. In fact, every school district should make its own decisions regarding discipline without mandates or guidelines from the federal or state level.

Most school districts have responsible (and hopefully, elected not appointed) school board officials. It is not unreasonable to assume that these officials will try other disciplinary methods, such as keeping children in at recess, withdrawing certain extra-curricular privileges, and contacting children's parents before resorting to corporal punishment. It is a measure of last resort—normally, one step before expulsion. As such, it is an effective deterrent to misbehavior.

At present, there are thirty one states which allow corporal punishment, nineteen states have abolished it including Oregon, New Jersey, Massachusetts, Maine and Hawaii. South Dakota is expected to abolish it within the year. (The National Parent Teachers Association along with the NEA, the American Medical Association and American Bar Association have mounted a national movement to restrict states rights in this area which, in my opinion, is a misguided and obtrusive action which could exacerbate the discipline problem further.)

Does corporal punishment violate the constitutional prohibition against cruel and unusual punishment? The NEA may think so, but the courts, and our common sense, tell us that unless a teacher goes overboard, corporal punishment is neither cruel nor unusual.

There are guarantees against corporal punishment abuses. They include criminal liability under law, which teachers incur if they act in excess. Second, most school districts have a policy that insures a witness is present, preferably an administrator.

Some schools, especially in urban areas, have been forces to deal with the problem of school discipline with more drastic measures such as armed guards, dope detecting dogs, metal detectors and surveillance cameras in the school halls. Armed guards at the school give the added benefit of time—instead of waiting for a patrol car to show up after an incident, these guards are able to "arrest the troublemakers on the spot and escort them to police stations for booking."[12]

"Is such sterner law inside the schools a good thing for education? In New York City it certainly is. Teachers who feel constantly threatened lose heart. And parents lose patience with schools that cannot guarantee the safety of their children. The sight of guards and the inconvenience of security procedures are a small price to pay for so basic a guarantee."[13]

Another good idea practiced at the large high school in Texas where I taught for three years is "in-house detention" or "alternative education settings." These areas within the school grounds were reserved for chronically disruptive and violent children whose behavior stops them from learning and is an impediment to the other children's opportunity to learn.

What about "children's rights?" I do not agree with the idea of children having rights. I agree with the Judeo-Christian concept that children are a gift to parents from the Creator, and that parents function as trustees until their youngsters leave the family and go out on their own.

As a result of this trusteeship, parents exercise authority, control, and responsibility over their children. Under this age-old system the rights which children will assume when they become adults are exercised for them by their parents.

This concept originated from humanist philosophy which is interesting because in the humanist's perfect, socialist world, individuals do not have rights, only the state or the collective has rights. Thus, it is somewhat ironic that the humanists are advocating the "rights" of certain individuals, such as children. It can mean one of two things: 1) the humanists are being inconsistent with their philosophy; or 2) the humanists are posturing and using advocacy of "children's rights" as a device to further destroy the family. I suspect it is more the latter than the former. Those advocating "children's rights" are flying in the face of over 3000 years of human history—not that that would deter them, of course.

People have always known intuitively that children lack the maturity to make the judgments necessary in exercising rights, especially when exposed to the no-absolute-values scam pushed by the humanists as a substitute for the traditional values of their parents. The proponents of "children's rights" are indulging in nothing more than rhetorical posturing to further their goal of destroying the family so they can usher in their dream of global socialism.

And what happens when parents refuse to do their fair share and control their children? The states have begun to crack down with anti-parent laws:

—**California**: Parents can be fined or jailed for allowing children to participate in gangs.
—**Wisconsin and Hawaii**: Parents can be forced to pay child support when children have babies.
—**Arkansas**: Parents can be fined when children skip school.
—**Florida**: Parents can be jailed if a child hurts another with a gun left accessible by the parent.

—**Lucas County, Ohio (Toledo)**: Juvenile courts fine or jail parents for encouraging drug use or when children skip school.

—**Twenty-nine states plus the District of Columbia**: Have won federal waivers to evict families from public-housing projects if one child is using or selling drugs. Many localities have similar policies. [14]

And look at what the humanist's "global socialism" has done to the public schools in the areas of discipline and violence. Both are a national disgrace. In many schools, especially those in large urban areas, a reign of terror is commonplace. How can children learn and teachers teach if the first order of business is survival?

In Crestview, Florida, according to a story in the Tampa *Tribune*, Vernell Williams, a high school girl, attacked a school bus driver with a broken bottle, slashing the driver. It seems that an altercation developed on the school bus and the driver, in an attempt to summon help, stopped the bus and got off. Miss Williams followed the driver off the bus and the attack occurred. The student was suspended, according to the story, whereupon she sued the school in federal court on the grounds that she did not get a fair hearing before she was suspended. U.S. District Judge Winston Arnow of Pensacola ruled that her rights had been violated and he awarded her a token $1. But the judge also ruled that the county school board must pay attorney fees and court costs in behalf of the girl. The school board's lawyer has recommended that the board pay up because, in his opinion, "an appeal probably would be unsuccessful and might cost more than $40,000-$50,000." [15]

Although violence is some form or another has always been a reality of the public school system throughout its history, it was sporadic and isolated. It usually reared its ugly head in the form of an occasional fist fight between individual students. However, today's violence has escalated to the point that our schools appear to be engulfed in a perpetual crime-wave.

In a move that has further fragmented the authority structure of school administrators, the American Civil Liberties Union (ACLU) has taken upon itself the role of child advocate. It is the contention of the ACLU that children's rights do not fall under the umbrella of their parents, rather they have rights that are completely independent.

In the area of school discipline the ACLU has a couple of policies to cover First Amendments rights. For example, "Here are some of the civil liberties the ACLU would guarantee to secondary and elementary school students, according to Policy #76 and #77: 'No student should suffer any hurt or penalty for any idea expressed in the course of participation in class or school activities. Whether in school assemblies or in extra-curricular forms, students should have the right to hear and participate in discussions of controversial issues. Restrictions may be tolerated only when they are employed to forestall events which would clearly endanger the health and safety of members of the school community or clearly and imminently disrupt the educational process.'"[16]

What is particularly disturbing about this blanket approach to free speech is that Policy #76 " . . . goes on to give students full access to public address systems and other communications tools within the schools, to hold meetings in school rooms or on school grounds."[17]

The result of such irresponsible meddling in parental affairs is often profane. The following is an example of a speech given by a student on behalf of his friend who was running for student body vice president. I must warn you, it is not pretty, but this is the kind of behavior the ACLU readily supports.

I know a man who is firm—he's firm in his pants, he's firm in his shirt, his character is firm—but most of all his belief in you, the students of Bethel is firm. Jeff Kuhlman is a man who takes his point and pounds it in. If necessary, he'll take an issue and nail it to the wall. He doesn't attack things in spurts—he drives hard, pushing and pushing, until finally, he succeeds.

Jeff is a man who will go to the very end—even the climax, for each and every one of you so vote for Jeff for ASB Vice President—he'll never come between you and the best our high school can be.[18]

This speech resulted in the expulsion of the student who gave it, which was appealed but upheld by the U.S. Supreme Court. But who is really to blame for this action? Certainly the student bears a large portion of the responsibility, but would this ever have happened without the gentle prodding of social change agents like the ACLU? Perhaps not. This is why it is vitally important for each parent to carefully review all aspects of their child's education. Unless you do, your child, just like the one who gave the speech, will suffer.

Thanks to the anarchic efforts of "student rights" groups like the ACLU, teachers have had to take more drastic measures to ensure harmony in their classrooms. With legal roadblocks preventing teachers from maintaining order, more and more are turning to sedation of children as the answer, and the drug of choice is Ritalin. Ritalin is easy to prescribe since it is considered to be an innocuous solution to the problem of hyperactivity or, its clinical name, Attention Deficit Disorder. All that is required for prescription is the diagnosis of a school psychiatrist that a child is hyperactive. One major problem associated with this concerns the parameters in which hyperactivity is defined. It is so vague that many children appear to have been misdiagnosed, yet they continue to be drugged as a means of controlling their supposedly abnormal behavior.

For example, the American Psychiatric Association defines an attention disorder, of which hyperactivity is a part, this way:

The essential features of this disorder are developmentally inappropriate degrees of inattention, impulsiveness, and hyperactivity.

Some people, however, show signs of the disorder in only one setting, such as at home or at school. Symptoms typically worsen in situations requiring sustained attention, such as listening to a teacher in a classroom, attending meetings, or doing class assignments or chores at home. Signs of the disorder may be minimal or absent when the person is receiving frequent reinforcement or very strict control, or is in a novel setting or a one-to-one situation . . .

In the classroom or workplace, inattention and impulsiveness are evidenced by not sticking with tasks sufficiently to finish them and by having difficulty organizing and completing work correctly. The person often gives the impression that he or she is not listening or has not heard what has been said. Work is often messy, and performed carelessly and impulsively.

Impulsiveness is often demonstrated by blurting out answers to questions before they are completed or making comments out of turn.

Hyperactivity may be evidenced by difficulty remaining seated, excessive jumping about, running in the classroom, fidgeting, manipulating objects, and twisting and wiggling in one's seat."[19]

I do not know about you, but this sounds like just about every elementary school student I have ever met. All children embody one or more of these qualities, yet this is the criteria currently being used to determine whether your child is hyperactive and, hence, should be drugged.

In fact, "One million children across the country regularly take drugs, such as the strong stimulant known as Ritalin, to control their hyperactive behavior. While the medication helps increase the amount of time a child can spend 'on task,' (subdued) it often produces no improvements in learning, according to studies.[20]

In 1987, *Newsweek* characterized the situation like this:

Weary teachers and parents might occasionally fantasize about sedating rambunctious youngsters with a magic pill. In the bedroom communities of Atlanta (Georgia) they're actually doing it, thanks to doctors who are prescribing a powerful drug called Ritalin. Ritalin is an effective treatment for hyperactive children afflicted with Attention Deficit Disorder (ADD), a baffling condition characterized by an inability to concentrate. But not every unruly kid suffers from ADD. Since January, Georgia's composite State Board of Medical Examiners and the federal Drug Enforcement Administration have been investigating charges that children who might need nothing more than counseling are getting heavy doses of Ritalin instead.

. . . pharmacies in a few wealthy Atlanta suburbs accounted for 45 percent of the sales, leading some investigators to speculate that Ritalin was becoming a quick fix for teachers intent on orderly classrooms and parents bent on academic achievement. "In affluent areas we've found school pressure to medicate kids with marginal behavior problems," says Andy Watry, executive director of the Board of Medical Examiners. "We're concerned we may be creating a bunch of little addicts."[21]

The article goes on to assert that,

. . . hyperactivity is notoriously easy to misdiagnose. While Ritalin can be tremendously helpful for youngsters with ADD, it can have dangerous side effects, including insomnia, nervousness, weight loss and nausea. Experts believe an increasing number of non-ADD children are receiving the drug—at great risk.[22]

The situation has gotten so bad that Mr. Watry has found that some teachers actually steer parents to doctors who are known to prescribe the sedative without asking too many questions. This is cause for great concern because in addition to drugging children needlessly there are harmful side effects to the use of Ritalin when it is being used incorrectly, among them addiction and depression, possibly suicide.

Are there truly hyperactive youngsters out there who need Ritalin to cope with their problems? Of course there are, but not that many. "Scientific estimates on the prevalence of the condition vary markedly—from 1.19 percent to between 10 and 20 percent of all children . . . And the criteria for diagnosing the disorder are largely arbitrary: Many of its characteristics . . . occur just as frequently in non-hyperactive children. Such issues . . . spark 'a flicker of doubt about the integrity of the diagnosis itself.'"[23] If a doctor diagnoses your child with ADD, make sure you immediately take him or her to a specialist for a second, or even better, a third opinion.

The solution to discipline problems in schools is not drugs, or student advocacy unions, it is old-fashioned, common sense law and order. Joe Clark, New Jersey's famous high school principal showed all of us that by eliminating the trouble makers, and fostering a sense of academic enrichment, students can and will learn, and do not need to be drugged to behave. We could all learn a thing or two from Mr. Clark, but we will never succeed in our battle against the educational anarchists unless we actively participate in the education of our children.

CHAPTER 12 FOOTNOTES

1. *Education Week*, November 22, 1989: page 3.

2. *Education Week*, page 3.

3. Senator Throm Thurmond, "What Administration Is Doing About School Violence," *Human Events*, September 1, 1984: page 23.

4. "School Violence and Vandalism, Hearings Before the Subcommittee to Investigate Juvenile Delinquency," Committee on the Judiciary, U.S. Senate, U.S.G.P.O., 1976: page 19-20.

5. School, page 20.

6. Discipline: How Parents Can Help, NEA publication.

7. NEA Handbook 1982-83, (Washington, D.C.: NEA publication, 1982) page 201.

8. NEA Handbook, page 238.

9. "The Public's Attitude Toward the Public Schools," Gallup poll commissioned by Phi Delta Kappa, 1983.

10. *Today's Education*, May 1983: page 11.

11. Michael A. Rebell and Arthur R. Block, Educational Policy Making and the Court, (Chicago, IL: University of Chicago Press, 1982) page 27.

12. *New York Times*, The Editorial Notebook, 8-11-82: page 21.

13. *NY Times*, page 21.

14. Joseph Shapiro, "When Parents Pay for Their Kids' Sins," *U.S. News & World Report*, July 24, 1989: page 26.

15. *The Presbyterian Journal*, December 1, 1982: page 4.

16. Daniel J. Popeo, Not Our America . . . THE ACLU EXPOSED! (Washington, D.C.: Washington Legal Foundation, 1989) page 97.

17. Popeo, Not, page 98.

18. Courtesy of the National Council for Better Education.

19. Diagnostic and Statistical Manual of Mental Disorders, Third Edition Revised [or DSM-III-R], published by the American Psychiatric Association, May 1987: page 50.

20. *Education Week*, Commentary section, November 22, 1989: page 19.

21. "Behavior Pills—Disciplining Unruly Kids With A Potent Drug," *Newsweek*, April 20, 1987: page 20.

22. *Newsweek*, page 20.

23. *Education Week*, Commentary Section, November 22, 1989: page 19.

MODEL DISCIPLINE CODE FOR JUNIOR AND HIGH SCHOOLS

The code of conduct at_____School is based on the rules of Judeo-Christian morals and ethics. It exists to protect the rights of students, to promote the practice of fraternal charity and good order within the school community. In addition, it insures the good name of the school and safeguards school property. Needless to say, this code of conduct should lead to the proper learning atmosphere so necessary for student success.

GENERAL RESPONSIBILITY:

1) <u>Principal and Assistant Principals</u>: The overall conduct of the school in all areas of student activity is the responsibility of the Principal and his Assistant Principals. The expulsion of a student from the school is the responsibility of the Principal. This is done after consultation with the Assistant Principal and the student's parents. Either the Principal or the Assistant Principal may suspend a student for serious violations of the rules.

2) <u>Faculty responsibility</u>: The faculty shares with the Principal and his Assistants the obligation of providing good order for a good learning experience and the positive development of each student. We emphasize that every faculty member has authority over each student in the matter of discipline and has the responsibility of seeing that the good order of the school is maintained. In matters of serious violations of school rules, a faculty member may recommend expulsion or suspension and in matters of lesser offense should give demerits and private detentions when they are warranted.

3. <u>Student responsibility</u>: A student comes to_____School in order to learn and prepare himself for life. His is the responsibility to set a good example.

CONDUCT IN PUBLIC PLACES:

It is the responsibility of each student to conduct himself/herself in an appropriate manner at all times, whether on or off the school grounds. School authorities will hold students strictly accountable for any action which damages the good name of_____School. In light of this, the following regulations are in effect:

1) Students are not to loiter, congregate or smoke in the vicinity of the school at any time.

2) Students who violate this rule will be suspended or are liable to suspension.

ABSENCE:

On the day of the absence, the parent or guardian must call the center office to report his child's absence. A follow up phone call from the school will be forthcoming the same day. Any abuse of this will result in suspension of the student.

When a student has been absent from school for one or more days, he must report to the central office with a note signed by his parent on the proper note form provided by the school. It must contain the following information:

1) Student's full name and parent's full name

2) Date or dates of absence

3) Reason for absence

4) Signature of parent or guardian (Must match signature on file in central office)

*Failure to use the proper note form warrants a disciplinary demerit. Any unexcused absence is considered truancy and the student will be suspended.

For absences of five or more consecutive days, a doctor's certificate may be required. A parent who wishes to check a student out of school for three or more days, should alert the central office in advance so that the appropriate "make up work" can be assigned beforehand. The teachers do not have to make up missed assignments, tests and etc., and may give the student a '0' grade for work missed unless prior arrangements have been made between the parents and the central office.

Excessive absences will be reflected in the student's grade and may make the student liable to repeat the year's work. This would mean the student could not return to_ School. Make up work for each day's absence is the responsibility of the student. Students should not be permitted to stay home to do school work.

ALCOHOL AND DRUGS:

Students using, possessing or selling drugs (or placebo drugs) or alcoholic beverages during school, school activities or on school property will be expelled and charges will be filed with the proper law enforcement authorities.

AUDITORIUM OR GYMNASIUM:

These buildings are out of bounds for students except when in use for formal school activities in which they are participating. After school when various groups of students are using these buildings for specific purposes, other students are not to enter without the direct permission of the faculty member in charge.

AUTOMOBILES:

The following rules are to be observed by the student. Non-compliance can signal forfeiture of a student's right to drive.

1) Students who drive to school must register the vehicle and receive a decal if they are to use the school parking lot. This includes motorcycles.

2) The speed limit is 5 mph on school property. Student parking is restricted to designated areas.

3) Students may not park in designated faculty parking area.

4) After school hours, students are not allowed to drive through school property except when attending school sanctioned activities.

5) Cars are not permitted on busport driveway.

6) Students are not allowed to go to the parking lots, get into their cars or leave between the first bell in the morning and the dismissal bell in the afternoon without permission from the front office.

7) On school properties and surrounding areas, the following are also violations of state traffic laws:

a) failure to give a pedestrian the right of way

b) failure to stop when entering a street from school driveway

c) any manner of driving which endangers the life, limb or property of any person (formal charge is reckless driving). The school will report all such matters to local police and such action will result in a student's privilege to drive a car to school.

DRESS CODE:

The dress code at_ School is designed to encourage neatness and good order among the students. In this light, students are expected to be properly dressed, observing school regulations when they arrive at school in the morning and when they leave at the conclusion of the day. The dress code is to be observed on field trips unless specifically stated otherwise.

General Dress Code: All students must be neat and well groomed.

Self-styled clothing must be neat and in good taste. Any clothing appearing to be resembling or part of the U.S. flag improperly displayed is prohibited.

Patch flags properly displayed are allowed but not to be worn below the belt.

Any patch, shirt, etc., containing sexually suggestive, profane or drug/alcohol suggestive is prohibitive.

Students must wear shoes at all times.

No see through or mesh apparel will be allowed.

BOY'S SPECIFICS:

—Must be neat and well groomed at all times.

—Moustaches and beards are not permitted at any time.

—Sideburns are not to extend below the ear lobes.

—Socks or stockings must be worn at all times.

—T-shirts or tank tops may only be worn as underwear and never as shirts.

—All tailored shirts must be worn tucked in at all times.

GIRL'S SPECIFICS:

—Must be neat and well groomed at all times.

—Tight or revealing clothes are prohibited.

—Lingerie worn on outside of clothing is prohibited.

—No clothing may be worn which a bra cannot be worn with.

—Blouses without a square cut that are meant to be tucked in must be so at all times.

—Strapless apparel is prohibited.

—Straps must be at least 1-2 inches wide.

—Low cut, revealing apparel will be prohibited.

BUILDING:

Students are expected to keep the building and its furnishings clean and in good order. Keep the classrooms and corridors clean by placing your waste paper in the proper containers.

The marking or defacing of school property is strictly forbidden and is punishable by suspension and/or expulsion. Serious cases will be handed over to law enforcement officials. In addition, the student who damages school property must pay the cost of repairs.

On weekdays, students who are not involved with school sanctioned extra-curricular activities must be out of the building by 4:30 PM. Those participating in non-athletic activities by 5:30 PM. Students involved in athletic activities shall be out of the building by 6:30 PM unless otherwise scheduled by athletic director.

CAFETERIA REGULATIONS:

1) Students are expected to show good manners.

2) Each student is responsible for disposing of his own paper bags and trash in the containers provided.

3) No food is to be taken out of the cafeteria at any time.

4) No students are to leave school property at lunch time. Students who leave unauthorized are regarded as truant.

5) There is to be no gambling on the school grounds.

CHEWING GUM:

Chewing gum in the school building is not permitted. We believe this regulation improves the general appearance of our school (floors, desks, railings) as well as the appearance of our students.

DANCES:

At school sponsored dances, students are to dress properly and modestly. They are expected to conduct themselves in a becoming manner. The code of conduct as posted at the dances is to be observed. Any student violating one or more of these regulations may be expelled or suspended from school. It is as follows:

1) No one will be admitted during the last half hour of the dance.

2) No smoking is permitted in the building.

3) No one is permitted to leave and re-enter the dance.

4) Once leaving the dance, students must leave the property.

5) No loitering in the school parking lot or on school premises.

6) No drugs or alcoholic beverages are permitted on the school property. Any student suspected of using either will be made to leave the dance immediately.

7) I.D. cards are required.

8) During the dance, students are not allowed to go to any other part of the school other than the building where the dance is being held.

9) Guests passes are required in advance. Students must obtain a guest pass from the front office for any non-student attending the dance escorted by that student. One pass per student.

EARLY DISMISSAL:

Permission to leave school from classes is discouraged. Parents should use the utmost discretion in requesting permission for their child's dismissal from school. Because of the disruptions caused by these dismissals the school reserves the right to deny these requests.

In order to obtain an early dismissal pass, a note written by a parent on the proper note form must be submitted during homeroom.

Early dismissals and late arrivals will be counted as half-day absences unless prior arrangements have been made between parents and school authorities.

SCHOOL SPONSORED FIELD TRIPS AND EXTRA-CURRICULAR ACTIVITIES:

The dress code of_____School is to be observed on all field trips unless otherwise stated. The rules of the school apply on field trips.

Students participating in school trips must have written prior parental permission. This written approval is given to the person in charge of the activity. Extra-curricular activities such as retreats, athletic events and various trips must be approved by the principal and scheduled to have a chaperon (approved by front office) before authorization is given for the activity.

Only school vehicles with school approved and licensed drivers may be used for field trips.

Activities involved will be charged with clean-up and damage to any school vehicle or property.

FRATERNITIES AND SORORITIES:

Membership in fraternities and sororities is forbidden. School authorities will deal with students who violate this regulation. To break this rule exposes the student to the possibility of expulsion. Such membership would also deprive the student of any privileges, honors, or other recognition by the school.

The following characteristics would give the presumption that a group is a fraternity or sorority:

1) a set of laws and regulations
2) a group of officers
3) a record of attendance
4) a collection of dues
5) acceptance into or exclusion from the group by vote
6) initiation of members
7) a name or insignia that particularizes the group (especially the use of traditional Greek letters)
8) regularly scheduled meetings.

FUNERALS:

If the school provides a bus for a funeral, all students must use this transportation.

Students wishing to attend such funeral must bring in a written note from a parent on the morning of the funeral and present it during home-room.

LOCKERS:

Lockers, which are school property, must be kept neat and clean and should be securely locked at all times. A student may not go to his locker during class, study hall or lunch.

The principal and his assistants reserve the right to inspect occupied student lockers at their discretion. If a student refuses, locks will be cut off at the student's expense.

EXTRA-CURRICULAR ACTIVITIES:

Students are allowed to participate in extra-curricular activities under three conditions:

1) parental permission
2) permission of school administration
3) grade point average of_____

PUBLICATIONS:

At no time should publications be distributed by faculty or other students without the prior approval of the school administration.

SMOKING:

Students are not permitted to smoke or hold a lighted cigarette on school property, in the school buildings, on school buses or in any area in the vicinity of the school. The penalty is suspension.

The administration reserves the right to confiscate any cigarettes which are found on students.

STEALING:

Students who steal will be suspended and are liable to permanent expulsion. All theft cases will be reported with local law enforcement officers.

TARDINESS:

_____minutes are allowed between class changes. This is more than sufficient time for a student to go to his locker and make his way from one class to another in plenty of time to be seated when the bell rings. Anything short of this, will be considered tardy.

The tardy policy will be strictly and evenly enforced and demerits given to violators. Three or more demerits warrants one week in mandatory after-school study hall.

TELEPHONES:

Telephone messages will not be delivered to students during class time except for emergencies. No student may use a public phone during class time which includes study halls and assemblies without permission.

TRUANCY:

Being absent from any scheduled exercise, or unauthorized leaving of school, is considered truancy.

1) <u>School truancy</u>—unauthorized non-attendance at school, leaving the campus without permission, forged excuse notes are major offenses punishable as follows:

    a) first time—suspension

    b) second time—suspension

    c) third time—expulsion

    d) Each time will be reported to parents and truancy officers with local law enforcement agencies.

2) <u>Class truancy</u>—skipping class but remaining on school property is punishable as follows: three demerits for **EACH** class skipped plus possible private detention at the discretion of the school administration:

WEAPONS:

Any student caught carrying or possessing a weapon of any type will be expelled immediately. Said student will also have charges pressed against him by the school district. A partial listing includes knives with at least____inch blades, mace, bats, guns, ammunition, explosives, stun guns or other electrical gadgets.

PENALTIES

Violations of the rules at_____School will be met with the following penalties:

DETENTION AND DEMERITS:

1) <u>Private detention</u>—may be given by any member of the school administration or faculty (with administration permission) to a student who violates the school's rules. A student may be asked to remain after school by a teacher because of some violation of the rules or classroom misconduct the teacher wants to remedy as long as he has been given one day's prior notice. A student may not absence himself from this.

2) <u>Disciplinary Demerit</u>—a student violating certain rules of the school will be given a disciplinary demerit. The accumulation of five

(5) disciplinary demerits will result in the student's being suspended from the school.

SUSPENSION:

Suspension is a serious penalty. For breach of school regulations:

1) a student shall be sent home for a period of one to three days depending on the nature of the offense.

2) Before the student is allowed to return, the parents must confer with the school administration in charge of discipline.

3) In-school suspension: at the discretion of the school administration and in-lieu of an out-of-school suspension, a student may be required to spend one to thirty days at the In-House suspension center (located on school grounds) where he will be in a solitary, noiseless environment. He will not be allowed to speak to other students and will work on pre-assigned class work during the confinement. Students will eat lunch observing the same rules and follow the same school schedule.

Offenses for which a student may receive suspension are:

1) five (5) disciplinary demerits

2) truancy

3) smoking

4) using profanity

5) disrespect to a member of the staff

6) fighting

7) cheating and similar offenses

8) forgery

9) defacing or destroying school property

10) possession of weapon

11) stealing

12) failure to attend in-house suspension or after-school study halls

EXPULSION:

For serious violation of the rules a student may be asked to withdraw from_____School. Criminal charges will be pressed by the school district with local law enforcement agencies.

Expulsion **may** take place for the following reasons:

1) stealing

2) cheating

3) disrespect to a staff member

4) possession of a weapon

5) damage to school property

6) defacing and destroying school property

7) false fire alarms and bomb threats

Expulsion **will** take place for the following reasons:

1) using, possessing or selling alcoholic beverages during school, school activities or on school property.

2) using, possessing or selling drugs or designed drugs during school, school activities or on school property.

3) using or possessing weapons on school property or during school related activities.

**Any severe disruption of the school day may also make a student liable to suspension and/or expulsion.

**If a student receives three suspensions during the course of a school year, he is liable to expulsion.

WHAT PARENTS NEED TO KNOW ABOUT SCHOOL RECORDS

On November 14, 1974, The Family Educational Rights and Privacy Act (FERPA), commonly known as the "Buckley Amendment" was enacted as a federal law by Congress. It assures the right of all parents or guardians over 18 years old and any student over 18 years old "to see, correct and control access to student records." Schools are <u>required</u> to establish written procedures to carry out these rights, and the Department of Education (DOE) is required to see that they do."[1] Furthermore, schools are required by law to send parents an annual notice informing them of the procedure for viewing their child's records.[2]

Divorced and noncustodial parents also have the right to access their child's records under the Buckley Amendment.

Even though the Buckley Amendment does not permit a parent to view psychiatric or "treatment" records, you may have a doctor look at them for you.

The Buckley Amendment guarantees parents the right to have copies of their children's records made, although the school can charge a reasonable fee for copying charges.

A parent may seek to correct misleading or false statements in their child's records in the following manner: "First, ask the principal or dean to remove it and explain why. If he or she agrees, then you don't have to go any further. The school has a 'reasonable' period of time to agree or refuse. If the school official refuses, request a hearing. Put your request in writing and send it to the principal or the school official designated in your school's procedures. Be sure to keep a copy of your request.

"In this case a hearing means a meeting between you and school officials, presided over by an impartial individual known as a hearing officer. The purpose is to let each side present evidence about the school record in dispute and to let the hearing officer decide who is right. Each school must establish its own procedures for conducting hearings. These rules determine who is permitted to act as a hearing officer and how long it will be until you receive a decision. Hearing procedures must comply with DOE regulations."

A hearing must be held within a "reasonable" length of time after requested and you are allowed to bring someone with you to the hearing. If the hearing officer decides against you, your alternatives include filing a written statement of protest listing your objections. This letter of protest, by law, must be included in your child's file and released to anyone viewing your child's records.

Remember, these records can not be released without your prior permission to law enforcement officers, potential employers, etc., with the exception of school personnel. You may get a listing from the school of <u>who</u> has asked for your records and <u>who</u> has reviewed them. By law, they must keep a record of this with your child's file.

If a school district refuses to allow you to view or have copies of your child's records you may file a formal complaint with the Department of Education (DOE), who is responsible for enforcing the Buckley Amendment. Send your complaint to:

Family Policy and Regulations Office
U.S. Department of Education
400 Maryland Avenue SW
Washington, D.C. 20202

The FERPA office will contact the school on your behalf and ask them to respond. If DOE decides the school is in violation and has not responded lawfully, they can take action to have all federal funds to the school stopped.

For additional information, write the FERPA office and request a free copy of the Buckley Amendment and any pertinent information.

FOOTNOTES
1. "Your School Records" by The Children's Defense Fund, September 1978, page 2.
2. Ibid, page 6-7.

A GUIDE TO DISCIPLINE
FOR TEACHERS

1) Define the boundaries before they are enforced. The most important step in any disciplinary procedure is to establish reasonable expectations and boundaries in advance. It confuses children if they are not sure what is or is not acceptable behavior.

How can a child be responsible for the rules and guidelines set down in his student handbook if he is not held responsible for those rules consistently? This precondition will eliminate the overwhelming sense of injustice a student feels when he is punished for mistakes and blunders. If the school has a tardiness policy (in your seats when the bell rings—not after it rings), enforce it and do it consistently. Do not expect students to understand why Mrs. Smith down the hall does not mind if he comes straggling in two minutes late but you do. Not only is Mrs. Smith undermining her colleagues, she is breaking the pattern, the continuity of teaching the child self-discipline. If it is defined— enforce it!

2) When a student defiantly challenges you, respond with confident decisiveness. Nothing is more destructive to teacher authority than for the teacher to disintegrate during a confrontation. When you react with tears, or other evidence of frustration, your student will begin seeing you in a negative vein, instead of a secure and confident leader worthy of respect.

Children will always challenge (and/or assault) authority. When this happens, it is important for the adult to win decisively and confidently. Once a child understands what is expected, he should be held accountable for acting accordingly.

3) Distinguish between willful defiance and childish irresponsibility. A child should not be spanked or punished for behavior that is not willfully defiant. If a second grader forgets to being his pencil to class or a high school junior tracks mud in the hall, it must be handled rationally and without undue emotion. In younger children this type of behavior is somewhat typical and should be handled with a gentle touch as you teach him to do better. With older children, or persistent younger ones, it may be appropriate to administer some well-defined consequences such as cleaning up the mud. The point is that childish irresponsibility is very different from willful defiance and should be handled more patiently.

4) Reassure and teach after the confrontation is over. After an episode of conflict during which the teacher has demonstrated his authority (particularly if it resulted in tears from the student), a younger child may want to be hugged or reassured. Even though we are warned against such behavior as educators, how many of us could not react thusly? Gently let him know why he was punished and how it can be avoided next time. With older children, I would never suggest a physical encounter. A moment of open communication should suffice and help to build respect and fondness.

5) Avoid making impossible demands on your students. Be sure that what you ask of your students, they are capable of delivering. If a child is truly not capable of academic success, he should never be chastised for lack of it. This type of impossible demand puts the student in an unresolvable conflict. Not only is a discipline problem inevitable, it could cause emotional damage to the child as well.

6) Be professional, kind and consistent. A teacher/student relationship characterized by these qualities will be healthy and conducive to learning, even though there are bound to be mistakes and errors on both sides.

PREVENTIVE DISCIPLINE TECHNIQUES:

It is far better to prevent discipline problems from happening than to have to correct them. Here are some rules for teachers to follow which should help problems from arising.

1) The well-organized teacher prepares her class thoroughly; begins teaching immediately and does her best to make it interesting. Students are constantly occupied. This teacher understands that unpredictable and arbitrary conduct leads to disciplinary problems.

2) The teacher must be the consummate professional. She should never argue with her students or use coarse language. She should never lower herself to their (age) level.

3) Students should have assigned seating. Copies of the seating arrangement per class should be left with the Assistant Principal (for substitute teachers) and in the teacher's desk drawer. Remember to revise the list if changes occur during the year.

4) Students should be expected and required to take their places as soon as they enter the classroom and be in their seats when the tardy bell rings. They should never be allowed to leave them without permission.

5) A class should never be left without supervision.

6) A teacher should have her desk arranged where she can see every student in her class at all times.

7) Materials which do not pertain to the lesson should not be allowed to remain on the students' desk.

8) If there is disorder in the class, stop the lesson until the students return to good order.

9) Begin and end the lesson on time.

THE LESSON:

10) When using the blackboard, the teacher should turn her back on the class as little as possible.

11) The teacher should be conscious of her voice during the lesson. Her tone should be moderate and clear. She might tape a lesson and play it back to evaluate her classroom technique.

12) The teacher should not lecture too much. Class participation should be encouraged.

13) The teacher should never crutch on audio/visual materials. They are a wonderful teaching supplement but should never take the place of solid instruction.

14) Work demanded of students should not be too easy or too hard. Challenge the students to the level of their capability.

15) A teacher should never use controversial speakers or supplementary materials without first clearing them with the front office and secondly, with the parents.

POLICY ON ASSIGNMENTS:

All work submitted by the students should be done neatly in ink or type. When then is insisted on, students will turn in their work promptly and well done. Homework should be given often; on occasion, it would be well to give study assignments which supplement that day's class work. Assignments should always be:

1) Clear and readily understood; it is best to write out assignments on the blackboard.

2) Motivated—students should be able to see why the work is being given; "busy work" is frustrating and a hindrance to the learning process.

3) Creatively help the student to apply class material to some phase of the subject not necessarily taught in class; i.e., reports, projects.

4) Follow up. Do not give assignments that will not be graded and returned to your students. Students must realize that all assignments will be reviewed and be considered a part of their grade, particularly when there is considerable creative effort on their part. It is a good practice to return corrected work promptly.

5) Classroom assignments should be timed to fit and coincide with a teacher's lesson plans.

6) Always consider when giving assignments that the student has a limited amount of time he can devote to your subject. When your assignment requires a disproportionate amount of his time it takes away from his other classes.

CLASSROOM ENVIRONMENT:

1) Attention should be paid to ventilation, temperature and lighting.

2) Insist on cleanliness and order in the classroom. Before dismissing a class, be sure floors are not littered and desks are in straight lines.

3) Students should maintain good posture at all times. Never let a student get by with sleeping in your classroom.

4) Students who do not adhere to dress codes should be referred to the principal's office immediately. What teacher in her right mind wants to compete with some sultry sixteen year old dressed like Madonna?

CORRECTIONS:

1) The more frequent the punishment, the less effective.

2) Correction should be unobtrusive and should not disturb the class.

3) Punishment should be just, not vengeful. The teacher should be careful not to act in the heat of the moment out of emotion or anger.

4) Correction, however, should be immediate.

5) Extremely long punitive exercises may interfere with a student's completion of his regular school work and should not be assigned; nor should humiliating or bizarre assignments.

6) Students should be sent to the front office infrequently and only for serious reasons.

7) No teacher has the authority to suspend or drop a student from her class without approval from the front office. Any special class arrangement with a student should be discussed with the principal and the parents of the student before being put into effect.

8) Parent/teacher conferences (even by phone) are still the most effective way of dealing with an unusually disruptive student.

9) Corporal punishment (if part of your school policy) should be administered with a witness (fellow colleague) and preferably by the administrators in charge of discipline.

CONCLUSIONS:

1) A teacher should make sure that her students clearly understand what is expected of them.

2) At first, use reminders, punishments may follow for repeated offenders.

3) The goal of discipline is to help the student avoid the fault, not the punishment.

4) Praise students who do well.

5) Be a cheerful and zealous teacher.

6) The teacher should not expect to meet antagonism and ill will, but rather cooperation and good will.

7) Teachers must be available for extra help on a daily basis.

PHONICS VS. LOOK-SAY—THE FREEDOM OF LITERACY

One of the major factors contributing to the alarming rise in illiteracy in this country is the fact that children are passing through our school system without being taught to read properly.

The education elitists are quick to blame the children. They trot out pseudo-scientific explanations to buttress their far-fetched claims. Children are failing to read because of television, poor eyesight, a nervous stomach, poor posture, heredity, nebulous social conditions such as broken homes, undernourishment, sibling rivalry (even, an Oedipus complex) or dyslexia. You name it and the witch doctors of American education will toss it out as an explanation for Johnny's failure to learn to read.

Let us take a look at one of the more frequently talked about reading or "learning disabilities." Dyslexia is a reading disability which causes a child to see letters upside down or backwards—as if he is looking into a mirror. A true dyslexic child has a very hard time learning to read. This problem is the perfect alibi for the educational establishment because it sounds so mysterious, and teachers, of course, cannot be blamed for "medical problems." It has become the favorite scapegoat for elementary school teachers who are not teaching their children how to read.

Literally one million people in the United States suffer from true dyslexia. This relatively small number represents about 2 percent of the overall population. Yet, some education "experts" attribute all reading difficulties to some "learning disability" like dyslexia. Instead of admitting that these functionally illiterate children are "teaching disabled," the so-called experts would rather take the easy way out, medically label these children and pass them off as statistics.

As proof, *U.S. News and World Report* pointed out that "the total number of learning disabled children grew from 796,000 in 1976-77 to 1.9 million in 1986-87, the mentally retarded category shrank from 959,000 to 643,000."[1]

As a history teacher in Texas, I was informed that a dyslexic 17 year old would be enrolling in my class. This young man barely had an overall passing average but was determined to get his high school diploma. Refusing to believe he was dyslexic, I had him tested and, sure enough, he was not. Never had been. Somewhere down the line, somebody did not do their job and rather than get him the help he needed and, perhaps admit they did a less than satisfactory job, they chose to write him off as "learning disabled."

We enrolled him immediately in a reading program at the high school and, even though it took him an extra year, he passed his classes, graduated and went on to a vocational college. He now runs his own successful business.

Actually, the reason why Johnny cannot read is very simple—it is the fault of the teaching method used, not the children. Reading is being taught by the "look-say," or hieroglyphic method, instead of the old-fashioned, reliable intensive phonics approach. Probably the same method used to teach you how to read.

"Look-say" is sometimes called the "hieroglyphic ideographic system" because, like the Chinese or Ancient Egyptians, reading is taught as a series of word pictures representing objects, feelings, actions and ideas and has nothing to do with sounds made by the tongue. I can not begin to tell you what a travesty of justice this is. The one thing that should be guaranteed to parents is that their children will be reading (and reading well) by the time they leave elementary school. By using the "look-say" method—public schools can not guarantee parents anything. It is truly a hit or miss method. Some children learn through this method, those who have good minds for memorization, but most can not keep up with the demands, and not only is their reading ability severely impaired, they can not spell correctly either.

In the "look-say" method the written word is treated as a picture that can be interpreted by the reader in any way he wishes. Of course, the child might confuse the proper image with the word. For example, with "look-say" it is easy for a child to confuse the "image" of the word zebra with that of a horse, but the "look-say" proponents say that is okay, the child is simply being creative. It is not what the author has to say that is important but what the reader thinks he has to say. Each reader can interpret differently the message of a written page.

This would be laughable were it not reality. No wonder children are not learning to read properly when subjected to this type of education malpractice.

How was such an educational con game ever foisted on American education? "Look-say" was developed by the famous educator of the deaf, Thomas H. Gallaudet. Since deaf-mutes have no reference to a spoken language they cannot learn phonics or a sound system of reading. They have to read by means of a purely sight method consisting of pictures and whole words. As far as the deaf were concerned, the written language represented ideas and had nothing to do with sounds made by the tongue and vocal chords.

Gallaudet thought his method might also work with people who can hear and in 1837, under the influence of Horace Mann, Gallaudet's method was officially adopted for use in Boston's primary schools.

However, seven years later a group of Boston schoolmasters had had enough of Mann's new-fangled experiment. A bitter dispute broke out between Mann and the schoolmasters over the experimental teaching method which lasted for a year. It resulted in Mann backing down and sanity returning to Boston's public schools as the sound-based alphabetic method (phonics) of reading was returned to the classroom.

Phonics is based on the fact that there are complications in the English alphabet. It uses the letters which represent 44 sounds. Because of this there are important distinctions to be made between the letter names and letter sounds. Because the English language has many quaint irregularities, it must be taught in a logical, organized sequence starting with the simplest combinations and working toward more complex combinations.

It is a logical short step from learning the alphabet phonetically to reading with understanding. Once a child is trained in translating written sound symbols into the spoken language the symbols represent, precision in reading becomes automatic. A child might not understand all the words he reads initially but at least he has a firm foundation for comprehending the printed word that does not rely on some unnamed image popping into his head.

Why has such malpractice had such a survival rate in American education? The finger once again gets pointed at John Dewey. If you will remember, Dewey was determined to change education's direction from developing individual educational skills to the development of cooperative social skills.

Many conservatives believe Dewey, in keeping with his dream to remold the competitive, capitalist man into a docile, subservient serf of the socialist state, purposely dumped the phonetic method in order to create a more malleable people. These people believe that in Dewey's view, a highly literate society could be a serious roadblock to the imposition of socialism. A private consciousness, the greatest enemy of socialism, seeks knowledge in order to exercise its own judgments rather than blindly conforming to a group or collective.

I have to agree that this logic makes a certain amount of sense. Socialism stands a better chance of being foisted on an illiterate rather than a highly literate society. A solution could be to forcibly (by taking control of the school system) induce illiteracy through bad teaching methods. Socialism needs illiteracy and Dewey admitted as much in his writing:

> It is one of the great mistakes of education to make reading and writing constitute the bulk of school work the first two years. The true way is to teach them incidentally as the outgrowth of the social activities at the time. Thus language is not primarily the expression of thought, but the means of social communication . . . . It is not claimed that by the method suggested, the child will learn to read as much, nor perhaps as readily in a given period as by the usual method . . . [2]

Dewey never explained how somebody with poor literacy would be able to function in a complex society. In fact, the individual apparently was not to function that way at all; rather he was to depend upon a socialist educational elite for guidance and control.

One of Dewey's disciples, G. Stanley Hall, even went so far as to make illiteracy a virtue. He said:

> Very many men have lived and died and been great, even leaders of their age, without any acquaintance with letters. The knowledge which illiterates acquire is probably on the whole more personal, direct, environmental and probably a much longer proportion of it practical. Moreover, they escape much eye-strain and mental excitement and, other things being equal, probably more active and less sedentary. It is possible, despite the stigma our modern age puts upon this disability, for those who are under it to lead a useful, happy, virtuous life but to be really well educated in many other ways. Illiterates escape certain temptations, such as voracious and vicious reading. Perhaps we are prone to put too high a value both upon the ability required to attain this art and the discipline involved in doing so, as well as the cultural value that comes to the citizen with

his average of only six grades of schooling by the acquisition of art.[3]

Thus the tenet of Deweyism, which has become like a Mosaic commandment in education is that the development of literacy in school children is not only unimportant but socially undesirable.

With such an attitude no wonder you have a public school system that is geared to, and keeps turning out, illiterates. The U.S. Senate Republican Policy Committee recently released a report on illiteracy which states, "As much as a quarter of the American labor force, anywhere from 20 to 27 million adults, lack the basic, reading, writing, and math skills necessary to perform in today's increasingly complex job market." This is attributable to the fact that, "one out of every four teenagers drops out of high school, and of those who graduate, one out of every four has the equivalent of an eighth grade education."[4]

In 1969, the National Academy of Education appointed a blue ribbon commission on reading to study the illiteracy problem in this country. It's 1979 report was not kind to the nation's education system. The report said, "We believe than an effective national reading effort should bypass the existing education macrostructure. At a minimum, it should provide an alternative to that structure. That is, the planning, implementing, and discretionary powers of budgeting should not rest with those most likely to have a vested interest in maintaining the status quo, especially given their unpromising 'track record.'"[5]

The operative words here are "bypass" and "vested interest." A government report telling parents to "bypass" their own school systems because those with a "vested interest" want to see the "status quo," illiteracy, maintained. In other words, according to this commission, the greatest obstacle to literacy in the United States is our educational system. And, if we want to eliminate illiteracy in this country we have to do it outside the public school system.

I have included several things at the end of this chapter to help you as a parent to "bypass" that system. First, I have included a revised edition of the Morrison-McCall Spelling Scale, usually referred to as the Ayres Spelling Test. With the easy instructions given, you can determine the current reading/spelling level of your child. If he is in the third grade and is reading at the second grade level, you will know he needs immediate help. Do not let a school official tell you it is normal for a child to read one grade level below his classroom status—it is not. Phonics guides and aids, such as flash cards, can be found at most bookstores with the biggest selection usually found in religious bookstores. Look for "intensive phonics" only. "Eclectic phonics" is simply a mixture of "look-say" and phonics and is only one step above "look-say."

Read to your child on a daily basis and when he old enough, have him read to you. Always make readily available books and a library card. Encourage your child to check books from the library. Not only does it teach him to read, it teaches him responsibility as well. There is a **"Suggested Reading List for Elementary and Secondary Levels"** at the end of this chapter. Please look this over and use it as a guide to choosing books for your children. I have tried to choose non-controversial classics, which can sometimes be difficult.

Most of us would agree that the classics are classics because they are culturally valuable literary works that have stood the test of time. As such, most parents would encourage their children to read them so they can gain a broader understanding of preceding generations.

It is important to remember, however, that previous eras had a much different view of children than we do today, and this is reflected in much of their literature.

A couple of centuries ago children were viewed as miniature adults and were expected to learn and live as their elders. Today, we realize that children can be quite sensitive to certain events, so we as parents must be careful to screen the material they read.

In a January 14, 1990 article in the *Los Angeles Times,* it is pointed out that *Grimm's Fairy Tales* include particularly violent passages in which, for example, " . . . a treacherous maid is put stark naked into a barrel stuck with nails and dragged along by two white horses . . . until dead." The article also points out that in a later Grimm version of Little Red Riding Hood, she is eaten and " . . . unappetizingly rescued through an incision in the wolf's belly, which is subsequently filled with rocks."[6]

There are many examples like these throughout the classics, and while they might not cause problems among adolescent children, they may be a bit too strong for children in their pre-teens. It is up to you, as a parent, to make that determination, so it is vitally important that you are familar with the books your children read. If you take the time to read with them and help them to understand the context in which these great books were written, reading can be an enjoyable and rewarding experience for both you and your child.

The next positive step you can take is to contact your child's teacher and find out what method is being used for reading in his classroom. Here is a **short check-list of "phonics" indicators.**

1) Examine your child's reading primer, called a "basal." Keep in mind that most major publishers use the "look-say" method and there are only a few pure "phonics" approaches such as Spaulding.

2) Does the text emphasize the sounds of individuals letters and frequent letter combinations such as "ight"?

3) Does the text emphasize the blending of sounds?

4) Does the text explain the rules that govern sounds of letters: for example, are words presented as syllable units? If not, the child will never learn whether "baby" is pronounced with a long a or a short a sound.

5) Does the text emphasize multiple sounds of letter combinations, like "psy"?

Keep in mind that the younger the child is the less likely it will be that all five of these phonics indicators will be found. But, by the fourth and fifth grade, the child should have encountered all of them.

I can not emphasize enough how important it is for you, as a parent, to constantly monitor the academic progress of your children. In the unreliable setting of today's classroom, the chances are your child needs your help. It may be up to you to be the master of your child's destiny, but do not fear—it is a simple task. If you can read, you can certainly teach your child to read. Take the time to help your child because each year it becomes more and more critical that he or she can read.

This is due in large part to what author John Naisbitt claims is a shift from an industrial society to an information society. He asserts, "In an industrial society, the strategic resource is capital; a hundred years ago, a lot of people may have known how to build a steel plant, but not very many could get the money to build one. Consequently, access to the system was limited. But in our new society, as Daniel Bell first pointed out, the strategic resource is information. Not the only resource, but the most important. With information as the strategic resource, access to the economic system is much easier."[7] Therefore, reading and writing will become absolutely essential commodities in the not so distant future.

Even though we hear about expected shortages of scientists and engineers, experts say the real shortage will be in the mid-level jobs which do not require a college education but a full grasp of reading, writing and reasoning skills. It is expected that the three jobs most in demand in the 1990s will be nurses, sales people, waiters and waitresses.

Will these children whom the left experimented on throughout their school years be left to fend for themselves? Will they be able to compete, much less live, in the world of the 21st century? "Probably not. High-school graduates and dropouts fare abysmally on standardized achievement tests when matched against their counterparts in other industrial nations. National surveys show that a large percentage of the forgotten half lacks the reading, math and writing skills needed to handle even the most rudimentary problems in the modern workplace.

—One out of three high school juniors cannot describe, in a reasonably cogent paragraph, the kind of job he or she would like.

—A third of young high school graduates cannot order two items from a lunch menu and then figure out how much change they are owed after paying a waiter $3.[8]

How bad is the problem? In 1987, 57,000 people took the New York Telephone Company's entry-level examination for employment. It included simple math, reading and reasoning. 54,900, or 96 percent, of the people failed!

"Qualifications for today's middle and low-wage jobs are rising even more rapidly than in the past. In 1965, a car mechanic needed to understand 5,000 pages of service manuals to fix any automobile on the road; today, he must be able to decipher 465,000 pages of technical text, the equivalent of 250 big-city telephone books . . . . The secretary who once pecked away at a manual typewriter must now master a word processor, a computer and telecommunications equipment."[9]

U.S. News & World Report has developed a chart which estimates the amount of time spent reading by several widely diverse occupations. Average time reading equals time spent per day:

Occupation	Avg. time reading	Type of Material Read
Secretary	168 minutes	Reference books, lists, letters and handbooks
Account clerk	120 minutes	Correspondence, lists, ledgers and tables
Electrician	120 minutes	Technical references, blueprints & schematics
Nurse	78 minutes	Charts, tables, card files, reference books
Auto mechanic	60 minutes	Technical references, memos & work orders
AC mechanic	45 minutes	Manuals, blueprints, memos[10]

Catherine Barrett, the former president of the NEA, declared in 1972 that, "We will need to recognize that the so-called 'basic skills' which currently represent nearly the total effort in the elementary schools, will be taught in one quarter of the school day. The remaining time will be devoted to what is **truly** (emphasis added) fundamental

and basic."[11] NEA leaders are not suffering from mental illness.
They are enjoying it thoroughly!

CHAPTER 13 FOOTNOTES

1. *U.S. News & World Report*, March 13, 1989: page 61.
2. "University Schools," as published in University Records, I (1896) pages 417-422.
3. G. Stanley Hall, Educational Problem II, (New York, NY: 1911) pages 443-444.
4. ILLITERACY: An Incurable Disease or Education Malpractice?, published by U.S. Senate Republican Policy Committee, September 13, 1989: page 1.
5. Samuel Blumenfeld, The Victims of Dick and Jane, Reason Foundation, 1982: page 19.
6. "Textbooks and Fairy Tales: The Value of Classic Myths," *Los Angeles Times*, January 14, 1990: page M4.
7. John Naisbitt, Megatrends (New York, NY: Warner Books, Inc., 1982) page 15.
8. David Whitman, "The Forgotten Half," *U.S. News and World Report*, June 26, 1989: page. 46.
9. Whitman, page 46.
10. Whitman, page 46.
11. Allan C. Brownfeld, "Public School System Sliding Toward a Shambles," *Human Events*, December 31, 1977: page 8.

AYRES SPELLING TEST

Dear Parents and Concerned Citizens:

As we all know, our country has changed drastically since 1914. The developments in science and technology alone have completely altered our way of life. With America making so much headway in so many areas, we should expect our children's reading and spelling ability to also improve. With that in mind, please take a few minutes to test your child with the Ayres Spelling Test. The test will give you a good idea of your child's spelling level which is directly linked with his reading level. (According to Dr. Albert J. Harris, former President of the International Reading Association, "Readers who are poor in word recognition are rarely, if ever, good spellers.")

DIRECTIONS FOR ADMINISTERING TEST:

This test is designed for children in grades 2 through 9. However, for children in grades 2 and 3 it is only necessary to test the child on the first thirty (30) words. The same scale is used for measuring all grades, but norms for upper-grade children are higher than those in the lower grades. Please use a pencil and show your child where on his paper to write the words. Read each word, then the sentence following it and repeat the word once more. Ask your child to spell the desired word after you have done this, pronounce each word at a rate best suited for your child.

DIRECTIONS FOR SCORING TEST:

Mark each word either right or wrong. Pay no attention to capitalization. Count the number of words that are spelled correctly. The table below represents the average achievement level for 57,337 pupils tested in rural and village schools during a study done in 1914. It will give you a good indication of your child's abilities. EXAMPLE: If your child spelled 16 words correctly, his ability would be close to the third grade level.

SCORING TABLE

Grade	2	3	4	5	6	7	8	9
# words spelled right	11	18	24	30	35	39	42	44

1.	run	The boy can run	run
2.	top	The top will spin	top
3.	red	My apple is red	red
4.	book	I lost my book	book
5.	sea	The sea is rough	sea
6.	play	I will play with you	play
7.	lay	Lay the book down	lay
8.	led	He led the horse to the barn	led
9.	add	Add these numbers	add
10	alike	These books are alike	alike
11.	mine	That bicycle is mine	mine
12.	with	Mary will go with you	with
13.	easy	Our lessons are not easy	easy
14.	shut	Please shut the door	shut
15.	done	He has done the work	done
16.	body	The ear is part of the body	body
17.	anyway	I shall go anyway	anyway
18.	omit	Please omit the next verse	omit
19.	fifth	This is my fifth trip	fifth
20.	reason	Give a reason for being late	reason
21.	perfect	This is a perfect day	perfect
22.	friend	She is my friend	friend
23.	getting	I am getting tired	getting
24.	nearly	Nearly all of the candy is gone	nearly
25.	desire	I have no desire to go	desire
26.	arrange	Please arrange a meeting for me	arrange

27.	written	I have written a letter	written
28.	search	Search for your book	search
29.	popular	He is a popular boy	popular
30.	interest	Show some interest in your work	interest
31.	pleasant	She is very pleasant	pleasant
32.	therefore	Therefore I cannot go	therefore
33.	folks	My folks have gone away	folks
34.	celebration	There will be a celebration today	celebration
35.	minute	Wait a minute	minute
36.	divide	Divide this number by ten	divide
37.	necessary	It is necessary for you to study	necessary
38.	height	What is your height?	height
39.	reference	He made reference to the lesson	reference
40.	career	The future holds a bright career for you	career
41.	character	He has a good character	character
42.	separate	Separate these papers	separate
43.	committee	The committee is small	committee
44.	annual	This is the annual meeting	annual
45.	principle	The theory is wrong in principle	principle
46.	immense	The man is carrying an immense load	immense
47.	judgment	The father's judgment was good	judgment
48.	acquaintance	He is an acquaintance of mine	acquaintance
49.	discipline	The army discipline was strict	discipline
50.	lieutenant	He is a lieutenant in the Air Force	lieutenant

SUGGESTED ELEMENTARY READING LIST

A Christmas Carol
Adventures of Huckleberry Finn, The
Aesop's Fables
Aladdin and the Wonderful Lamp
Alice in Wonderland
Arabian Nights
Beauty and the Beast
Canterbury Tales, The
Casey at the Bat
Bible, The Children's
Chronicles of Narnia, The (by C.S. Lewis)
David Copperfield
Dr. Jekyll and Mr. Hyde
Dr. Seuss
Emperor's New Clothes, The
Goldilocks and the Three Bears
Goose with the Golden Eggs
Gulliver's Travels
Gunga Din
Hans Christian Andersen
Hansel and Greta
Hare and the Tortoise, The
Hiawatha
Jack and the Beanstalk
Johnny Appleseed
King Arthur and the Knights of the Roundtable
Legend of Sleepy Hollow, The
Little Red Hen, The
Little Red Riding Hood

Never Ending Story, The
Night Before Christmas, The
Oliver Twist
Pied Piper of Hamelin, The
Pinocchio
Princess and the Pea, The
Rip Van Winkle
Robin Hood
Robinson Crusoe
Rumplestiltskin
Sleeping Beauty
Three Bears, The
Three Little Pigs, The
Tom Sawyer
Treasure Island
Twenty Thousand Leagues Under the Sea
Ugly Duckling, The
Winnie the Pooh
Wizard of Oz, The

**I would like to take this opportunity to warn parents of elementary and junior high children about Judy Blume books. Mrs. Blume is one of the most popular and prolific authors of children's books. In my opinion, much of her writing contains inappropriate subject matter including masturbation and voyeurism. Please look over her writings before you allow your child to check them out of the school library.

SUGGESTED SECONDARY READING LIST:

Aeneid, The
Adventures of Sherlock Holmes, The
Agamemnon
Animal Farm
Antigone
Antony and Cleopatra
Atlas (World)
Beowulf
Bible, The Holy
Brave New World
Candide
Chrysanthemum and the Sword, The
City of God
Connecticut Yankee in King Arthur's Court, A
Democracy in America
Divine Comedy, The
Don Quixote
Federalist Papers, The
Gone With the Wind
Great Expectations
Hamlet
Henry V
Hunchback of Notre Dame, The
Iliad, The
In Praise of Folly
Invisible Man, The
Julius Caesar
King Lear
Last of the Mohicans, The
Legend of Sleepy Hollow, The

Les Miserables
Little Women
Look Homeward, Angel
Macbeth
Main Street
Merchant of Venice, The
Moby Dick
Montaigne's Essays
Odyssey, The
Oedipus Rex
Old Man and the Sea
Once and Future King, The
Othello
Pilgrim's Progress
Plutarch's Lives
Poor Richard's Almanac
Pride and Prejudice
Prince, The
Pygmalion
Ramayana
Red Badge of Courage, The
Republic, The
Richard III
Richard IV
Ring Trilogy, The (By J.R.R. Tolkein)
Romeo and Juliet
Screwtape Letters, The (C.S. Lewis)
Song of Roland
Sound and the Fury, The
Tale of Two Cities
Three Musketeers, The

Tom Jones
Trial, The
Uncle Tom's Cabin
Witness (By Whittaker Chambers)
Wuthering Heights

STANDARDIZED TESTS

In 1972, the NEA began what the rival AFT calls an "all-out war on testing."[1] The attack initially was on standardized tests but eventually included all testing in general. The NEA demanded they "be dispensed with once and for all."[2]

"The NEA mounted a massive legal, legislative and public relations campaign to arouse public suspicion and hostility towards all standardized tests."[3]

The most famous of all their ads was of a little girl crying. Supposedly she had just taken her first standardized test. Though she was "bright and happy" before she took the test, the ad explains that now she has been "branded," "categorized," "labeled" and condemned to inferiority.

The NEA is not just against standardized tests, they are against all standards in education. This is evidenced by a 1972 NEA resolution on testing which calls for "a national moratorium on standardized testing."

In addition, NEA Executive Director, Terry Herndon's address to The Commonwealth Club, December 19, 1975, insisted that "standardized testing must go." Adding, standardized tests are "similar to narcotics."[4]

A 1979 Gallup poll of parents on standardized tests showed that 81 percent of parents felt they were "very useful" or "somewhat useful," with 17 percent rating them as "not too useful." Among non-white parents taking the poll, the ratio was 6-1 in favor of the tests.[5]

But NEA officials did not let parental opinion get in their way:

—They "maim" children.[6]

—Comparing the testing companies to "armament manufacturers."[7]

—Describing SAT college admissions tests as "wasteful and destructive."[8]

NEA leadership is out of step (once again) with parents and their
own members on this issue: According to an NEA poll, 66 percent of
their teachers feel that standardized tests are "useful in diagnosing individual student learning needs."[9]

What is it the NEA does not want you to find out? How about the
most recent Congressionally mandated NAEP (National Assessment
of Educational Progress) scores which showed that "between 1970 and
1980 seventeen-year-olds declined in their ability to understand written materials, and the decline was especially striking in the top group,
those able to read at an "advanced level."[10]

Or maybe it is that standardized testing now reveals that the problem
we face with our education system is effecting not only our disadvantaged students "but also our best educated and most talented young
people are showing diminished verbal skills. To be precise, out of a
constant pool of about a million (SAT) test takers each year, 56 percent
more students scored above 600 in 1972 than did so in 1984. More
startling yet, the percentage drop was even greater for those scoring
above 650—73 percent."[11] (1200 is a perfect SAT score.)

"The evidence for the decline of shared knowledge is not just anec-
dotal. In 1978 NAEP issued a report which analyzed a large quantity
of data showing that our children's knowledge of American civics had
dropped significantly between 1969 and 1976. The performance of
thirteen-year-olds had dropped an alarming 11 percentage points. That
the drop has continued since 1976 was confirmed by preliminary results from a NAEP study conducted in 1985. It was undertaken both
because of concern about declining knowledge and because of the

growing evidence of a casual connection between the drop in shared information and in literacy."[12]

Studies prove that teachers are for standardized testing: As a report from the University of Pittsburgh concluded, "Feeling strongly that they know their own students, teachers think of the tests as yet one more piece of evidence, one further measure of how a child is doing in school. The tests are particularly helpful, the study noted, in assisting teachers in identifying those students who do better on the tests than the teacher had predicted based on his or her observations and experiences with the child."

Another reason for keeping standardized tests: "In education, as well as in private employment, the military and the civil service, the use of objective tests reflected an effort to locate talent and ability regardless of its social origins. The selection of individuals to do a job on the basis of ability rather than social characteristics also expressed the American commitment to equal opportunity."[13]

Standardized tests have their faults but they are objective indicators of achievement and therefore, of great value. They are not perfect and should not be used solely to determine a child's progress.

As you are undoubtedly aware, the use of standardized tests can work two ways: for your child, or against him. As a parent and taxpayer, you are entitled to know what kinds of tests are being used and the purposes for their use.

You also need to be aware of your child's strengths and weaknesses with regard to test-taking, as well as his attitude towards the tests, to help ensure the highest possible score. Because standardized tests have the reputation among students of "not being very important" (since they do not directly affect a grade), the child's attitude toward them can be so lax that he makes a poor showing. On the other hand, some students become overly anxious and perfectionistic to the point where they waste time over questions they are not sure of, therefore making a poor showing.

I have included questions and tips for you as a parent so you can prepare your child. Remember, these test scores will become part of his permanent record. Check with the school at the beginning of the year and find out from the principal on what date tests will be given. If he does not know, have him call you at least three weeks beforehand so you and your child can prepare.

CHAPTER 14 FOOTNOTES

1. "The AFT vs. The NEA," AFT publication #31, May, 1983: page 5.

2. NEA President John Ryor, *The Washington Post*, August 25, 1977, page A8.

3. Ryor, page 5.

4. NEA Executive Director, Terry Herndon, as quoted in "The War on Testing: David, Goliath and Gallop," by Barbara Lerner, *The Public Interest*, Summer, 1980: page 131.

5. *American Psychologist*, March, 1981: page 272.

6. NEA Executive Director, Terry Herndon in a speech to the 1979 NEA Representative Assembly.

7. "NEA Opens Attack on the Testing Industry," (Washington, D.C.: *NEA Now*, November 19, 1979) page 1.

8. NEA Vice-President, Bernie Freitag, as quoted in *NEA Now*, April 20, 1981.

9. NEA Nationwide Teacher Opinion Poll, 1979: page 22.

10. E.D. Hirsch, Jr., Cultural Literacy, (Boston, MA.: Houghton Mifflin Company, 1987) page 4.

11. Hirsch, Cultural, page 5.

12. Hirsch, Cultural, page 7.

13. Daniel Resnick of Carnegie-Mellon University, "Testing In America: A Supportive Environment," *Phi Delta Kappan*, May 1981: page 626.

STANDARDIZED TESTS: HOW TO FIND OUT WHAT YOU NEED TO KNOW

**Here are some questions and tips that you should consider with regard to standardized tests.

1. How much time will the tests take?

2. How much do the tests cost?

3. What are the tests supposed to measure?

4. How does the test supplement other forms of assessment already available?

5. How will test results be kept?

6. Who will see the test results?

7. How can students and/or parents prepare for the tests?

In assessing your child's test score results, ask:

1. How does this score compare with previous scores in the same academic area?

2. In what areas does your child appear to need help?

3. Is there a great disparity between the standardized test score and the teacher's test scores in the same academic field?

4. How does your child's percentile ranking compare with the local and national norm?

5. Are several subject areas lumped together to compile and average the score, or is the scoring done on a per subject basis?

Tips to help prepare your child for standardized tests:

1. Make sure your child gets a good night's sleep before taking the test.

2. Find out how seriously the child is taking the test in question.

3. Is your child good at following directions? If not, he may lose points on the test.

4. How neat is your child? Will he be careful about filling in the "bubble" with his pencil? The computer is unforgiving.

5. Is your child a reflective thinker? This is an admirable trait, but it may waste too much time on standardized tests.

6. Is your child prone to giving things "a lick and a promise" so he can be done with it? If so, he may be rushing into lost points by not reading questions carefully.

7. Have you been spot checking your child's academic progress frequently? If not, you may wind up unwittingly encouraging him to "cram" for these kinds of tests when you discover that he does not know the material you think he should have already covered in the subject. Standardized tests, unfortunately, do not lend themselves to the "cramming" method of study.

8. Go to a bookstore and find your child sample tests (multiple-choice, true-false, matching and completion) that are appropriate to his age level and let him practice his test-taking skills occasionally. You can help him find the best approaches for working.

CHAPTER 15

TEACHERS: PARTNERS
OR PAWNS?

The frightful state of public education that has come to public attention in the last decade has focused on some long-overdue attention on
the classroom teacher. This is to be expected as it is the teacher who
is most exposed to the public during the education process. She is the
one doing the actual work, trying to teach little Johnny in the classroom. So, it is usually the teacher who is in direct contact with the
parents concerning their offspring's school work. Other school officials such as the principal or superintendent rarely meet the parents
unless their youngsters are into some serious trouble at school. Even
then, this trouble is more likely to be of a disciplinary nature than an
academic one.

The point is that the teacher best represents the school both from an
academic and a public relations viewpoint. Public perception of the
educational system either rises or falls on the efforts of the teacher.

In some ways this is not entirely fair. If a bankrupt system of education is forced upon a teacher, even the most capable cannot make a
silk purse out of a sow's ear. In short, all is not well in the public
schools and teachers know it despite the propagandizing of the NEA.

The present crop of teachers is clearly dissatisfied. More than one-
third say that if they had it to do over again, they would not choose
teaching as their career. In 1983, 15 percent of teachers said they
would definitely bail out of the profession if given the chance; 30 percent said they would "probably" do so.

That means that you as a parent have at least a one in three chance that your child's teacher is a dissatisfied classroom caretaker who would just as soon be somewhere else doing something different.

We are forced to draw the inevitable conclusion that education is still in a lot of trouble. The NEA feels differently. The leadership of the union routinely tells anyone who will listen that today's students are the most sensitive, intelligent beings the planet has ever seen. One wonders when NEA leaders will return from their ozone expedition.

Most of us remember education the way it used to be. By this, I do not intend to be overly sentimental or nostalgic; the past had enough of its own problems which do not need resurrecting—racial inequality being the most acute. But it is an indisputable fact that education used not to be in such a desperate state. Indeed, public education used to be pretty good. It was something we could rely on to make our children bright and decent adults, productive and honorable members of society.

What is more, public education achieved this with a small amount of money. Teachers have never been a highly paid lot; in fact, in the past they were relatively worse off than they are now. This is not to say I favor paying teachers substandard wages; but it is true that despite low salaries teachers performed well in the past. From this one might conclude that high salaries are not the determinant factor, perhaps not even a relevant factor, in the issue of teacher performance.

Consider that between 1952 and 1979, education's share of the national budget more than doubled. During the same time, the number of employees in public education per 100 students increased 84 percent—from 6.8 to 12.5. Meanwhile, productivity and results, as measured in test scores, went down. According to the Department of Education's 1989 Digest of Statistics, SAT scores fore college-bound seniors were an average of 54 points lower in 1987-88 than in 1966-67.[1]

I once heard columnist Pat Buchanan put the issue into perspective by comparing our public school system to the Boeing Company. He said if Boeing had twice as many employees as they did in 1952, with three times the government funding, and could not build a plane that could fly as high, as fast or as far as the old B-52, would that be an argument for additional funding?

The NEA would naturally say yes. But not because its members, having graduated from public schools, are unable to reason. Rather, the NEA has a vested interest in more funds for education. So it calls loud and often for additional funding no matter how bad the system becomes. Is education in good shape? The NEA would say yes, we are doing a splendid job so give us more money. When someone counter argues, no it is not and asks what they are going to do about it, the NEA simply responds, the problem is education is under-funded, just give us more money and we will fix it. They sound like a broken record.

This continues to be the case today, even though statistics show that increases in education-related expenditures have not produced a compatible increase in the quality of public education. In fact, right after Secretary of Education Cavazos released the latest dismal education results (January 1990), a liberal group called the Economic Policy Institute had the audacity to manipulate the expenditure numbers to give the appearance that the United States spends less on education that most of the other industrialized nations. Why? Because this group, like most liberals, thinks that more money is the answer to all our education woes.

Let us assume that we doubled or even tripled salaries of all education personnel. How would that change things? Would education go through a miraculous recovery overnight? We certainly would be paying teachers more, no question about that. But incompetent teachers would still continue to wander the corridors of our public schools, only better dressed. And, the system would still be churning out illiterate children.

The "more money" solution has been hopefully and aggressively attempted for more than twenty years and it has hopelessly and spectacularly failed.

We must keep in mind that teacher's salaries have been raised considerably in the past ten years. Today, the average starting salary in America for a teacher is $18,557; the average teacher in this country makes $29,900 per year for approximately nine months of work.[2] Do I think teachers deserve even higher salaries? In some cases, yes, if they are being paid more because they are doing outstanding jobs. But I also think there is a lot of dead wood which could be eliminated in any given school district and this would allow more money to be pumped into teacher salaries. I have never met a teacher who would not like to see a few "test facilitators" and guidance counselors eliminated; these people draw significantly higher salaries than do even tenured teachers. Their salaries range from $40-80,000 annually!

What is particularly sad about the situation is its effect upon the students. Charles Silberman describes it in <u>Crisis in the Classroom</u>:

> Adults fail to appreciate what grim, joyless places most American schools are, how petty are the rules by which they are governed, how intellectually sterile and barren the atmosphere, what an appalling lack of civility obtains.[3]

Children do not feel good when they are pandered to by unenthusiastic teachers, some who are barely literate themselves, or have no sense of discipline or order. The students do, however, feel good about themselves when they operate under certain rules, certain restraints. They feel good about themselves when they accomplish goals, acquire skills and participate with others in serious, structured activity.

Yet all the NEA wants to do is throw more money at the problem. Robert Poole, Jr., the editor of *Reason* magazine, refutes the "more money" clamor:

> It need not cost a penny more to require homework, discipline, performance testing, and academic rigor. Even paying

more to attract math and science teachers (who are more in demand) could be accomplished by not giving raises in other fields and utilizing savings from declining enrollments. But these sensible reforms are being staunchly resisted by the teacher's unions and educational bureaucracy. Instead, additional billions are being proposed to perpetuate today's flawed system.[4]

It does not take a lot of common sense to realize that much can be done to raise the quality of education without spending a dime. Teachers never have been and never will be attracted to the profession solely on the basis of money. A dedicated teacher is someone who wants to make a difference in a child's life and receives a great deal of satisfaction from knowing a child is learning under her tutelage. She makes a positive difference in the child's life by molding their character and enhancing their minds. This is best illustrated by the fact that private school teachers do a better job even though they make considerably less than their counterparts in the public school arena. Basic to success in teaching, is not only dedication but competence.

What about the competency level of our public school teachers? That too often leaves a great deal to be desired. As a result the teaching profession has become not only less attractive but actually attracts a less competent caliber of teacher. Incompetency becomes a vicious circle.

"College students who plan to become teachers now score 80 points below the national average on the Scholastic Aptitude Test (SAT—required test for entrance into college). A college diploma doesn't always correct the problem: In California last December, 30 percent of prospective teachers failed the state's new competency test."[5]

Uneducated children have grown up and become our uneducated teachers. Said the National Commission on Excellence in Education: "Half of newly employed math, science and English teachers are not qualified to teach these subjects; fewer than one-third of U.S. high schools offer physics taught by qualified teachers."[6]

Not only are many teachers inadequate but in two important disciplines there is an acute shortage of them. Said the National Commission:

> Despite widespread publicity about an overpopulation of teachers, severe shortages of certain kinds of teachers exist; in the fields of mathematics, science and foreign languages, and among specialists in education for gifted and talented, language minority and handicapped students. The shortage of teachers in math and science is particularly severe.[7]

A 1981 survey of 45 states revealed math shortages in 43 states, critical shortages of science teachers in 33 states and shortages of physics teachers in every single state.[8]

The state of Minnesota reportedly trained only one physics teacher in 1983; in New York, out of 15,000 teaching graduates in 1981, only 61 were certified to teach chemistry.

What is the reason for these shortages? Simply that math and science teachers earn only about $15,000-$18,000 as teachers, while they can make $25,000 or more if they join a private business, especially computer firms, which are snapping graduates up with lucrative salary offers.

The obvious solution is to let the market take over. Pay whatever is necessary to attract quality teachers in these areas. In other words, make education a bit more receptive to the free market. Pay teachers what they are worth in the terms of the laws of supply and demand. If math and science teachers are paid more, perhaps more students would become math and science teachers, attracted by higher, more competitive wages, and the shortages would not persist.

The public wisely agrees. But, of course, the NEA fights this idea tooth and nail. They believe the only solution is across the board compensation. In other words, forget that there is a glut of history and English teachers on the market and a shortage of math and science teachers. Pay everyone the same salary and hope for the best. They say having better teachers wouldn't be worth the lowering of teacher morale or violating their egalitarian stands on financial equity.

The same old song of more money! But will this really solve the problem? That is not how it works in the private sector. There, people who do jobs which are in higher demand get paid more. Computer scientists get paid more than janitors because fewer people are qualified to be computer scientists and there is a great demand.

Nobody in the private sector recommends paying everybody the same for the same job, and then if shortages develop in certain areas, recommends paying all workers more money so that all areas in general become more attractive. No one recommends such egalitarianism—that is, no one except the socialists.

Why isn't the NEA against paying math and science teachers more? For the same reason that it is against "merit pay," an innovative solution to the problems of teacher incompetence.

Merit pay simply states that teachers who do the best job should get paid more. Why? Because it encourages more teachers to teach better. In that way, excellence is subsidized and incompetence is punished.

The NEA opposes merit pay for the same reason it opposes competency testing, professional evaluations for re-certification and other incentives. The NEA wants to protect incompetency. They have much to gain from a teaching profession filled with incompetence. As former NEA staff executive Bill Boynton once explained, the NEA is an organization that thrives on its ability to attract members. The key ingredient to that is to deal with members as an angry group of people. Now that angry group must be alternately stirred up and then placated by the NEA to keep membership high and the NEA in its favor.

Sooner or later, an astute teacher will see through this ploy as *Education Week* reported, "Nearly two out of three teachers responding to a national survey on the issue of merit pay said they support the idea of paying better teachers more money . . . . Only 17.6 percent of the teachers in the survey said they support the current system of linking salary increases strictly to seniority and academic credentials . . . . 62.1 percent of those [respondents] who belong to the N.E.A. said they approve of the idea of linking pay to performance." [9]

"But the NEA says no [to merit pay] . . . They say merit pay is a political smokescreen, a way to ignore the miserably low salaries of most teachers." [10]

This should not surprise you. The NEA has never worried much about being in step with their rank and file members on key education issues. And their rank and file members have never been too worried about being out of step with parents on key education issues.

The results of a *Newsweek* poll on education prove this: 71 percent approve of a constitutional amendment that would permit prayers to be said in public classrooms; 45 percent approve of a tuition tax credits for children attending private or parochial schools; 90 percent approve of competency testing for teachers; 80 percent support a merit pay system for teachers; 71 percent approve of changing or abolishing the tenure system so you can get rid of bad teachers. [11]

The NEA wants teachers who will not question their teacher training, who will rely on tenure instead of the job market, where they might have to compete. They want teachers who will not be familiar enough with the free enterprise system to question equalization schemes which the NEA expects them to transmit to their classrooms.

In short the NEA would have everything to gain from a teaching profession filled with incompetents—especially if the entire profession were under the NEA's legal control, from credentialing to the accreditation process. For this is exactly what the NEA wants. Remember, George Fischer, past NEA president said,

> Within ten years, I think this organization will control the qualifications for entrance into the profession, and for the privilege of remaining in the profession.
>
> A model Professional Practices Act has been developed, and work has begun to secure passage of the Act in each state where

such legislation is needed. With these new laws we will finally realize our 113-year-old dream of **controlling who enters, who stays and who leaves the profession**. Once this is done, we can also control the teacher training institutions—which would require another whole speech to describe—but don't worry, we'll get there too.[12]

Former NEA president, Mary Hatwood Futrell, fourteen years later proved this was a long term NEA objective when she said, "Until we gain control over the training arm [of the teaching profession] we will only be seen as practitioners."[13]

Let us look at two forms of proposed plans for performance-based pay which could have a positive impact on bettering the quality of teachers who are in our public schools: merit pay and a career ladder.

"Merit pay is a system that rewards exemplary teaching by either a bonus or an increased annual salary. The career ladder system creates levels of teachers from apprentice teacher through several intermediate steps to the highest level of master teacher. Different salaries and responsibilities are associated with each step on the career ladder."[14]

Merit pay bases pay on performance which could be rewarded monetarily or with sabbaticals, cash bonuses or help towards tuition for higher education goals.

In a tiered system which you would have with a career ladder, teachers would start as entry level apprentice teachers and move up the ladder to a "Professional Teacher" with five years' experience, to a "Senior Teacher" with a Master's Degree and finally, the best ones could become "Master teachers." "A master teacher might have responsibilities which include developing curriculum, aiding other teachers in the classroom and serving on panels to evaluate others to be master teachers."[15]

This kind of system would allow for the professionalism that so many teachers yearn for in the education field. Staying after school to grade papers or work on a bulletin board would no longer be considered a perversive act on the part of an enthusiastic young teacher who is accused of "union-busting" by her peers (i.e, disobeying contract provisions requiring that all teachers must leave school by a certain time). In other words, no one should have the opportunity to "look better" than anyone else by staying later.

This is in the interest of education? No, of course not. The NEA chucked the whole idea of education as a learned profession years ago in favor of having it viewed as a unionized skilled labor. And teachers wonder why their stature has dropped so dramatically with the public. You can not have your cake and eat it too.

How can teachers have the respect they once did when the organization which represents them is blatantly and unapologetically political? "The NEA was identified during a Congressional debate as the second most powerful lobby in Washington. While this is the highest ranking ever given to our effectiveness, I will not be satisfied until we are the most powerful lobby," said past NEA president George Fischer.[16]

With all this crass politicking, it is no wonder that the *New York Times* found that "[t]eachers feel that they no longer command the respect they once did, from students, parents, and the community at large."[17]

How did America's school teachers, one out of every two, get so duped by the NEA? To answer this you must remember that the NEA started as a professional organization dominated by principals and school administrators. A different situation exists today. The NEA's membership is primarily dominated by teacher members who have alienated themselves from school administrators with their attitude of belligerence and their Machiavellian tactics. NEA membership was in trouble in the 1960s because teachers did not feel they were getting their money's worth from the national office. So, instead, the bulk of them decided to only join their local and state affiliates, where all the work for them was actually being done. The national NEA office, in a real financial quandary decided to take drastic action. In the 1970s the NEA instituted a Machiavellian policy designed to force teachers to financially support the national office. Their "unification" policy simply stated said teachers would no longer be permitted to join only the local or the state affiliates. Instead, if you joined one chapter, you must join all three. The NEA's membership went from 713,994 members in the late 1960s to 1,709,673 in the early 1970s. It may have been unethical but it worked.

Collective bargaining has led to a dramatic increase in teacher strikes. The NEA moans and groans about the lack of respect teachers get as a profession and wants to be elevated to the rank of doctors and lawyers. They ignore the rigid standards of competence that have to be met, entrance examinations which must be passed, additional years of schooling and severe penalties for malpractice that exist in these two professional fields. They also ignore the fact that most "professions," are not in the habit of engaging in militant labor union practices such as strikes. When was the last time your doctor walked out of an operation to protest hospital fee hikes? When was the last time your lawyer walked out of a courtroom because he wanted a raise? When was last time you saw them picket a hospital or courthouse to protest alleged bad working conditions?

Such occurrences are an extreme rarity. Yet it is common place as the start of each new school year approaches to wonder how many schools will open on time because of various threatened teacher strikes.

Who suffers when teachers go on strike? Not the school board, the voters or parents—they have all had their education. It is the children, the very ones the teachers are supposed to be helping, who suffer the most. And God help any teacher who crosses a picket line and resumes her duties. According to the NEA, they are "scabs" and, if they are NEA members, lose their membership immediately. If they are not, they are barred from ever becoming an NEA member (see below). This is nothing compared to the treatment this "scab" will have to endure for the rest of her time in the school district from NEA teachers.

Collective bargaining has empowered and drastically changed NEA recruitment tactics. It has also forced the NEA leadership to show its true colors to many of its teacher members. Take the case of Susan LaVine, a tenured Illinois educator who was evaluated thusly by her school supervisor: "I need an entirely new list of superlatives to express adequately my professional and personal opinion of her. She is an outstanding teacher. Her students love her and learn from her."[18]

A few months after this evaluation, Susan LaVine was fired from her job. The reason? The school district had signed a contract imposing compulsory NEA membership on the teachers. Susan LaVine, being an independent sort, refused to join. Union officials pressured school administrators and school board members to charge Mrs. LaVine with "deficient and unsatisfactory performance as a teacher."[19]

Upon her dismissal, Mrs. LaVine said succinctly, "I just strongly feel that no one should be fired for reasons other than quality."[20] The problem was the NEA did not care about quality. Quality was secondary to control, so outstanding teacher LaVine became a casualty of the NEA's drive for monopoly control, as did Charleen Sciambi, a California teacher who won the 1983 Outstanding Foreign Language Teacher Award. Sciambi also refused to join the NEA's forced-membership scheme. All because she lived in one of the 16 states which routinely fire teachers for the only reason they refuse to give their hard-earned money to the NEA.

It should be sobering to all of us when we read polls which show that 82 percent of all educators favor "right to work" laws. Of this 82 percent, 72 percent are union members.[21]

Right to work laws permit employees to work regardless of whether they support the union or not. People in right to work states believe union membership should be voluntary for all employees who believe the union represents their best interests and is therefore worthy of their funding. In a free country, people's arms should not be twisted, their jobs terminated and their paychecks substantially reduced just because they do not wish to join a political union. Only a sovereign government should have that type of power (the same power the NEA possesses in non right to work states) and even then, on a very limited basis.

As Thomas Jefferson once wrote, "To compel a man to furnish contributions for the propagation of ideas which he disagrees with is sinful and tyrannical."

To show you the radical transformation the NEA has undergone through the years, you must remember that in the beginning the NEA vehemently opposed the process of collective bargaining and in many cases favored school administrators over teachers. What does collective bargaining mean? Simply that if the NEA has been voted into your school district (with a majority vote), even though you voted against them, as your "collective bargaining agent," you will be forced to support them with compulsory union dues—money that teachers are forced to pay on threat of losing their jobs. Now the NEA does not like to call these monies "dues." In fact, they say it is a "fee" that a teacher must pay because whether she likes it or not, she is getting the benefit of their representation with the management (school administration) because the NEA has the burden of being all the district teachers' "collective" bargaining agent. (Forget that they lobbied long and hard for this "burden" on the federal and state levels.) What they do not like to tell you is that this "fee" is 40-95 percent of what NEA "dues" would be. So, you are basically paying the dues whether you like it or not, so, why not go ahead and join the union, thus, getting all the benefits, i.e., health and life insurance options, travel discounts, etc., that a bona fide member receives?

—In seventeen states and the District of Columbia, teachers can be required to join or support a union in order to teach in the public schools.

—In 36 states, teachers can be required to accept unwanted representation by teacher union officials.

—In 1980, NEA-union officials adopted a resolution demanding the "ultimate appeal" of Right to Work Laws.

—In 1984, NEA-union officials adopted a proposal prohibiting membership to any teacher who has engaged in "scab employment in any school district in which teachers are on strike." (1984 Bureau of National Affairs)[22]

The NEA leadership continues to pound away at teacher credibility by insisting that teachers must evaluate and govern their own profession. Keep in mind, this is the same organization that has publicly denounced teacher competency exams, merit pay for outstanding teachers and abolishing tenure laws so districts can rid themselves of bad teachers. All would expose the failure of the education system.

The NEA tries to stifle the growing cry for competency testing of teachers by proclaiming it should control all teacher training and testing. It proposes to do this through an autonomous agency which would approve teach preparatory programs in colleges and decide which prospective teachers would be certificated or not. They would like this board to be run by a majority of teachers who are members of the largest national teacher's organization—handily, naming themselves.

But the NEA's idea of teacher education programs in colleges so contradicts standards of merit, is so ideologically biased, and is so filled with incomprehensible jargon (as opposed to substance) that most universities have been hard pressed to take the NEA seriously. The low level of intellectual challenge in existing teacher education programs, thanks to the NEA, is one reason so many intelligent young people are staying away from the teaching profession as it is.

It is fair to say, albeit a probable understatement, that the NEA has an attitude problem. It stems from their belief that teaching is a right, not a privilege. From this premise, they defend their rights not to be tested or held accountable in any respect.

The public has grown weary of their constant bullying. The majority of states require competency exams for their prospective teachers even though many of them are so easy as to make a mockery out of the process. Teacher evaluation processes in school districts many times are not any better.

One effective method of testing and evaluating teachers is one used in some California schools. There teachers are given a set of objective goals and a lesson plan. They are then placed in a classroom with students unfamilar to them. Their goal—to teach these children the lesson in a designated time period. (She is given time to prepare for the lesson beforehand, the students are not.)

At the end of the time period, the students are tested to see how much they learned. Their grade becomes the teacher's grade because how well they learned is, in large measure, a reflection of how well the teacher taught them. The teacher, of course, is also graded by an administrator for her presentation, ability to control the class and keep order and rapport with her students. I have no doubt the NEA would ballyhoo this idea very quickly because it does not fit in with their automatic entitlement view.

The NEA has been very bold in some instances with their staunch criticism against testing of any kind—teachers or students. In an NEA publication entitled, "Testing—It's Uses and Abuses" they call for a world without testing. Here are some of their stated objections to evaluative tests, cited verbatim from their booklet:

—Tests don't help teachers teach. In fact they are often obstacles to good teaching.

—They do not enable teachers to diagnose students' learning problems.

—They do not help teachers prescribe remedies for student's learning problems.

—They take inordinate amounts of time to prepare for, administer and score.

—They are often constructed so that the questions are too ambiguous to be answered with a single word or phrase.

—They often contain inaccurate information based on incorrect sources. [23]

Now most of this is pure nonsense. Tests do not "often" contain inaccurate information; that is why an SAT or other standardized test has a single error, out of several hundred questions, it makes newspaper articles.

Other stated objections are simply irrelevant. Perhaps tests do not by themselves diagnose why students learn slowly, or propose remedies. But neither do tests tell why Dewey lost the election to Truman. The point is: tests serve admittedly limited objectives, but serve them well.

The point to remember about testing is that there is a difference between standards and arbitrary privilege. Tests are not elitist, as their opponents say, because they do not measure social class any more than a football tryout does. The fact that some groups score less well than other groups does not, by itself, prove heinous racism. The ability to assimilate facts is an objective measure of talent, and talent reflects neither social standing nor race. Thus testing compares favorably against other criteria of advancement.

The other prime objective the NEA has in avoiding accountability for its teachers by raising questions of racism and sexism is you can only be an advocate for someone (in this case, teachers) if there is someone to advocate against. It is in the NEA leadership's best interest to keep as much animosity going between school administrators and teachers as possible. They have even gone so far as to "teach" their educators how to fuel and fan the fire.

I am talking about the infamous "Alinsky Report," written by radical-leftist organizer, Saul Alinsky and which was used extensively in a modified version by the NEA and its state affiliates. To show you the ill will the NEA needs to breed to insure their position, here are a few quotes from the NEA version:

237

> Alinsky would not recommend exchanges of letters or private discussions with the superintendent . . . Such meetings or such correspondence might solve the problem.

> . . . getting the superintendent to insult or assault your people, he [Alinsky] would regard as of higher value than ten weeks of formal training.

> The [teacher] organizer must not resolve issues even though he might be able to.[24]

In the original version, Alinsky says, "Forget the older teachers four or five years from retirement. They will fight organizing."[25]

Again we see the NEA's blatant disregard for any member who does not fall in line with their agenda. The older and usually more conservative teacher can wither away or lose their jobs. It is the militant, radical, globalists and secular humanists who will find job fulfillment and advancement within the NEA.

Curriculum Director Robert Dorian gives some insight into the brand of teachers the NEA wants in the profession when he quotes from an organization directive entitled, Education for the 70s and Beyond: "Schools will become clinics whose purpose is to provide individualized, psychosocial treatment for the student, and teachers must become psychosocial therapists."[26]

News columnist David Broder has estimated that more than 40 percent of NEA teacher members are Republicans. Yet the NEA routinely excoriates the Republican cause and its leaders and unabashedly affiliates itself with Democratic Party officials and political positions, as immediate past president Futrell proved when she addressed a pre-convention caucus at the Democratic Convention in 1984, "Whatever flag you waved during the long political spring, we must all wave the same flag this fall, and that must be the flag of the Democratic party's team for the White House."[27] This is bi-partisan representation?

Before prospective teachers join the NEA they should remember several things. One, union officials in Washington consider the NEA "their organization." They know what is best for teachers. The views of members, especially the more traditionally minded ones, are considered to be a minor nuisance that is most safely ignored.

Secondly, the NEA has a top down structure which repudiates democracy and is not accountable to its members. Elected officials exercise little or no real power. Even the former NEA president, Mary Hatwood Futrell, a black woman, was mostly there for token purposes. You see, the NEA by-laws state that a minority must hold the position of president at least once every seven years. If they have not, then in the next election only minorities are allowed to run for the office. Mrs. Futrell presided over meetings and proved to be an effective spokesman for the organization but she had little real power. She was, in practice, subservient to the professional staff led by the Executive Director, Don Cameron, who wields the bulk of the power.

NEA rules give the executive director, who is not elected, the "primary responsibility for implementing the policies of the Association," including the power to "employ, direct and supervise all Association staff."[28] Who chooses this director? Not the members, rather, it is a 'politburo' of nine people, meeting in closed session.

The NEA's cavalier attitude towards teachers and blatant disregard for their political views has begun to cost them their membership. They lost more than 50,000 members in the mid-1980s. (The NEA quickly recouped by making membership available to "all school personnel," including bus drivers, cooks, nurses and janitors.) An American Federation of Teachers (AFT) document explains why:

> We think the NEA has been promoting views which teachers do not agree with. Many NEA policies have done serious harm to teachers, students and our schools. We think that, rather than advancing the cause of our profession, the NEA has actually contributed to a negative public image. And rather than bolstering support for public education, NEA activities have frequently undermined it.[29]

What kind of impact does this NEA influence have on our teachers as they face the challenge of educating our youth? A very negative one, as we have seen.

Prospective teachers must either be ready to lock step with the NEA or clear out of their way, as Suzanne Clark, a teacher at a Bible college in Tennessee found out the hard way. Mrs. Clark was sued for $100,000 by the NEA when she responded to an opinion editorial written by Terry Herndon (then Executive Director of the NEA) and Walt Mica (Virginia state affiliate president) which appeared in her local newspaper. In her rebuttal letter to the editor, Mrs. Clark quoted directly from NEA material which advocated one-worldism, values clarification and sexual license.

Chalk up another one for free speech and let it dispel the myth that the NEA stands for all teachers and for education in general. The NEA stands for its own private power and hell hath no fury like a union which has been scorned.

Nat Hentoff, a columnist for the *Village Voice* newspaper and director of the New York Civil Liberties Union had this to say about the NEA's action against Mrs. Clark: "It seems clear from the basic facts underlying the suit that this is a reprisal. They (the NEA) had their fair chance to respond."[30] He went on to call the suit "appalling."

The NEA eventually dropped the case when they received such bad publicity and, more importantly, when it became apparent that Mrs. Clark could force them to open their financial records in a court of law and prove that they do indeed spend the bulk of their money on left-wing politicking.

I have taught with and know some fine teachers. Some of those teachers are (voluntarily) NEA members, although not the more militant ones you see at the NEA's annual conventions. I want to impress upon my reading audience that there is nothing wrong with joining a union. There is also nothing wrong with a union being political. The problem that I have with the NEA is their constant deceitfulness in dealing not only with the public and the media but with their own membership.

Any teacher who is considering joining the NEA, or for that matter the AFT, should get a copy of their handbook first and truly scrutinize it. If they do not have a problem with their union using their dues money to support ultra-leftist politics on the national and state levels, then all the power to them. On the other hand, if they wisely decide against membership but are in a non-right-to-work state where the NEA has been voted in as their collective bargaining agent, they should get help before they let the NEA forceably extract their money from them. The oldest and most effective of all organizations fighting compulsory unionism is the National Right to Work organization in Springfield, VA. They may be able to offer assistance in this kind of situation.

Remember, the NEA, much to its chagrin, is not omnipotent. Teachers should not be afraid to challenge them if they find their leftist antics morally reprehensible, but should be sure not to wander blindly into a lawsuit. At the end of this chapter I have prepared a "Tips for Student Teachers" supplement which is designed to make young teachers aware of the pitfalls they may experience, but any teacher can benefit from it.

I am confident that once teachers know their rights, they will choose to break free from the NEA's tyrannical stranglehold on education, and begin to make truly meaningful strides towards improving education.

CHAPTER 15 FOOTNOTES

1. 1989 Digest of Statistics, D.O.E., U.S. Government Printing Office, 1989: page 120.
2. Digest, page 79.
3. Charles Silberman, Crisis in the Classroom, 1983.
4. *Reason,* October 1986, editorial by Robert Poole, Jr., page 32.

5. John C. Quinn, "The best teachers deserve merit pay," *U.S.A. Today*, June 2, 1983: page 8A.

6. A Nation At Risk, NCEE, U.S. Government Printing Office, April 1983, page 23.

7. Nation, page 23.

8. Nation, page 23.

9. Thomas Toch, "Survey Indicates Teacher Support for Merit Pay" *Education Week*, August 31, 1983: page 1.

10. Toch, page 8A.

11. Dennis A. Williams, "The Merits of Merit Pay," *Newsweek*, June 27, 1983: page 61.

12. George Fischer, NEA past president speaking at the 1970 NEA convention.

13. Mary Hatwood Futrell, past NEA president speaking at the 1984 Convention of the American Association of Colleges for Teacher Education.

14. Merit Pay Task Force Report, Committee on Ed and Labor, October 1983, page 4.

15. Merit, page 5.

16. George Fischer, NEA past president speaking at the 1970 NEA convention.

17. *New York Times*, May 1982: page A21.

18. *Instructor*, September 1981 edition: page 4.

19. *Instructor*, page 4.

20. *Instructor*, page 4.

21. "The Evolution of the NEA," briefing paper from the National Right to Work Committee, September 30, 1980: page 5.

22. "NEA Fact Sheet," produced by National Right to Work's Concerned Educators Against Forced Unionism, May 1984.

23. "Testing—It's Uses and Abuses," NEA Publication, National Education Association, Washington, D.C.

24. Michael Arisman, "Alinsky for Teacher Organizers," NEA, June 1972: pages 6 and 7.

25. The Alinsky Report by Saul Alinsky.

26. Robert P. Dorian , "Direction of Education," *Bangor Daily News*, February 11, 1980: page 13.

27. Mary Hatwood Futrell addressing a preconvention caucus, Democratic National Convention, July 1984.

28. NEA Bylaws, Sections 10-1 and 10-3.

29. "The AFT vs. The NEA," AFT Publication, Item #31, May 1983: page 3.

30. *Pro Family Forum Newsletter*, March 1983, page 1.

TEACHERS' BILL OF RIGHTS

1) A classroom teacher has the right to be safe and secure in the classroom and on school grounds. **(THE SAFETY CLAUSE)**

2) A teacher has the right to fair compensation for the fruits of his/her labor. **(THE COMPENSATION CLAUSE)**

3) A teacher has the right to his/her compensation and should not be forced to share them with any other person, group or organization. A teacher further has the right to refuse membership in or payment to any organization that is inimical to his/her beliefs without that fact affecting his/her employment or employment status. **(THE MEMBERSHIP CLAUSE)**

4) A teacher has the right to expect respectful demeanor, both in speech and action, from his/her students and to have that right energetically pursued at the administrative level. **(THE RESPECT CLAUSE)**

5) A teacher has the right to discipline unruly students and to expel from his/her classroom any student who habitually misbehaves and compromises the progress of the other students in his/her charge. **(THE DISCIPLINE CLAUSE)**

6) A teacher has the right to be free from excessive form-filing and red tape procedures that take away valuable time from the classroom, and to have some input into what is designated as "excessive." **(THE BUREAUCRACY CLAUSE)**

7) A teacher has the right to decide, after parent consultation, how learning materials in his/her classroom shall be taught. **(THE PRESENTATION CLAUSE)**

8) A teacher has the right to have input as to the materials and textbooks used in the classroom. **(THE RIGHT-TO-INPUT CLAUSE)**

9) A teacher has the right to inform authorities concerning what, in his/her judgment, may be dangerous activities on the part of a student (such as possession or use of drugs or weapons) without fear of reprisal. **(THE EXPEDIENCY CLAUSE)**

10) A teacher has the right to expect professional status, as teaching is a noble pursuit essential to the transmission of knowledge in American society. **(THE PROFESSIONAL STATUS CLAUSE)**

TIPS FOR STUDENT TEACHERS

1. **Be a leader** by inspiring confidence in your students. Your own confidence level will increase by, 1) being well prepared in your lessons for the day; 2) being a disciplinarian; 3) showing respects for your student's views and giving them advice when they need it; 4) welcoming questions from your students and really listening to them when they answer; 5) being sensitive to the needs of others; 6) asking for advice when you need it; and 7) getting your students to follow your directions without generating contention.

2. **Be fair,** patient, cheerful, kind and thoughtful, not only with your students but with your colleagues as well.

3. **Be enthusiastic** and you will automatically motivate your students.

4. **Challenge your students** by asking them to give their opinions and then to back up those opinions. Whenever possible, ask higher level questions which, in turn, tend to stimulate higher levels of thinking.

5. **Use audio-visual aids and other instructional materials** but only when they are appropriate to the day's discussions and you have previewed them first.

6. **Prepare lessons and lesson plans in advance.** Your lesson plans should include your major objective for the week, then for the day with a summary of the major points you wish to teach your students.

7. **Use the chalkboard** to emphasize a point, add interest and present diagrams.

8. **Keep a current bulletin board** with pictures and interesting items which parallel your studies. Each display should present one theme or message that is short and direct.

9. **Be well groomed** and display good taste in your dress.

10. **Never socialize with your students** after school hours. Student teachers are still in college and likely to frequent local hang-outs. Al-

ways remember, the title *teacher* carries with it both honor and responsibility, at all times.

This list has been extracted from a **must-read book for any prospective teacher called, <u>Hot Tips For Student Teachers</u> by Fillmer Hevener, Jr., R & E Publishers, 1985.

CHAPTER 16

VOUCHERS: THE ISSUE IS PARENTAL CHOICE

In November of 1985 the United States Congress began debate on an issue which could reverse the course of elementary and secondary education in America.

The issue: educational vouchers. The debate: whether or not the elements of choice and competition are to be injected back into the American education process. The success or failure of the November proposal will determine whether, at long last, the ball will really start rolling on education reform.

It was a bit of a gamble on the part of the powers that be. Those who cast their votes in favor of vouchers were making an important assumption about the American parent. They were assuming that, given a choice, American parents would seek the highest quality education available for their children. "Yes" voters also assumed that the American parent has the ability to recognize and reject the gimmicky, the insubstantial and the mindless—in other words, the kinds of trivia that have been passed off as solid subject matter for the past several decades.

In 1985, under the Reagan Administration, the Department of Education introduced a voucher initiative called TEACH, the Equity and Choice Act of 1985. It was designed to allow recipients of the standard federal assistance package for the disadvantaged, called Chapter One or the compensatory education program, to use an education voucher to secure alternative educational services at another public school within their own district, at a public school outside their own district, or as partial tuition at a private school of their choice. In other words, the intent of the TEACH bill was to voucherize special education aid for disadvantaged children by allowing their parents to purchase remedial mathematics and reading help (which is what Chapter One funds have traditionally been used for) from either the public or private sector.

Because the federal government was already funding Chapter One, it was able to prescribe the conditions under which such funding would be disseminated. Had federal funds not been involved, the federal government would have been inhibited from initiating any choice proposals. It is somewhat ironic that those who had worked the hardest over the years to ensure the federal government did become involved in education (as the NEA's lobbying for Carter and a DOE) became the loudest critics of this, and all positive steps aimed at education's improvement.

But with the election of Ronald Reagan in 1980 and again in 1984, the tables were turned. Instead of a mouthpiece for their own left-wing political agenda and a rubber stamp for their outrageous spending initiatives, NEA union leaders got instead a dedicated champion of high standards, Secretary William T. Bennett, who dared to suggest that the goal of education should be excellence, not simply fun, and that parents deserved a say in how their children were educated.

Until 1985, education reformers had all but despaired of ever designing a plan capable of energizing America's ailing education system. All the legal avenues to reform seemed to have been plugged by an overbearing and condescending bureaucracy which told grassroots America, in effect, that they were too stupid to make education decisions for their own children.

With the voucher initiative, Secretary Bennett and the DOE managed to capitalize upon President Reagan's "let the system work" philosophy and at the same time defuse the liberals' favorite oppositionist maneuver of denouncing any conservative-administration program as an attack on the poor, or, as the NEA called it "a cruel hoax."

For here was an idea specifically targeted to help disadvantaged families. And, if it worked for the disadvantaged, its success would undoubtedly encourage the states and locals, sooner or later, to come up with the voucher or choice plans of their own—something all parents can use. The 1985 choice plan, which was admittedly only experimental, could serve as a first step toward a full-scale transformation of public school expenditures into educational vouchers. And this was the very reason the NEA was so adamantly against it.

For example, the NEA quickly released a five page statement in October of 1985 condemning the voucher initiative. Among the many bogus arguments used was that the voucher plan "could undermine public support and funding for public schools, ultimately weakening and destroying them"; that it "could potentially violate the principle of separation of church and state"; that it "could lead to racial, economic and social isolation of children," and that it shifts attention away "from the nation's most critical issue: the lack of adequate funding for high quality public education."

Apparently, the assumption of the first argument was that, given a choice, all parents would flock away from the public schools as fast as possible and place their children in private and parochial schools. Aside from what such an assumption says about union leaders' view of public education (and what the parents think of it), the TEACH proposal was not intended to cover the entire cost of tuition at a private school, since it applied only to the amount allotted for Chapter One compensatory education funds. Secondly, in many areas of the country, private schools are not available, so, in that case parents would be left with only two options: transferring their children to another public school inside their own district, or transferring their children to a public school outside their district

The 1985 voucher plan was intended to generate competition among public schools. And, let us face it, the public schools are the ones that need it; private schools already have that benefit. That is why they do so well.

The separation of church and state argument was equally off-base. In the first place, the voucher was designed only to encourage freedom of choice, not to either aid or discourage those who choose religiously oriented schooling for their youngsters. And there is nothing unconstitutional about having a choice—at least not yet. In the second place, the argument of separation of church and state is fallacious, since that term never appears in the Constitution but, rather, comes from a private letter sent by Thomas Jefferson to the Danbury, Connecticut Baptist Association in 1802. Liberals and atheists have taken the term entirely out of context in an effort to remove theism, not sectarianism, from both our nation's schools and public places. The First Amendment was never intended to separate God from country. It was meant to ensure that a state church, such as the Anglican church of England, would not be imposed upon the entire population. But thanks to the excesses of the anti-God forces of this country led by the A.C.L.U., we now indeed have a state religion. It is atheism, or humanism as its advocates call it and it is imposed upon all the people regardless of their own beliefs.

To suggest that vouchers "could lead to racial isolation of children" was, perhaps, the most intellectually dishonest of all the charges made against the idea. Education vouchers would produce precisely the opposite result because parents would, in fact, no longer have to beat the bushes finding the "right" neighborhood for their children's schooling. Since the disadvantaged can rarely move to the "right" neighborhoods, the 1985 TEACH proposal was especially beneficial to them. No, the real fear for education liberals has nothing to do with "racial isolation" or the plight of the poor; what the liberals are afraid of is that with choice in education they may eventually lose their ability to pit racial, economic, and social groups against each other because they all will begin to mingle more naturally.

Finally, there was the charge that the voucher issue shifts attention away from the supposed lack of adequate funding issue. Notice that naysayers like the NEA never remind us about all the wonderful things we have received with "adequate" funding—such as bilingual education, whereby a child goes through twelve years of schooling without ever learning how to speak English; or teen health clinics, whereby Mommy's little girl can have a sample of her urine carted over to a Planned Parenthood clinic for analysis; or MACOS (Man: A Course of Study), a social studies text that specialized in denigrating the United States.

The "give us more money" liberal educationists always claim to be progressive while they are busy denouncing every positive or constructive suggestion to come down the pike. Their solution to education's problems is a tired, broken record that we have all lived with for a number of unimpressive years. Indeed, the NEA has raised "shifting focus away from an issue" to the level of a new art form, so it is with some audacity that union leaders and their cohorts should charge the pro Choice forces with disguising, or clouding the issue.

Fortunately, both President Bush and Education Secretary Cavazos have come out in favor of Choice programs. Mr. Cavazos has called parental choice the "cornerstone" of the Bush Administration's educational policy and President Bush has labeled Choice the "single most promising idea" in education today.

Promising it is. "Minnesota, Arkansas, Iowa and Nebraska already have in place statewide 'open enrollment' plans giving parents wide discretion in choosing schools. Scores of cities around the country have for years offered magnet and alternative schools that extend options beyond neighborhood schools," and these are the schools that have been the most effective in raising student test scores. [1]

Minnesota is one state that takes particular pride, as well it should, in the Choice programs offered in its public schools. In Minnesota a child or parent "can choose a school in any district, restricted only by available space and considerations of racial balance. Juniors and seniors in high school can attend classes at colleges, universities or vocational schools. Dollars follow students, forcing schools to be competitive in what is legitimately described as educational 'entrepreneurships' requiring truth in marketing." [2]

Statistics seem to indicate that this is a popular notion with both parents and students. For example, "In 1987 only 137 students used the open-enrollment law in Minnesota. About 440 students used it the following year. This year (1989), 3,500 students applied to schools outside their districts, usually choosing better courses, better teachers and higher standards.

"It's easy to see where Minnesota, whose graduation rate of 91.4 percent is the highest in the nation, might benefit from school choice. But it works in less prosperous places, too. When choice was introduced in a district in East Harlem, the graduation rate in one high school rose from 7 percent to more than 90 percent."[3]

Even though school Choice programs have exhibited remarkable success in addressing the myriad problems that exist in the current structure of the NEA-guided public schools, President Bush will face stiff opposition to his policy of gradual inclusion of Choice.

The biggest problem President Bush or anyone else will have to face in getting a Choice plan through Congress is that we have let the liberals frame the debate not only on the Choice issue but on the voucher issue as well. Like the NEA, to whom several key members of Congress (including Congressman Augustus Hawkins, Chairman of the powerful House Committee on Education and Labor) erroneously believe they owe their careers, many of the liberal camp do not want Choice in education. A few of these, of course, sincerely believe the average American parent just has not enough sense, or judgment, or expertise, to exercise such a choice. But the greatest, and most vocal, of those who oppose Choice do so because they know that competition in education will signal an end to the education monopoly in this country. And if the monopoly is broken, that means a lot of those people who have a stake in the status quo will lose their power. Remember, former Indiana legislator Joan Gubbins did not call public education the most reform-proof special interest in the country for nothing.

Like the union leaders of the NEA, these people are not interested in improving education, reforming education, or bringing new ideas to it. Like the NEA, they do not care about education. They care about keeping the power structure intact, and the sooner the American people understand this, the better able they will be to significantly change what is wrong with the American educating process.

It is relatively easy, once one knows what to look for, to see through these kinds of questions to the real objections to Choice. In the case of the NEA, one needs to look at its annual legislative agenda. There is found year after year a blanket condemnation of any and all voucher and tuition tax credit concepts—in other words, all "Choice schemes," as they like to put it. Looking further, the reader will find that what the union leaders are objecting to in reality is competition—merit, grading, testing, professional evaluations, and so on.

The sad fact is that many in our country find the ideal of competition uncomfortable. That becomes particularly critical in an education environment, where we are supposed to be teaching youngsters how our system, economic and otherwise, works. Competition is one of the bases of our democracy, and the values that go with it—like initiative, perseverance, determination, self-reliance—are what make our free enterprise system work.

So, Congress and the American people need to think long and hard about what a Choice plan, even a limited one like the Bush proposal, will mean to them and to the future of this country. For the outcome of this issue will in many ways be a statement about the course we want to pursue as a nation.

CHAPTER 16 FOOTNOTES
1. Lee A. Daniels, "Choice," *New York Times*, October 18, 1989.
2. Suzanne Fields, *The Washington Times*, September 21, 1989, page A14.
3. Fields, page A14.

PARENTS' BILL OF RIGHTS

1) Parents have the right to have the final say as to what their children will or will not be taught.

2) Parents have the right to demand that their children will not be subjected to either physical or psychological abuse in the classroom.

3) Parents have the right to insist that their children will not be treated as laboratory specimens testing some new theory of education.

4) Parents have the right to send their children to whatever school they may choose free from the dictates of federal judges, or administrators who choose to bus children all over the landscape.

5) Parents have the right to demand accountability in their local schools.

6) Schools reflect the morals, ethics and mores of the local community. As such they reflect the values of the parents living there and local control of the schools is an unalienable right of the parents.

7) Parents have the right to know that their children will not be subjected to instruction which encourages their children not to tell their parents about the school's curriculum.

8) The parents have the right to remove their children from the public school if they feel the schools are indoctrinating their children against the wishes of the parents.

9) The parents have the right to forbid their children from taking part in school conducted classes on political activism. The schools are not to be used as social experimentation labs for espousing political creeds in opposition to those of the parents.

10) The parents have to be satisfied with the progress their children make in school before assenting to grade advancement or graduation.

HOW TO WRITE EFFECTIVE
LETTERS TO ELECTED OFFICIALS

DO'S:

1. Always be kind, courteous and respectful.

2. Only address one issue per correspondence.

3. Be specific and add the name of the legislation or bill number if you know it.

4. Make your letter personal and include a complete return address.

5. Be specific as to why you are writing and ask direct questions.

6. If he has voted right on issues you are concerned about in the past, thank him for those votes.

7. Ask for a prompt reply.

8. If you receive a reply that seems to bypass your question, write again thanking him for his reply and ask him to specifically answer your question.

9. Feel free to send mailgrams. By using Western Union, your message will be delivered in one day's time and the charge will be added to your phone bill. (Western Union 1-800-325-5300)

DON'TS:

1. Do not be rude or threatening.

2. Do not mix issues. Stick to one subject.

3. Do not use form letters, postcards or petitions when you can help it.

4. Do not use irrational or irresponsible language in your letter.

**This "model letter" was extracted in part from, *"How To Write Effective Letters To Your Legislators,"* by Mrs. H.J. Cameron.

CHAPTER 17

EDUCATION ENTERPRISE ZONES: HOMING IN ON EDUCATION'S MISSING LINK

E ver since the National Commission for Excellence in Education released its report, A Nation At Risk, the American parent could not get enough bad news. Poll after poll showed a loss of confidence in public education. Drugs were up, praying was out, test scores were down, and teachers were on strike.

Responding to the furor, experts went back to the drawing board and dumped on implausible excuses—running the gamut from hyperactivity to cultural deprivation—to explain why Johnny could not read or write. To add insult to injury in the end they decided it was because little Johnny could not cope. Indeed, if all the reports of the 1960s and 1970s were taken together, nearly every child in the nation could boast a statistically valid learning disability.

For example, in 1982-83 the federal government provided funding for 31,196 blind students, and more than 1.7 million "learning disabled" children. Over a seven year period, that is an increase of 119 percent. The hoax was that most of these children were not learning disabled at all; they were "teaching disabled." That is, most of the 1.7 million youngsters acquired their handicap in the public school classroom because of widespread educational malpractice—all at the taxpayer's expense.

So back to the drawing board and along came the brainstorms to save education: Less pressure, more social activities, fewer regulations, and "mini courses." When that did not work, and parents and teachers started blaming each other, experts went to work on what they viewed as the heart of the matter—social pressures— and injected more sex education, nuclear war curriculum, and drug-abuse education courses into the school day. Textbook companies added their own supplemental literature to existing subjects like English and history to further fuel these social issues.

Declaring that no price was too high, self-styled experts like the NEA leaders carried the banner for high dollar federal programs: bilingual education, special classes for the handicapped and emotionally disturbed, and more. For the NEA, it was a dream come true; the programs proved multi-million (and billion) dollar subsidies such as Title I, Head Start, Special Education, and the Office of Basic Skills.

Schools suddenly found that to obtain federal money for things like libraries and construction,they would have to hire psychiatrists, guidance counselors, and something called "test facilitators." Other interested parties, primarily ex-football coaches turned administrators, thought perhaps a heightened emphasis on sports—and increased school spirit—would make the difference.

Finally in the mid 1980s, having utterly failed to decelerate the nation's headlong plunge into ignorance, the education establishment threw up its collective hands in exasperation and called for longer school days, longer school years, mandatory kindergartens, more pressure, more homework, grade point prerequisites for participation in sports and "back to basics." The heat was on, and the ball was in the educator's court.

GOVERNMENT SCHOOLS OR COMMUNITY SCHOOLS?

It was not until recently, though, that anybody took a hard look at the basic premises behind the public school system. Surprisingly, it is not based on the noble Jeffersonian ideal about free and accessible education for all; rather, the public school is a self-serving mechanism that operates not in the interests of children or their families, but in the interest of itself—and, of course, of the government that keeps it solvent.

Simply put, public education in this country is a welfare program—a "make-work" program that does not work.

Public schools are, in reality, government schools, or "state schools"; they are owned, operated and funded by the government. Consequently, the children who attend them belong not to their parents, but to the school or government. Taxpayers' dollars, while necessary to the process, are viewed much in the same way as tax dollars for any other purpose—public roads, for example, or food stamps. Because the taxes for the purpose of education apply to all, the dollars are not seen as representing a constituency.

And like any other welfare program, public education is operated on the premise that those it serves do not—and cannot—know what is good for them. Thus, it has grown beyond anyone's ability to make it responsive to the people who pay for it.

Moreover, it is not surprising that there is a built-in conflict of interest between the home and the school. What has masked the true nature of the public school as an institution is that there has always been a kind of lip service, however grudging, given to the concept of parental involvement and support. Too, schools in the private sector always did—and still—operate on the basis of parental involvement, so that over the years, Americans have assumed that this, in fact, is the true nature of the school/home relationship. Parent conferences, PTAs, and back-to-school nights have reinforced this view, despite clear indications that these are little more than token symbols of interaction between parents and a child's instructors.

The fact is the public school simply does not exist to fulfill the expectations of parents, and it does not have to. It exists to protect its own interests, and the students are caught somewhere in between.

PARENTS: THE FORGOTTEN CONSTITUENCY:

In the days when public schools were still small, independent and unconnected entities with no big programs which owe their existences to the federal bureaucracies that created them, both parents and teachers had no trouble communicating their concerns to one another.

But with the 1930s and the Second World War came the push toward consolidation and collectivization which changed the way people conducted business. The individualistic, independent basis shifted toward a layered bureaucracy at all levels of endeavor—from independent grocers to steel workers. Education was no exception. Eventually, people were expected not to speak on their own behalf; instead, the collective emerged, with its designated spokespersons, who for a fee took up the cause of the individual—making his contracts, settling his disputes, and even disseminating his opinions in the form of ever-larger collectives known as lobbying organizations.

This is where parents lost out. They never had an organization; they never had a spokesperson. And though, perhaps, the largest interest-group in America, parents suddenly did not have a voice, either.

When government considers parents as a group, it does not see them as a class of citizens, and only recently has there been any visible interest in addressing parent issues (called "family issues"). Yet it is parents who must meet with and coordinate the various experts and institutions that affect the upbringing of their children.

Parents are like executives of a large firm—responsible for the smooth coordination of the many people and processes that must work together to produce a final product. But parent "executives" labor under enormous restrictions. While any business executive would have authority to influence the decisions of those whose work he oversees, the same individual, as a parent, has no authority over those with whom he must share the burden of raising his family. Parents always work from a position of inferiority. Teachers, doctors, social work-

259

ers—all of whom deal with only a "piece" of the child—have status. Parents, on the other hand, have no authority to make anybody listen to them.

Yet parents supposedly have the responsibility for their children's upbringing. If anything goes wrong, parents are blamed. Parents alone must answer for the mental and moral character of their sons and daughters. They do this despite influences from the street, the so-called peer group, the mass media, teachers and a well marketed and "packaged" youth culture which they can neither escape nor contend with. Responsibility for children has, in many ways, become a test of endurance, and no amount of money or subsidies can solve the problem.

For more than two decades now, leaders at the NEA and other proponents of a larger federal role in education have questioned whether the family is truly fit to assume the role of major caretaker of society's young people. They question this in spite of the family's endurance, in step with the history of mankind. They begin with the premise that parents are either ignorant or irresponsible.

But if parents are to be charged with the responsibility for raising their children, they must be allowed to do so in ways consistent with their children's needs and their own values.

It is parents who are the key link to excellence in education. No one understands this better than the Japanese. When you cut parents out of the educating process, you undermine and eventually destroy the entire effort.

It is time to start working from the natural premise that parents are responsible, caring, and in the best position to make judgments relating to their own offspring. Schools must, therefore, be returned to parents and local communities. Furthermore, the school cannot continue to be the laboratory system for social change. Schools must be reinstated as institutions that teach children basic academic skills. The longer we delay these reforms, the closer to outright collapse public education will come. It is already dangerously close.

THE EDUCATION ENTERPRISE ZONE:

In 1983, I developed a concept for education reform that frankly, even my conservative peers thought was too radical for any type of widespread acceptance. The Education Enterprise Zone (EEZ) could well be the vehicle that gets public education back on the right track. Never having been one to let a little criticism get in my way, I proceeded to have my idea placed in the Education Plank of the 1984 Republican Platform (obscure as it may have been). Although the idea has received more than its fair share of media attention, it was not until early 1989, when Governor Pete DuPont became interested in the reform measure that it began to gain the acceptance I had long hoped for. Governor DuPont is working to establish EEZs in Delaware during the 1990s. I wish him the best of luck.

I still believe this bold concept is as fresh today as it was in 1983 and, if acted upon, would cut through the centralized, bureaucratic control of education, would remove burdensome union and state regulations, and would promote meaningful dialogue between the parent, the school, and the community.

The most important aspect of the EEZ, is its contention that the kind of instruction children receive is the responsibility of parents—an idea that has met with overwhelming approval from the taxpaying public. The EEZ is based on the premise espoused by most Americans: that a school is an extension of the home. Under the EEZ concept, both the social and academic training of a child belongs to the parents, and it assumes that when parents send their children to school, they are delegating, not abdicating, responsibility.

I have always believed that the first target for an EEZ should be a small, rural test area which is willing to serve as the site for a pilot project, or demonstration area. The parents and school would enter into an arrangement that would leave the parents in control of instruction. Today's public schools have little incentive to improve largely because they enjoy a monopoly situation. Parents are forced to send their children to public schools, unless there happen to be good, affordable, and accessible alternatives, which in many areas there are not. The lack of accountability on the part of teachers further adds to the lack of incentive for reform or improvement.

The model for the EEZ is the private school, as well it should be. There is much that the private school can teach its government subsidized counterparts about quality, excellence and discipline. If that were not so, how could private institutions, even those with less money and lower paid teachers, so consistently turn out better educated children? James Coleman, a leading sociologist at the University of Chicago, has reported on over 60,000 high school students in both public and private schools. Even with the controversy and heated discussion that surrounded his report, one finding could not be refuted: students and teachers in the private schools work harder than their public school counterparts. Teachers expect more—and get more—in private schools than they do in public schools.

ORGANIZING THE EDUCATION ENTERPRISE ZONE:

The EEZ has prompted a lot of interest from school districts in the Southwest. Parents in these districts are fed up with what they view as trendy courses and behavioral teaching strategies that distort and disparage the free enterprise system, along with the fundamental American values that make it work. But because of the structure of the public school, they have been ignored.

Before an EEZ can be established in any area, I would suggest a few prerequisites. Parents in the area should be formally petitioned in order to demonstrate support for the project. Then, with 75 percent or more of the school district in support of the idea, a lobbying effort would have to be started targeting the state legislature and governor's office. An EEZ could also be sponsored by the Department of Education as a "demonstration project." This leaves you with a locally oriented project that can be adapted later on a national basis.

BUILDING A FRAMEWORK:

The first rule of the EEZ is full participation by parents and community members. For this to happen, working committees and sub-committees are formed under the broad headings of curriculum development, textbook selection, teacher policies and student policies. Under the guidance of the elected school board, a rotating advisory body is selected from interested parents, community members and teachers to staff the committees in each of the four topic areas above. The emphasis is on shifting the basis of public schooling from an entertainment center and babysitting facility to a well-planned set of educational objectives tailored for and agreed upon by the local community. While current educational policy consists of little more than a hodgepodge of meaningless programs, held together loosely by something called "academic credits," schools in an EEZ will be built around a well-planned, specific and consistent framework.

For example, an EEZ community might decide that:

1) Education should result in a citizenry that is capable of independent thought, which are prerequisites for self-government.

2) Education should provide the tools for personal financial independence and stability.

3) Education should uphold existing community standards of honor and decency.

Now, this is a workable framework. Anything that cannot be directly related to one of those three goals could be considered secondary, not basic. It is something from which standards, curriculum, textbook selection, and student/teacher policies can be formulated.

Obviously, what parents in Idaho Falls, Idaho, might consider paramount would be different from the framework proposed by a community in San Francisco, California. This is fine. The point is that whatever set of goals the community comes up with will affect the way the school is controlled; the way curriculum and textbooks are selected; the establishment of discipline codes; the policies for students and teacher accountability; and expulsion, hiring and firing policies.

This is precisely why the public schools have failed in later years: because they are no longer built around any consistent, agreed-upon framework.

Public school policies today, if they reflect anything at all, mirror the philosophy of the NEA, the Alan Guttmacher Institute, Planned Parenthood and the ACLU. It is their philosophies, widely publicized, which have filtered down into the classrooms as:

—hostility toward values such as competition, merit and free market;

—a call for the redistribution of the world's wealth and goods through a socialist government;

—hostility toward individuality in favor of collectivism (i.e., group ethics, collective conscience);

— promotion of peer pressure used as a teaching technique;

—equalization schemes so that no one person can be labeled "better" than another.

What about social problems—drug abuse and teenage pregnancy? Again, this is for the parents and communities to decide. If a community thinks its children will benefit from courses or lessons in these areas, then they should certainly be able to select a program,

But, that is the key: community selection. In some areas of the country parents are going to look at the teenage pregnancy statistics and decide that birth control is not the point, morality and self-control are what is needed. Which ever they decide, no program should be thrust upon a locality, especially in sensitive areas like these from an "all-knowing" educational bureaucratic elite in Washington. Parents and educators should be able to go back to their school boards or committee and tell them when a program is not working out so it can either be reworked or scrapped.

What about handicapped children, foreign-born students and special equipment in an EEZ? Are locals going to be able to foot the bill for all these things? And if they cannot, does that mean they have to accept government regulations when they accept federal funding?

The fact is, there was a time when communities, left to their own devices, did handle these things for themselves. For one thing, a district does not always have the same needs from year to year. One year a school may have twenty handicapped students. Another year, it may have only one. The club used by groups like the NEA and the ACLU to force locals to accept programs they do not want is to get them dependent upon federal dollars for programs they do want. Soon, both are out of control and local communities have no voice in how they are run.

In an EEZ, federal and union regulations will be lifted (for a grace period of two to five years) to give the local communities a chance to try it on their own. They might find that if they were not required to fund things they do not want or need, they would have extra money to be used towards projects they feel are more worthwhile. We're not talking about dismantling existing civil right or handicapped laws. They would be left untouched in an EEZ. An example would be schools who are required to match federal monies and build elaborate ramp systems for handicapped children they do not even have. This happens often.

LIFTING THE BURDEN:

A study, by the National Council for Better Education, is currently underway to determine exactly which provisions of state and federal codes in Texas and Oklahoma (where the most interest has been shown) need to be lifted in order to implement an EEZ. Credentials, tenure laws, and teacher compensation are three areas which may require revision.

For example, parents and school boards in an EEZ may want to hire people who are experts in their subject fields, but who do not necessarily have "teaching credentials" i.e., an education certification. The difference amounts to four to eight classes in college on education theory, method courses and child psychology which are of no use to anyone in a classroom setting in the first place. The term "credentialed teacher," therefore, is often a misnomer in that it implies a better knowledge of the subject being taught. Consequently, communities should not be bound by such a restriction.

It may also be that communities want to see competency testing used more extensively in their district. Or, an EEZ may decide that it wants all new teachers hired on a probationary status and supervised by a senior or mentor teacher for the first year or two. Many communities will decide not to keep the policy of tenuring because of declining enrollment or the desire to have more control over their hiring and firing policies.

In any case, it is clear that parents are done a disservice when their children are placed in the position of being held captive audiences by instructors they feel are unsuitable. It is time we start considering parent morale as much as we do teacher morale.

Then, of course, there is the salary issue. In keeping with free enterprise initiatives, the market should, if desired, be permitted to determine how much is paid. If a district thinks it can get and keep good teachers for less, more power to them. If they cannot, they will need to offer more competitive salaries. What could be simpler than that?

Moreover, the purpose of the EEZ is not, as liberals contend, to substitute conservative mandates for existing ones. It is simply to return a significant portion of the educating process to the people who pay for it. It is an attempt to improve parent morale, to encourage their interest rather than to keep them away from the schools.

The bottom line is that a powerful teacher union or a top-heavy federal bureaucracy, preoccupied with its own material well-being and continued existence, is not going to put the good of America's children first. Only parents can do that and America's schools need to utilize this resource.

CHAPTER 18

THE CURE

Today, the whirlwinds of the humanist's socialist agenda are hastening the demise of learning in the United States. The only cure is a sense of purpose, vision and a return to excellence. Only these things can turn the tide and restore education to its once-honored role among men of noble purpose.

The cure will involve answering two basic questions: 1) Can the public schools be salvaged? and, 2) Who is responsible for the education of the individual?

It may appear to be backwards but let us first look at the second question. We do this because the question concerning educational responsibility is critical to any understanding of the crisis facing this nation.

Did you know that virtually none of our nation's most brilliant minds of the past had a formal education? How many of the education elitists can match the intellectual genius and versatility of Benjamin Franklin? He had only two years of formal schooling, yet his brilliance was recognized and honored both here and in Europe. He was presented doctorate degrees by two universities in England, and was honored by kings and statesmen in Europe.

How many of our so-called learned of today, possess the wisdom, eloquence and humility of Abraham Lincoln? His formal schooling totalled less than one year.

We marvel at the technological gadgets that enhance our lifestyle today. Yet, where would many of them be without the numerous discoveries and inventions of a man whose classroom instruction totalled three months: Thomas Alva Edison.

Many more examples could be cited of successful individuals in various fields, from entertainers to business executives, who were the equivalent of public school dropouts. This raises an important point to consider: as long as a child's education leaves him academically proficient and morally upright, what difference does it make where and by whom the child is educated?

To answer this, one must resolve an even more basic question that underlies the entire educational process: Who has the final responsibility, and thus jurisdiction, over a child's education—the government or the parent?

Obviously, the answer to this question carries enormous implications and is crucial to the question concerning the salvageability of the public school system. If, for example, it is agreed that the parent has the primary responsibility of educating their children, a valid argument can be made to junk the public school system.

Some, like author Samuel Blumenfeld, have made that very proposal:

> The pursuit of education, like the pursuit of happiness, is an individual affair. It can start with parents, but it ends with oneself. The state has no logical role to play in it except to provide the conditions of freedom in which individuals can work out their own destinies in their own way.
>
> Ideally, in our free society, government should be . . . uninvolved with education.[1]

Obviously there have been many parents in the United States who have completely given up on public education. Enrollment has skyrocketed in private schools over the past two decades and there is currently a boom underway to start new private schools, especially parochial or religious schools.

I personally, do not agree with those who would abolish the public school system. In a perfect society it is true you would not need a state supported system but we do not live in a perfect society. As long as the state respects the rights of parents to make the best decisions concerning their children without interference from the state, a public school system is palatable.

On the other hand, I feel strongly that the education of the child is the parent's primary responsibility and that each parent should have the freedom of choice of where or if, they send their children to a formal school. That is why I have always been a strong proponent of private/parochial alternatives as well as home schooling.

The NEA educrats vehemently disagree on that point. They believe the state has the primary responsibility for educating the child. They produce volumes detailing how the state can best control the education process. But it all boils down to the same issue: control over content. Keep in mind when reviewing the arguments that if the public schools were abandoned, the NEA would stand to lose all of its control over education. Therefore, they not only have a great economic stake in continuing the current system, bad as it is, but they have an even more important political stake.

When Abraham Lincoln said, "The philosophy of the classroom is the philosophy of the government in the next generation," he could have actually gone a step further. The philosophy of the classroom not only affects the government in the next generation—but the home, the church and society in general.

The NEA knows this and realizes that it must control education if it expects to continue its quest to transform America into a socialist paradise. They are interested in consolidating their power knowing, if they lose, they lose the battle for the hearts and minds of the children. No one understands this better than the NEA. That is why they lead the fight against home schoolers and private schools. They know they must control education if they expect to transform society into their socialist paradise.

Now, to answer the first question: Can the public schools be salvaged? The answer is yes but only if parents are willing to jump into the fray and take back their rightful control. Make the schools stick with the traditional teaching doctrines. That is what we are going to discuss now. Just what are traditional teaching doctrines and how do we re-implement them into our schools?

Traditionally, the goal of learning has been to teach children how to think for themselves. Instruction that fails to accomplish this is nothing more than wasted effort on the part of educators. So, at the outset of the education reformation a distinction must be made between two conflicting theories of methodology, or ways of teaching.

The reformed way, or skill developing mode, has as its task the development of skills on an individual basis in the classroom. Developing the child's skills is not the same thing as cramming as much subject matter as possible into their craniums. By developing the individual's learning skills at the elementary school level, the high school years are spent acquiring knowledge in the various academic disciplines, such as math and science.

The current mode of teaching, imparting knowledge, however, has a fundamental flaw. It assumes the teacher's role is to indoctrinate the child. This has been the NEA's way for well over thirty years. The chaotic results are painfully visible to all.

Education should begin by developing in the student the ability to learn for himself. This way, the student takes an active part in the education process because he is gaining self-sufficiency in life., The indoctrination method favored by the NEA causes passivity in the student. Let me give you an example. In November of 1989, a cataclysmic event took place in Eastern Europe, the Berlin Wall fell. Swarms of East Germans had escaped to the West and rather than see the entire country go under, the East German government capitulated. This was truly a monumental event, perhaps, the most monumental event our schoolchildren will see in their lifetimes. What was their general reaction—confusion and apathy. Quoting from a *Washington Post* story entitled, "U.S. Students Left Flat by Sweep of History":

. . . the response was flat. Some students got a kick out of

> the sight of the wall being dismantled and sold brick by brick, but they were confused about what this meant to the world and somewhat bewildered by the emotional reaction of the school's faculty. The teenagers had trouble with context: They could not relate what was happening to their own lives . . . [2]

But, of course, these teachers had no one to blame but themselves for not teaching their wards enough about world history where they even had a grasp of what communism was.

> These last few weeks appear to have been frustrating ones for many history, government and geography instructors in high schools throughout the U.S . . . . There is to begin with, little understanding of communism. "They don't understand what communism is in the first place," said Donald Van Orman, U.S. History teacher at Pasadena's Blair H.S. in southern California. [3]

On the one hand, the "indoctrination method" of teaching assumes the educator is the prime interpreter of life; in the reformed method, the student is learning the principles of interpretation so he can arrive at an individual perspective intelligently. while his value system remains in place. Attention to proper method in American education then will prepare students to think for themselves, or become self-sufficient in learning. Self-sufficiency in learning is the outgrowth of training in skills, in the tools of learning such as reading, writing and arithmetic.

The first tool of learning is grammar. At the grammatical level the child is introduced to a given body of knowledge by looking at various established facts associated with it. General principles are not mastered here, but particular time is spent mastering details. How these details fit together into a system of knowledge follows this first step. Here the memorization of facts and details, such as memorization of the multiplication table, characterizes educational efforts.

The second tool of learning is logic. Here all the particular facts are put into a system in the same sense that one emerges from a clump of trees, looks back and realizes he has been in a forest; that is, a generalization is made about all the particulars learned during the grammatical phase. Things are viewed as a system and pulled together into a whole, so that each detail is seen as part of the whole. The consequence of seeing how things fit together promotes questioning and a wholesome spirit of contradiction. This is the process of seeing through the logic of a matter for oneself. This cannot be done without some kind of dispute as to how all the details fit into the system. The amount and depth of disputation depends upon what is being learned and an open atmosphere of inquiring created by a given teacher.

THE JAPANESE MODEL:

Part of the cure must be the realization by all Americans that we as a nation no longer have the technological edge which assures us of the superpower status we have enjoyed since the close of WWII. Hardly anyone would disagree that this edge has been lost almost completely because of the failure of our public education system. When it comes to Japanese education—we just do not seem to be able to compete.

Two years ago, I spent ten months in Osaka, Japan, where I studied the Japanese education system first hand. What I observed impressed and amazed me as it has most educators, liberal or conservative, who have lived and studied in Japan. One well known authority on the subject, Professor Merry White of Harvard University wrote in her latest book, The Japanese Educational Challenge (a must read for anyone interested in the Japanese education system), "The visible outcomes of Japanese education . . . include stunning literacy rates, a highly sophisticated general population, and a well-socialized and committed work force. Less than 0.7 percent of the Japanese population is illiterate, compared to 20 percent in the United States."[4] This, when the Japanese language is considerably harder to master than the English language.

Many western critics of the Japanese system try to paint a picture of the Japanese child as a modern day "kamikaze pilot . . . hell-bent on

Japanese supremacy." They contend that "childhood as we know it does not exist in Japan: the playgrounds are empty, mothers are homework tyrants; weekends and vacations are devoted to organized study . . . . Failure is shame and may lead to death: the juvenile suicide rate is seen to be tied to academic shortcoming . . . Japanese education is dehumanizing and unfair, both to Japanese children and to the American economy."[5]

There is much truth to these allegations, as far as I was able to observe. But, let us face it, what is wrong with a mother being a homework tyrant? Mine was. What is wrong with children and parents being devoted to education as a way to prosperity both on a personal and national level?

For too long the American public has allowed the liberal-dominated media and their cohorts in the New Left to frame the debate on key issues. The Japanese frighten me too, but not because of the overblown allegations made by the left. The most frightening thing about the Japanese culture is its prioritization of education as the key issue facing the nation, its focus on that issue and its commitment to excellence instead of the American public's capitulation of our own system to mediocrity.

In Professor White's book, she gives a shocking example to show the difference between Japanese parent's high expectations and American parents' considerably lower ones. "In a recent survey mothers in Minneapolis [Minnesota] and Sendai [Japan] were asked to evaluate their children's school experiences. The Minneapolis mothers consistently answered queries by saying that the schools were fine and that their children were doing well. However, the Sendai mothers, very critical of their schools, were worried their children were not performing up to potential. Whose children were, in objective tests, doing better? The Sendai group—in fact, so much better that the **poorest performer in some classes in the Japanese group was well ahead of the best in comparable classes in the American group**."[6] (emphasis added)

Parental expectations probably have more influence on a child than any other factor in their adolescent years. In yesteryears, if parents made it known to their children from the time they reached the age of reasoning on that they were expected to finish high school and attend college, the chances were very good their children would do just that. Of course there were exceptions. Some parents "made it known" to the point they actually drove their children away from the idea. Successful parents, in this area, did not have to nag their children on the issue. It was merely a situation of elevated expectations. If, on the other hand, parents never spoke about college one way or the other, they simply expected their children to fend for themselves when they turned eighteen, their children most likely had lower academic expectations.

Now it goes without saying that financial limitations of many families were enough to convince the parents not to make promises they could not keep. Those days have changed and lack of funding is simply not an excuse for foregoing a college education. Between state scholarships, federal loans, tuition equalization grants and work-study programs most young people can make their way through college.

The point still being that parents who have high expectations usually have children who are high achievers. Not only do the Japanese people understand this basic fact, they have incorporated it into their culture.

"[Japanese] parents strongly feel that schools must provide their children with everything possible to help them climb the occupational ladder."[7]

Part of the Japanese child's education experience during elementary and secondary years includes *juku* or an after school tutoring class in major academic subjects which serves as a supplement to their regular class work. We are not talking about twenty or thirty percent of the school population—we are talking about virtually all Japanese students. These cram schools have become a part of the Japanese culture even though the government frowns on them.

"*Juku* range from small classes of two or three students meeting in the home of a teacher to large schools with dozens of classes, hundreds of students and branches all over the country. The content of the courses ranges from remedial to highly accelerated. Some are synchronized with school courses, some are given over to material one or two months ahead of the school curriculum, and some concentrate on techniques and information most likely to earn a high score on entrance exams. Hence the purpose of a course may vary from simply raising a child's math grade to preparing for a specific entrance exam to a targeted prestigious national university."[8]

Once again, it all boils back down to high expectations. First, on the part of society and parents which rubs off on the children. It is a national mindset.

American critics respond with an attack on the lack of creativity in Japanese students. They say the system purposely inhibits the growth of creativity in children and turns out Japanese adults who prefer to imitate other countries products because they lack the creativity to create and produce their own. There may be some truth to this criticism. Perhaps the Japanese do go to an extreme with their emphasis on rote memorization of basic education skills (a system of teaching known as "mastery learning") but wouldn't you prefer to have a child with a solid background in basics than some "free spirit" child who, although they may be truly gifted musically or artistically, never learned how to read and write well enough to get them any further than high school? Once again this Dewey/Rousseau influence of promoting "free spirited" children is a detriment to education.

A Japanese classroom would surprise many of its critics with its emphasis on creative problem solving, in my opinion, to a more frequent degree than in American classrooms. Japanese children are also required to take art classes, learn to read sheet music and play at least two musical instruments. Creativity just may be in the eye of the beholder.

Another advantage the Japanese child has is a mother who is devoted to the education of her child to the point of annoying the child's teachers or potential teachers. When a Japanese child turns three, usually the mother begins prepping him for his school career. She does this by teaching him to read and write the phonetic alphabet, count to 100 and compute—all before the first grade. Japanese mothers purchase teaching aids (which are also available to American mothers) to assist them in their endeavor. They approach their child's learning in a step-by-step process. Never heaping too much on a child at one time but setting their goals in do-able increments. Now we are not necessarily talking about mothers who are home all day because they do not have an outside job. Even working mothers make the time to tutor their children. Once again, it is simply what is expected by society.

Now many people might say, sure but these guys have been doing it this way for hundreds of years. It would take the same length of time for Americans to incorporate that kind of commitment into their culture. Not true. Almost all of this is as recent as post-World War II. In fifty years, the Japanese, who could not conquer us militarily, have almost succeeded in conquering us educationally.

Another lesson American parents could learn from their Japanese counterparts is how they handle their teenagers. Whereas the overwhelming preoccupation of American teenagers is the opposite sex, Japanese teens are focused on academic success.

Never will you hear of a "children's rights movement" in Japan. It is understood by one and all that only parents have rights and their children's rights fall under that umbrella. American children are simply taught independence too early. They view their academic success as no one's business but their own and feel it is unfair when parents tie in their academic achievements with their "rights" i.e., allowances, dates and free time. On the other hand, a Japanese teenager is still considered an adolescent, is treated as one, and acts accordingly.

The Japanese elementary student is expected to engage in at least two hours of homework per night and this increases to five or more hours during their secondary years.

What is the down side of the Japanese system? The pressure placed on Japanese students during exam time (from their families, society and themselves) can be overpowering to many young people. In 1984, a twelve year old elementary level girl had a nervous breakdown during an exam for entrance into a prestigious secondary school and was taken away from the testing center in an ambulance.

During these major exams, hundreds of families will gather outside the testing center for the long wait while their child takes the entrance test. You frequently hear stories of family members breaking down during these waits or attacking test proctors when they leave the building. One rather famous story concerns a father who, believing his daughter was not well enough prepared to take her college entrance examination, dressed as a woman, complete with facial makeup, and took the test for her, in fact, doing quite well. The test proctors knew it was a man dressed as a woman but were too embarrassed to say anything to him during the test. Afterwards, he was drawn aside by testing officials and admitted to his fraudulent activity on behalf of his daughter.

The major problem associated with Japanese education practices involves the incredibly high suicide rate among Japanese juveniles. Many critics associate this high rate with the grueling examination process. It is interesting to note that the United States leads Japan in teenage suicide rates (15-20 year olds) with 12.5 per 100,000 as compared to Japan's 10.8 per 100,000.[9]

While the Japanese system of education is not perfect, it certainly warrants a long look from U.S. educators. I am not suggesting we go completely Japanese, but we do need to return to the traditional methods we once used. After their defeat in World War II, the Japanese simply modeled their education system after the U.S. model and, as you can see, they are beating our pants off with it. While American educrats have developed "touchie-feelie" methods of teaching to the detriment of our schoolchildren, the Japanese have stuck with _our_ traditional method and have created the most literate and highly accomplished schoolchildren in the world. It should be crystal clear—if the U.S. wants to compete in the 21st century we must return to the basics.

CHAPTER 18 FOOTNOTES

1. Samuel L. Blumenfeld, How to Start Your Own Private School (New Rochelle, NY: Arlington House, 1972) page 344.

2. David Maraniss and Bill Peterson, "U.S. Students Left Flat by Sweep of History," *The Washington Post,* December 2, 1989: page A-1.

3. Maraniss, page A-1.

4. Merry White, The Japanese Educational Challenge (London, England: Collier Macmillan Publishers, 1987) page 2-3.

5. White, Japanese, page 2-3.

6. White, Japanese, page 165.

7. White, Japanese, page 76.

8. White, Japanese, page 77.

OFFICIAL FORM
for
ACADEMIC EXCELLENCE
[Request for School Accountability]

In the interest of high quality education and the general well-being of students attending

---

[name of school(s)/school district]

[Superintendent]

is hereby officially requested by:

[name of concerned citizen/citizens group]

to fully justify the selection and use of instructional materials designated below by completing this Official Request for School Accountability.

[Signature of Petitioner]

(To be completed by Citizen/Citizens Group initiating this Official Request)

TYPE OF MATERIAL IN QUESTION:

☐ Textbook   ☐ Supplementary Material
☐ Curriculum Program   ☐ Occult/Witchcraft
☐ System   ☐ Fantasy Role Playing/D &D
☐ Library Book   ☐ Film/Filmstrip/Tape/Record
☐ Teaching Method   ☐ Pilot or Experimental Materials
☐ Sex Education   ☐ Other

TITLE _____

AUTHOR _____

PUBLISHER _____

JUSTIFICATION FOR SELECTION OF INSTRUCTIONAL MATERIALS

*[Questions 1-14 to be completed by appropriate school official [s].
Where space is insufficient additional information may be attached.]*

1. DESCRIPTION:

Provide a brief descriptive synopsis of questioned materials:

_____

_____

_____

2. GRADE LEVEL:

At what grade level is material actually being used or taught? _____

3. LOCATION:

List name of school[s]/and school district(s) using (or intending to use)
questioned materials:

_____

_____

4. PERSON(S) RESPONSIBLE:

List the name and title of person(s) responsible for selection of material:

_____

_____

5. TEACHER EVALUATION:

A. Were teachers using this instructional material given ample opportunity and time to properly review and evaluate entire material before approval or adoption for local classroom use?　　☐Yes　☐No

B. If not, why not?

_____

_____

_____

_____

C. If so, list all teachers who reviewed material:

_____

_____

_____

D. Teacher evaluations and all criticism of material: *[List or attach]*

_____

_____

_____

_____

6. CITIZEN/PARENT PARTICIPATION:

A. Were parents/taxpayers asked to review questionable material prior to approval and/or use?　　☐Yes　☐No

B. If not, why not?

_____

_____

_____

C. If so, list citizens and/or groups asked to review material:

_____

_____

D. Citizen evaluations and criticisms.

_____

_____

_____

7. CONTENT:

A. Is the basic purpose of this material **ACADEMIC** or **SOCIOLOGICAL?** *[Circle appropriate word]*

B. Is the material positive, wholesome and uplifting? *[Cite page, paragraph, lines, and/or other references.]*

_____

_____

_____

C. List all aspects of this material that are negative, downgrading, or critical of (1) individuals; (2) ethnic, racial or religious groups; (3) institutions; (4) cultural, social, political, and/or economic beliefs, practices of traditions; (5) our own American heritage:

_____

_____

_____

D. Where violence is included, advise:

(1) All instances where violence is included in the material.

[Cite page, paragraph, lines, and/or references.]

_____

---

(2) Is violence treated in the context of cause and consequence?

☐Yes ☐No

[If so, document and specify page, paragraph, lines, and/or other references.]

E. Description of profanity and immoral conduct used.
(1) List all instances of profanity and immoral conduct included in the material.

---

(2) Are profanity and immoral conduct treated in a context of cause and consequence? ☐Yes ☐No

[If so, specify page, lines and/or other references.]

---

(3) Justify the materials' inclusion of profanity and immoral conduct in a controlled and compulsory classroom situation, where all children are required to use and be exposed to the material regardless of their own unique, individual family backgrounds and preferences.

F. If the basic purpose is ACADEMIC, advise:

(1) How specifically does this material improve students' basic academic skills and knowledge essential for them to become successful citizens in our competitive world of work? *[Attach detailed explanation for each subject in curriculum.]*

(2) Is this particular material superior to other available material in teaching basic academic skills? ☐Yes ☐No

If so, by what standards and by whose determination?

_____

_____

If not, why was this material selected for use in this school district?

_____

_____

_____

8. INVASION OF PRIVACY AND POTENTIAL PSYCHOLOGICAL HARM:

A. Have proper guarantees been provided to ensure that none of the questioned material invades privacy of children or exposes them to psychological, emotional, or other harm? ☐Yes ☐No

Explain:_____

_____

_____

B. Is any testing pertaining to student attitudes, parent or guardian attitudes, or any collecting of personal information pertaining to a student or student's family, including personality profiles, value appraisals, or psychological inventories administered or undertaken in connection with this questioned material? ☐Yes ☐No

C. If *yes,* is specific prior written approval and informed consent obtained from parents or guardians before personal inventories or testing pertaining to student or family attitudes beliefs are administered?

☐Yes ☐No

If *not*, why not? _____

_____

_____

9. TEACHING METHODS AND OUTCOMES:

A. Could any content, exercise, question, or other aspect of the material in question be used to change attitudes, or religious or political beliefs of students? ☐Yes ☐No

B. Are psychological techniques—such as personality or attitude profiles, questions or interviews in areas of social, emotional, mental, or personal problems—used in connection with this material?

☐Yes ☐No

10. EXPERIMENTAL MATERIAL:

A. Is any part of the material experimental in nature? ☐Yes ☐No

B. If so, describe the objectives and techniques of the experiment.

_____

_____

_____

C. What do researchers stand to gain from the experiment?

_____

_____

_____

D. What do students stand to gain?

_____

_____

11. CONTROVERSIAL MATERIAL:

A. Were you aware of controversy over this material in other school districts and/or states prior to local approval or use? ☐Yes ☐No

B. If yes, what specifically was done to determine the extent of controversy or dissatisfaction over this material in other communities or states?

_____

_____

_____

C. If controversy over this material was known, what overriding benefit over other available material justified adoption or use for this school district?

_____

_____

_____

12. SAFEGUARDS:

A. List all specific alternative programs provided for students who parents refuse their participation in programs using material they consider objectionable. *[The criteria and purpose may be furnished in an attachment.]*

B. What specific action is being taken to protect students from feeling odd, peculiar, different or isolated from their peers when any parent or guardian questions school subject matter?

_____

_____

_____

C. Who will assume the responsibility for any damage—emotional, mental, moral, physical, or otherwise—that may be caused from use of the classroom material? *[Indicate where it is school district, super-intendent, teacher, or other.]*

_____

_____

_____

13. COST AND FINANCING:

A. What is the cost of this questioned material to the taxpayers of this school district?

     Per student cost: $_____

     Total Cost: $_____

B. Was the Federal government involved in any way in the development or implementation*

of this material? *[If the answer is "Yes" complete the following questions.]*   ☐Yes ☐No

1) Name of federal agency involved?

_____

2) Total amount of federal taxpayer dollars spent for implementation of this material nationwide: $_____

3) Total amount of federal taxpayer dollars spent for implementation of this material in this school district: $_____

C. Were any conditions involved with the use of these materials? *[If "yes," list or describe such conditions in attachment.]*

        ☐Yes ☐No

D. Show amount of expenditures if any other than federal funds?

1) State expenditure for implementation of materials in this school district? $_____

_____

* *[The term "implementation" includes educator promotion conferences, teacher training, pre-service and in-service workshops, cost of materials, pilot testing of materials, and other costs associated with adoption thereof.]*

2) County or parish expenditures for implementation in this school district? $_____

3) Local expenditures for implementation? $_____

14. PARENTS'/TAXPAYERS' RIGHTS:

A. Who has the primary responsibility for what children are taught or not taught?

_____

B. Does the official policy of this school district uphold and practice the basic principles of parental rights? ☐Yes ☐No

C. If not, cite legal action (section of constitution, federal or state laws) transferring this responsibility from parents to the state?

_____

_____

D. List school officials and teachers who do not endorse the inherent right of parents over their children.

_____

_____

_____

_____

_____

_____

[Signature of school official who approved   *[Date]*
questionable instructional material.]

_____

[Signature of school superintendent]   *[Date]*

**Reprinted courtesy of the Mel Gablers, Longview, Texas.

SERVING ON YOUR LOCAL SCHOOL BOARD

TIPS FOR CANDIDATES

The local board of education is probably the most unique of all American institutions. It, having grown out of the town meeting, was designed solely for the purpose that public schools would have the flexibility they needed and a timely response from the community as they face the day to day chore of educating children.

As a member of a local school board you will show your commitment to local control and parental decision making in public education.

As a citizen considering running for a school board seat, you should:

1) be a qualified voter.

2) be a citizen of the United States.

3) not have any pecuniary (money) interest in the affairs of the school district.

4) contact the County Clerk's office to register, file the necessary papers and receive any instructions on your candidacy.

5) acquire a basic understanding of state education laws and regulations; school board policies; board procedures and teacher and student policies at each school. (A good place to start is by attending school board meetings.)

As a citizen serving on a school board, you should:

1) be prepared to devote the time needed to meet your new responsibilities.

2) have a sincere interest in public education, your local community, your state and country.

3) have respect for the need and feelings of all local citizens (parents or not) and have a well-developed sense of fair play.

4) be polite and accessible to parents and citizens who wish to speak with you. Do not have an unlisted phone number.

What does a school board member do?

Basically, your work will fall into four different categories:

1) communications (especially with parents)

2) policy development

3) quality and type of instruction

4) district management

As a school board member you will employ a professional staff of educators. However, you should always be a leader in:

1) assessing and reflecting the educational needs and wishes of the community.

2) developing an educational philosophy.

3) establishing education goals.

4) reviewing curricula and textbooks.

5) reviewing instructional methods used by educators.

6) reviewing and evaluating personnel.

**For a more in depth look at running and winning a school board race may I suggest you purchase an excellent (how-to) manual entitled, "School Boards: A Call To Action" by Wendy Flint of the American Freedom Coalition for $12.95. Their address is: 1001 Pennsylvania Avenue, N.W. #850, Washington, D.C. 20004-2505.

Index

NOTES

NOTES

NOTES

NOTES

NOTES

NOTES

NOTES

NOTES

NOTES

NOTES

NOTES

NOTES